Lake, Loch & Reservoir Trout Fishing

Lake, Loch & Reservoir Trout Fishing

Malcolm Greenhalgh

A&C Black · London

*Front cover: Trout fishing on Lake
Coniston, a natural trout water
(photo: Phill Williams)*

*Opposite: Bank House Fly Fishery,
an artificial modern put-and-take
trout stillwater*

To Peter, Geoff and Hugh for their encouragement

First published 1987 by
A & C Black (Publishers) Limited
35 Bedford Row, London WC1R 4JH

© 1987 Malcolm Greenhalgh

ISBN 0 7136 5597 6

British Library Cataloguing in Publication Data

Greenhalgh, Malcolm
    Lake, loch and reservoir trout fishing.
    1. Trout fishing
    I. Title
    799.1'755   SH687

ISBN 0-7136-5597-6

Printed and bound in Great Britain
at the University Press, Oxford

Contents

Preface

I have written this book in an attempt to put something back into the sport of stillwater angling in the vast range of trout lakes that occur throughout Britain. I hope that some who read it might be encouraged to turn to trout fishing. I hope that trout anglers may find something new and, possibly, the solution to a few problems. I hope that the experienced anglers amongst my readers will be encouraged to re-examine some of their ideas and attitudes in the light of what I have written. It is a book that summarises my experiences and findings: it is the crystallisation of many hundreds of days fishing and far more trout caught. It also includes the result of countless hours spent talking to anglers, and evenings reading anything I have been able to lay my hands on that deals with the sport of trout fishing. What the book is *not* is the last word on trout fishing: no book ever will be that!

Though I have written this book and am to blame for any errors that it may contain, many other anglers must be credited with contributing to its production and virtues.

I am fortunate in being a member of what is, in my opinion, the best fishing club in the north of England, if not the British Isles, Bowland Game-Fishing Association. With no exception the members of that Association have provided me with a great deal of support and encouragement in my angling writing. The Association also has many outstanding trout anglers who have, over the years, passed on tips, ideas, observations, experience and advice. It is difficult to single out just a few of them, but I must specifically present my thanks and best wishes to Albert Sanderson, Jack Morris, the two Brians (Hoggarth and Wells), John Bettaney, Brian and Harvey Buckley, Stuart Butcher (Wizard of the northern wet fly), John Dixon (a better all-round game angler you will not find), Bernard Downes, Eric Haygarth, Chris Heap and his wife Jean, Tony Hindle, and R. J. 'Josh' Hodgson.

I must also mention Jack Norris, a modest man who is surely the best tyer of a dry fly (Jack, unknowingly, has provided me with a lot of help and encouragement by his example); Jack's fishing companion, Eric Hirst; also, Peter Hemmings of Angus Stuart's Tackle Shop, Grantown-on-Spey.

As a person, though sociable enough indoors, I have always been a bit of a loner when outside 'doing my thing'. However, I have been blessed, in recent years, in having two regular fishing companions. The first is Geoff Haslam, an industrial chemist by profession who, during a long car journey, provides stimulating conversation and, on river or lake, is an excellent fisherman. The second is my son Peter who is now, at the age of sixteen, the best trout fisherman that I know, whether on stillwater or river.

Finally, all the diagrams and many of the photographs in the book have been produced in his usual meticulous fashion by Phill Williams, man of many talents.

Thank you all!

Malcolm Greenhalgh

> Cards, Dice and Table pick thy purse;
> Drinking and Drabbing bring a curse;
> Hawking and Hunting spend thy chink;
> Bowling and Shooting end in drink;
> The fighting-cock, and the horse-race
> Will sink a good Estate apace.
> Angling doth bodyes exercise,
> And maketh soules holy and wise:
> By blessed thoughts and meditation;
> This, this is Angler's recreation!
> Health, profit, pleasure, mixt together,
> All sport's to this not worth a feather.
>
> Thomas Barker, *The Art of Angling*, 1651

Note

In recent years the British or imperial measurements of weight and length have slowly been superseded to some extent by the international or metric units. It seems likely that, in the not too distant future, the last bastions of imperial measure will be a thing of the past. I remember, some ten years ago, helping to officiate in a team coarse angling cup competition that was, for the first time, being judged with the metric kilograms and grams rather than the traditional pounds, ounces and drams. Every angler who weighed-in some fish asked me, upon being told the *official* weight, 'But what is the *proper* weight?' And one angler, having had the top weight in his section, was still unsure as to whether or not he really had taken the top weight! Those of my generation often find metrication double Dutch.

In this book I have decided to accommodate, wherever possible and reasonable, both types of measure. So weights are given in pounds and ounces, and kilograms and grams; length is given in miles, yards, feet and inches, and kilometres, metres and centimetres. But how does one translate 'about a pound' into metric? It would be foolish to say 'about 454 grams'! I have retained such crude, near-cliché, measures, often based on my diary records of fishing days, without conversion.

1
Introduction

'He seeth the yonge swannes: heerons: duckes: cotes and many other foules wyth thyr brodes. And yf the angler take fysshe: surely thenne is there noo man merier than he is in his spyryte.'

Dame Juliana Berners, *A Treatyse of Fysshynge wyth an Angle*, 1496

'There is more to fishing than catching fish.'

Hugh Falkus, *Sea Trout Fishing*, 1975

A Hebridean loch

My son, Peter, and I parked the car in a tiny quarry close to the Stornoway—Tarbert Road. In front of us stretched a brisk climb into the hills and then a long trek through heather moor, bog and rock, past two tiny lochans and along a wet valley to our goal, one of the largest lochs of Lewis, Fadagoa. Distance demanded the minimum of tackle and the lightest of loads so Peter took the rucksack with provisions and I carried the fishing bag, net and rods.

As we negotiated the first extensive bog nesting curlews, redshank, lapwing and snipe took to the air before us, scolding us for disturbing their growing chicks. Marsh orchid, bog asphodel and crowberry flowers speckled the springy turf with splashes of pink, yellow and mauve and, in the wettest tracts, the white heads of the cotton-grass suggested an unseasonal snowfall. We skirted Loch an Tomain, a typically shallow Hebridean lochan with protruding boulders. In a tiny bay a red-throated diver 'quacked' at us and then slid beneath the ripple as we passed by. We continued our climb through a heather coll until we reached Loch an Sgàth—a beautiful little lochan, set in the hillside beneath the crags of Roineval. White water lilies choked one small bay; bog bean flowered along the margins.

Our trek then took us through the boggiest of bogs for over a mile. Dunlin replaced curlew, golden plover replaced lapwing and, most exciting, the very rare greenshank replaced the redshank of the lower level. Wheatears flitted from crag to crag, flashing their white behinds and chattering at us. Raven and hooded crow called from the rocky slopes. Finally, after an hour and a half of foot-slogging, we reached the gates of a trout fisherman's Eden. Large mazing lochs stretched before us. Mile after mile of rock and loch and not one piece of evidence of mankind. We set up base camp on a sandy beach at the head of Loch Fadagoa. Peter assembled the rods and I made coffee which we drank in a heathery hollow overlooking the loch.

Of that day's fishing neither of us can remember a great deal. Our diaries record the capture of 17 good trout, the best (caught by Peter) close to the two-pound mark. They were all taken on a size 10 Peter Ross or a size 12 Blue Zulu. In the late afternoon sun we laid out our catch on a big lichen-encrusted boulder. The fish were beautiful wild brownies, ranging in colour from one that was a black-speckled steel blue to three of the larger ones that were yellow and brown with bold red spots. As we packed the fish away and drank a last brew our day was brought to a close by a pair of black-throated divers planing into our bay and a male merlin hunting a meadow pipit along the loch shore.

What a day!

Two Highland lochans

On another occasion, in northern Scotland, Peter and I set off to fish two tiny lochans in the midst of mountain, crag and peat hag. A stream barred our way across the first valley and it took some negotiating for, although it was only just too wide for us to leap, its depth seemed bottomless judging from the extended landing-net handle. After a long detour we made a crossing with dry feet and proceeded through a side valley that climbed into the hills. Snipe, dunlin, curlew and golden plover called all around us, wheatears chattered from craggy outcrops, hooded crows croaked from the precipices and, overhead, a mewing buzzard circled.

We tackled up by the first lochan. We made our way along the bank, stepping and casting as we went and slowly bringing our teams of wet flies back with the ripple. Peter had a nice trout around the half-pound mark, then another. It was my turn next and I added three brownies to the bag. Peter had another. Then, as I was shaking a tiny fish from the hook I heard Peter shout. A shadow moved over me and, looking up, I was thrilled to see a golden eagle gliding low, very low, overhead. It disappeared from view over a hillside crag. I rushed along the shore to Peter.

'The best view I've ever had of an eagle!' I exclaimed.

'Did you not see the other one?' Peter asked. 'It landed on that boulder there, then took off and went that way.' He pointed with his fly rod.

Leaving Peter to continue around this pool I climbed over a heathery ridge and the few hundred yards to the next little lochan. As I approached, a fish moved close in. I flicked my team of wet flies across the waves and let them drift round, just below the water surface. The line drew and I tightened into a trout of about the pound mark. After an hour and three more trout I strolled back to see how Peter was getting on. There was no sign of the lad by the water; he was crouching amongst the heather.

The eagles had returned, one of them carrying some prey. We watched as one landed on a crag on the other side of the lochan. On the crag was an eyrie and in the eyrie an eaglet with only the last trace of its juvenile down.

A day we will both remember—not just for the excellent fishing, but also for the superb eagles.

A limestone tarn

Difficult days, when a problem presents itself and when one finds the solution, are always interesting and usually culminate with a feeling of elation that one has defeated the elements and the fish.

I arrived on a blazingly hot August day on a small tarn, set in the midst of some of the most beautiful limestone countryside in Britain. On such a day I would not normally have bothered before evening, but I had to leave the area that night so, if I was to fish, it had to be through the day. A light breeze rippled the water surface, but not a fish stirred. For almost four hours I went through the motions of giving one team of flies a go, then changing to another team, and so on. Exhausting work! I rowed back to the bank and sat, drinking luke-warm orange juice, watching the water. Where would the fish be? I had fished the margins thoroughly and plumbed the depths on several drifts. 'They must be deep!' I told myself.

At one corner of the lake some limestone crags formed a sheer drop into the pool, casting a shadow on the water. Possibly there might be a 'taking' fish in that area? So I pushed the boat out and carefully pulled on the oars until the boat lay some thirty yards from the rock face. Slowly I lowered the anchor. A fifteen foot leader replaced the ten foot one on the floating line. Two tiny black buzzer pupa imitations were tied to the droppers, and a Sawyer's Killer Bug to the point. The latter would sink quickly to the bottom, taking with it the two buzzers. I heavily greased the end of the fly line and leader butt (the Permagrease was a warm liquid oil rather than semi-solid grease!). Casting as delicately as I could I waited and watched the line as the flies sank. No offer resulted. Then, as the boat drifted around a little in the breeze, pulling on the line, the leader-butt dipped beneath the surface and I tightened into the first fish of the day: a splendid brownie close on the two-pound mark. In the next half-hour two more fish responded in like manner to the almost stationary deep nymphs. One became detached and the other joined the first in the creel. The deepest of the buzzers had done the trick, the fish having been taken in about nine feet of water and about two feet from the lake bed.

In five hours on the little lake the first four and a half had been fishless. However, the last half-hour had yielded a brace of hard-earned wild trout.

An English reservoir

Draycote was, for once, being exceedingly difficult. It was high summer and although I expected to catch a lot of fish that were feeding amongst the clouds of *Daphnia*, on a lure, I had only managed to extract a nice two-pound rainbow trout through the heat of the day. I was getting very tired and considered giving the fish best. Then, as the light began to fall a few fish began to break the surface in Toft Shallows. There was little evidence of a sedge hatch and few midges on the water, so I presumed that the fish were taking nymphs in the surface film. On the floating line I attached a big Red Sedge on the point and, on the top dropper, a Suspender Buzzer that would sit in the surface film and on the middle dropper a Sedge Pupa imitation that would bob to and fro just beneath the surface. I cast out and sat back as the line drifted round, keeping my eye on the dry sedge. There was a swirl close to the leader and the sedge bobbed under. I gave the rod a flick and found myself attached to a good fish that eventually came to the net: a nice rainbow that had taken the Suspender Buzzer.

In the next hour, five more followed that one into the creel on the same fly and two others became unstuck. Then came a lull in activity. I needed one more for the eight fish limit and time was running out. I headed into the bay for the last slow drift and, with the light almost gone, had my final fish, this time on the dry sedge. As I killed it, the red light flashed over the Fishing Lodge signifying 'Time Up'. As I chugged back into the gloom sedges fluttered over the surface and clouds of midges rose in the cooling night air.

A day that for the most part was a hard gruelling exercise, but in the end was outstanding.

Note: As I look back through my diaries a question arises. Is it not preferable to struggle hard to catch for most of the day and be rewarded in the last hour, than to take a fish early on and then continue for the remainder of the day without an offer?

Those four days which I have just described to you were four enjoyable days, either because of the quality of the fishing in terms of challenge and interest, or because of events completely unrelated to the fishing. But in not one case was it a matter of simply catching a lot of trout. Too often, for me and for many of my angling friends and acquaintances, a large bag made from easy trout results in feelings of let-down or anticlimax. Let me give a couple of examples.

A new fishery had opened in northern England where, I was told, some big rainbow trout were to be had. So I went to try it on the eight-till-four shift. I paid for the ticket and strolled to the dam where one of the four-till-eight early shift anglers was playing a large fish that turned out to be a rainbow of about four pounds. 'Fish from here,' he said. 'Use a fast-sink line, a big lure, and let it sink for ninety seconds. Dead easy!' A whistle blew, and he departed.

I tackled up as he suggested and cast out into the deeper water. At the prescribed time I began to tweak the lure back and a fish took immediately. It fought well for a few minutes before coming to the net. A two-pound rainbow. I killed it and dropped it into the fish bass. Next cast yielded one a bit larger. That one went into the bass. 'Pretty good!' I thought. By 9 o'clock I had landed seven trout and kept three towards my four-fish limit. Seven hours of fishing remained. So I determined that the fourth and last fish that I would kill to complete my limit would have to be a really big one: at least five pounds. An hour later and I had caught and returned another nine. Then, just before 11 o'clock, a big fish took the lure. I looked at it in the net: certainly a six-pounder. It went into the bass. By noon I was getting a bit bored. I had caught 29 rainbow trout, kept my limit, changed from lure to nymph and still continued to catch. The pub was open. I signed off and left.

Incidentally, the following week I took Peter (who was but eight years of age at the time) for the early morning session. A lad who has not been fly fishing long needs to catch some fish and this water, with its high density stocking of big trout, would be a real treat for him. I set his tackle up and he made a short cast. A five-pounder took his dry floating White Marabou as soon as it hit the water, first cast! And once more it was fish after fish after fish. Practice for a boy possibly, but hardly good fishing.

Malcolm and I set off from the moorings on our first visit to a new reservoir ticket water. A gale was piling up waves out in the body of the lake so we contented ourselves by drifting along the margins of a more sheltered bay close to the Fishing Lodge. We lost count of the number of rainbow trout that we returned when we had reached about the 80 mark. Certainly, we had well over the hundred between us on a wide variety of lures, nymphs and wet flies, and every one was a typical small stockie ($\frac{3}{4}$–$1\frac{1}{4}$ lb). A day reminiscent of feathering for mackerel!

Stillwater trout fishing is certainly the most widespread of the various types of angling in Britain. Coarse angling is largely restricted to the lowlands of England, parts of Wales, Ireland and southern Scotland. Salmon and sea trout fishing is primarily a sport of the rivers draining the uplands of the south-west, north-west and north of England, Wales, Ireland and Scotland. River trout fishing is widespread through the same regions as well as a few, though very important, chalkstreams of southern England. Stillwater angling, however, is on everyone's doorstep in some shape or form. It encompasses the often superb sport on the famous loughs of Ireland. Scotland prides itself on the thousands of trout lochs which extend from the far-flung islands of the Outer Hebrides, Orkney and Shetland, through the Highlands to the Border Country of Galloway and the Cheviot Hills. Most Welsh llyns hold trout, as do the lakes of Cumbria. Then through the Pennines there are a great number of trout reservoirs and a lesser number of natural tarns that hold a head of wild fish or that have been stocked for sport. Scattered across lowland England is a wide variety of trout fisheries varying in size from tiny pools and gravel pits to huge reservoirs, including the massive Rutland Water. You can fish for wild brown trout in remote mountain lochans and for stocked rainbow trout in lakes close to the centre of some of our largest cities, including London, Birmingham and Manchester. For us all stillwater trouting is just down the road and, when we go away on holiday, the fly rod can be put to good use even in the coastal resorts of Blackpool, North Wales, Devon, Cornwall and the south coast resorts of Bournemouth, Brighton and Hastings.

Trout fishing in the waters of upland Britain and Ireland is an old sport. In Ireland fly fishing has been documented since the eighteenth century:

'It may be assumed that fly-fishing was introduced to Ireland by the English officers who manned the early garrisons, and was further promoted by the sporting gentlemen of the leisured class at the invitation of the Irish landlords, but this new method certainly found favour with the sporting Irish...'

E. J. Malone, *Irish Trout & Salmon Flies*, 1984

This suggests that trout fishing in Ireland was by other methods before then, presumably natural baits and possibly artificial spinners; and that fly fishing on the British mainland was exported across the Irish Sea and therefore pre-dates fly fishing in Ireland. So it does; John Waller Hills in his excellent *A History of Fly Fishing for Trout* (1921), tracing the sport in mainland Britain back to the fifteenth century, says:

'There is nothing wrong with his [the 15th century angler's] flies, though it must not be forgotten that we do not know what they actually looked like, nor must it be assumed that because a modern dresser could make excellent flies out of the old dressings they were made with equal care over four centuries ago. But after making all allowances, it is safe to assume that his flies, though more coarsely dressed, larger in the wing and thicker in the body than those used now, still were fairly serviceable. The rod, from twelve to eighteen feet long, single-handed, so light and stiff yet springy, and with a following wind or on a still day would cast a hair line with delicacy...'

Up to the middle of the nineteenth century evolved the basic tackle and techniques, used on both river and lake alike, of fishing the fly on or just below the surface. And then a revolution occurred that tore stillwater angling and river angling asunder. The chalkstream dry fly revolution, promoted by F. S. Halford, C. S. Marryat, Francis Francis and others, banished large, gaudy and bushy wet flies in favour of delicate floating imitations of natural insects. Subsequently, the subsurface fly was re-introduced as the imitative upstream nymph, pioneered by the great G. E. M. Skues and, later, Frank Sawyer and Oliver Kite. On upland rivers the large non-imitative fly was superseded by a range of delicate, but sparsely dressed, tiny wet flies, fished just beneath the surface—the so-called traditional northern wet fly as described, for example, by T. E. Pritt, H. Edmonds and N. Lee. In the meantime, the larger wet flies continued to be used on stillwaters. New patterns were invented that were better than earlier ones and other older patterns were improved. A Mr Jewhurst of Kent invented the Butcher some time before 1838: 'On Scottish lochs . . .it takes more fish than any other fly' (Courtney Williams, *Dictionary of Trout Flies*, 1973). From this evolved the Bloody Butcher and Kingfisher Butcher. In Ireland Michael Rogan (1833–1905) perfected a very old pattern to produce the excellent Fiery Brown. And in Scotland a man *called* Peter Ross suggested improvements to the Teal and Red (a very old lake fly) to give rise to the fly we now know as the Peter Ross: 'the most killing lake fly throughout the British Isles' (Courtney Williams). Dry flies were dominated by the bob-fly (on the top dropper of a three or four wet fly cast) or by the large bushy dapping fly. In recent decades these types of fly and fly fishing have come to be called 'standard lake flies' and 'traditional loch or lake fishing'.

From about 1920, and increasingly since around 1950, a growing number of people taking up trout fishing as a pastime, especially in the English and Scottish lowlands, and a greater mobility of the British population, has resulted in an impact of river trout fishing styles on lake trout fishing. So, in one of the first and best books ever written on Scottish loch fishing (*Loch Fishing in Theory and Practice*, 1924) R. C. Bridgett introduced the idea of imitative nymph and dry fly fishing to stillwaters. Such imitative fly fishing, so reminiscent of the style that had evolved on the English chalkstreams, developed further when many chalkstream anglers turned to the new stillwaters that had sprung up in the south of England —Two Lakes, for example.

Then, coinciding with the boom of stocking stillwaters with American rainbow trout came a style that largely originated in the U.S.A., lure or 'streamer' fishing. This development has been a bit controversial in that the big, garishly adorned lures often bear little resemblance to natural trout foods so that in the eyes of many 'lure-stripping', as it became known, was 'unsporting', 'spinning with a fly rod', 'fishmongering', 'dreadful', 'the pits', and 'not worthy of the name fly fishing'! (Incidentally, I put these descriptions in 'quotes' because that is what they are—each has been said to me about lure fishing.) But it is an effective way of catching trout that cannot be caught by other means.

Today it is possible to visit almost any stillwater trout fishery in the British Isles and to see several styles in use at once. For example, on Draycote and Rutland Water, two of England's greatest reservoir fisheries, I have seen the traditional loch style, dapping, nymph, dry fly and lure-stripping being carried out simultaneously.

And on some Cumbrian lakes and Welsh llyns I have witnessed
several styles of fly fishing as well as the older techniques of bait-
and spin-fishing all in operation in one day. The good, all-round
angler should be capable of using each of these methods as
appropriate, depending, of course, on whether that particular
method is allowed by the fishery rules. Some waters have no restric-
tion as to methods of rod fishing; some other fisheries have some or
many restrictions. I know of small fisheries where the largest hook
that may be used is a size 12; on others big size 8 and 6 long-shank
lures can be used but not double-hooks or hooks arranged in tandem. In some, one may fish the fly or bait-fish with worm, but
maggot and spinning are banned. Whatever, the angler must abide
by the fishery rules. Where a method *is* allowed then, if needs be,
an angler should be capable of using that method if it is the only one
that will catch him a fish. For, after all, the real aim of fishing is
catching fish! A silly comment you might think but there are many
anglers who deceive themselves into believing that they go fishing
primarily to commune with nature or for fresh air, and they restrict
themselves to very narrow fishing styles and assume an air of
superiority over the realists. 'Oh! *I* stick to dry fly. None of this
chuck-and-chance it for me.' Indeed, only recently on Stocks
Reservoir, the very few anglers who were catching trout, all on
lures, were harangued by a loud-mouthed 'I'm-a-nymph-and-dry-
fly-angler' for being fishmongers! I'm sure that he enjoyed his day
even though he caught nothing.

The stillwater revolution has been maintained by the tackle
industry that now provides a wide variety of rods and lines which
enable the lake fisherman to get his flies quickly down to deep-lying
trout as well as fishing in the 'older' style close to or on the surface.
To go with the new rods and lines we now have new casting styles
that enable a fly to be propelled much further than was once possible. And for those who fish from boats there are several new
techniques which improve the chances of catching some trout.

An angler goes out to catch fish! Formerly this meant wild brown
trout. Then the wild brownies were supplemented in some fisheries
with trout that had been raised in 'stew ponds'. Today we also have
introduced rainbow trout and American brook trout (speckled
charr)—fish bred specially for angling, big fish, large numbers of
fish. For a lot of anglers it is the stocked rainbow that dominates
their sport and in many stillwaters huge numbers are stocked at
high density and frequency: 'Stocking policy input every 2–3 days',
said one advertisement in *Trout and Salmon* in February 1986.

Alas, newly stocked trout are usually very naïve and will often grab just about any fly you care to throw on the water. At its most extreme in some fisheries the angler actually catches his fish in the huge concentrations of the stock ponds. He pays a nominal sum to fish and then forks out so much per pound for the fish he catches. Now that *is* fishmongering. However, for a lot of anglers slaying such stupid fish is considered good sport. Some even plan their fishing trips to coincide with the arrival of the stocking wagon so that they can catch these tame trout. One even hears anglers boasting about how many stockies they have caught from such-and-such a water. Put many of these anglers on a wild brown trout fishery and how will they fare? Badly, I suspect. Put them on a stocked fishery when those trout that remain have learned what natural foods are and have grown wary of anglers and once more I believe that a large proportion of stockie-bashers will do badly. How noticeable is the decline in the number of anglers fishing a water once things have become difficult! And how many anglers moan when they fail to catch once the initial slaughter of the innocents is over.

I remember one incredible experience on the Pennine Trout Fishery in the hills near Littleborough. It had the reputation for high catch-rates of big trout, especially rainbow trout. One blazing August day the fish would look at nothing. We all struggled and, by mid-afternoon, only a couple of fish had been caught amongst 24 anglers. A group who had visited the water to drag out some easy fish began to argue with the proprietor, Roger Ditchfield. To try to placate them he went to the stock-pens and turned a few hundred big fish into the small lake. Three more fish were caught, but the group of moaners still failed to catch. They began to argue again. What could Roger do? To give him his due, he had tried very hard. They departed amidst a torrent of Anglo-Saxon adverbs, adjectives and nouns.

Why? Because they felt that the ticket cost was the price paid, not simply to go fishing in a well-stocked water, but to take some fish home. For such anglers this book is not written. I have no interest in simply catching a lot of daft fish. I look to fishing as being a challenge and where there is no challenge the sport ceases to have any interest.

Of course, most of us have, from time to time, to fish where stockies have just been put into the lake. We then find the fishing easy, but a bag of easy fish is a hollow victory.

Why has there been a trend, in recent years, on English reservoirs at least, to want to catch a lot of stockies? I think there are three reasons, each of them in its way a little sad.

First of all there is the demand of the home deep-freeze and/or the sale of fish to subsidise the costs of going fishing. Apparently it is possible to go to fishmongers' shops in several towns of the English Midlands and buy rod-caught rainbow trout from Draycote, Rutland and Grafham!

Secondly, there is the desire to boast. We all do it from time to time, even inadvertently, and if you keep going to waters that have just been stocked you will have more to boast about. Then if you go to a water that has just been stocked with really big trout you will have even more to boast about. Next year I will arrange for a hatchery to bring four twenty-pound rainbows and stock my bath (where there is a bag limit of four). Then I really will have something to boast about!

Thirdly, the fishing magazines and books are crammed with photographs of fishermen grinning at bag limits of trout, thereby encouraging everyone else to go and do likewise. Can you imagine a picture in a fishing magazine with the caption 'So-and-so with no fish—he had a blank'! Or someone writing about when he *didn't* catch some fish! I am as guilty as the rest. In my articles and books I tell of better days, of days selected from my diaries when I caught fish. This book contains the tales of many such days and some of the photographs illustrate them. But believe me, we all have blank days, only we rarely talk about them!

So, let us look at the challenging aspects of real trout fishing. Living as I do in northern England, with North Wales, the Pennines and Cumbria more or less on my doorstep, and with a job that allows me to spend long periods further afield from the farthest west, north and east to the deepest south of these Islands, we will consider the whole of stillwater trout fishing—loch, lough, llyn, lake and reservoir.

However, whilst we look at the fishing of stillwaters, let us not forget that one side of a day out with the rod is not the fishing. It is the fresh air, exercise, relaxation and change from daily routine that many of us need to recharge our batteries. There is the pleasure to be had from the other inhabitants of the lake and lakeside—from the plants, the birds, the mammals and the insects, many of which the trout find more interesting than we often do. To exclude them from our senses by concentrating solely on the fishing rod is to miss out on so much of the enjoyment that a day on the lake provides.

Stillwater angling is a popular sport. It deserves to be for, as Thomas Barker put it, 'All sport's to this not worth a feather'!

2

Lakes, Lochs and Reservoirs

'Does not much of the delight of angling ... spring from the peace and calm associated with placid lakes ... ?'

Garth Christian, *Tomorrow's Countryside*, 1966

The trout angler in the British Isles is extremely fortunate. These islands have an immense number of stillwaters that have a head of trout. From the loughs of Ireland, the lochs of Scotland, the natural lakes of Cumbria and the high-level tarns of northern England to the llyns of mountainous Wales and the man-made artificial fisheries that are scattered through every county of lowland England trout fishing is readily available, close at hand, for any who would care to have a try.

On the face of it stillwaters are simply bodies of water with no flow rate, containing trout that are waiting to be caught. However, such a view is the ultimate in simple-mindedness. Every body of water is uniquely different and must be considered so by the angler. It is no wonder that the vast majority of trout taken from a fishery are usually caught by 'regulars' who know the water intimately in all its moods and that an angler who visits the water several times in quick succession will find his catch rate increasing as he learns the idiosyncrasies of that particular water.

What the newcomer to a stillwater needs to know is where the trout are liable to be on the day, on what they will be feeding, what fly or flies are most likely to succeed and how these flies should be presented to the trout. By trial and error he should eventually find the answers for himself and so his catch rate will improve. Or a short cut may be possible. Another angler who knows the water well or a gillie, if one is available, may provide the advice as to where and how trout can be caught.

Very many anglers find it difficult to 'read a water'. This is a pity for such an ability can remove a lot of the heartache from visiting new waters. However, the acquisition of 'water sense' is not too difficult and once the instinct has developed you will gain a great deal of pleasure from fishing new waters. An individual may even earn the reputation of being a good angler, no matter where the water, but more likely the reputation will be that of a lucky angler. ('Jammy devil! He always catches more than his fair share!') (To anyone who feels that luck plays a major part in angling let me say this: as in everything, luck can contribute, but in 99% of cases skill accounts for success and lack of skill for failure.)

In this chapter we will look at the range of British stillwater trout fisheries and attempt to find the similarities and differences between them. We will try to discover what makes a very good trout water, where the fish are likely to be, when they will be feeding and on what they will probably be feeding throughout the trout-fishing season. In other words, we will attempt to read, on paper, a range of stillwaters.

Size, shape and depth   The most obvious variations amongst stillwaters are in size, shape and depth. Taking natural waters first, many of the largest are long, narrow and deep, and are set in spectacular mountain scenery. Most of these are glacial in origin, having been excavated by glaciers during the Pleistocene 'Ice-Ages'. The upper reaches tend to be rocky and, proceeding down the valley and lake, the rough terrain gradually gives way to shallower slopes and finer sediments at the mouth of the valley and lower end of the lake. Such valleys often have a natural dam of

A highland glaciated valley loch; it is narrow, steep-sided and oligotrophic

glacial moraine (boulders and clay) which retains the lake. All these larger waters have feeder-streams which drain the mountain slopes at the head of the valley and a river outflow that cuts through the moraine dam. Migratory salmonids (sea trout and salmon) often pass through such lakes, from the sea, to spawn in the lake's feeder streams. Table 1 gives examples of these.

	Length (km)	Breadth (km)	Area (sq.km)	Depth (m)
Loch Awe	42	1.1	39	90
Loch Muick	4	0.8	3	82
Loch Lomond	35	1.5*	71	180
Loch Tay	23	0.9	20	130
Loch Rannock	16	1.0	15	110
Windermere	17	1.5	15	67
Ullswater	12	1.0	9	63
Wastwater	5	0.8	3	79
Llyn Tegid	8	1.5	11	39

*excluding the bay at the southern end

Table 1 Statistics of some upland valley glacial lakes. It should be clear from these figures how steeply the shore drops away to great depths in these narrow lakes.

Similar in shape, but of different origin, are the lochs of the Great Glen. These are tectonic in origin; that is, they are the product of the shearing movements of the earth's crust which gave rise to a deep fissure in which the lochs lie. Loch Ness is the largest at 35 kilometres (22 miles) long by 1.6 kilometres (1 mile) wide and 230 metres (750 feet) deep. This depth is exceeded by that of Loch Morar, 310 metres (1100 feet), the deepest lake in Europe.

The most famous Scottish trout water, Loch Leven, is of glacial origin, but of quite different shape and depth. It began as a massive block of stranded ice that became surrounded by clay and boulders deposited by receding glaciers and their melt waters. The block of ice eventually melted, leaving behind a shallow water-filled depression, 5.7 × 4.1 kilometres (2.3 × 1.6 miles), and with a shallow average depth of only 4.5 metres (15 feet). Similar pools occur elsewhere in lowland Britain (e.g. some of the Cheshire and Shropshire meres), some of which are trout fisheries.

Set high in the mountains are small lochans or tarns that fill the cirques, cwms and corries—hollows in the mountainside scoured out by glacial action. Some of these high lakes, though tiny in area, are surprisingly deep and steep-sided (see Table 2).

	Altitude		Surface Area		Depth	
	Metres	*Feet*	*Sq.Km*	*Sq.Miles*	*Metres*	*Feet*
Blea Water	485	1600	.18	.07	12	38
Grizedale Tarn	464	1530	.15	.06	14	46
Red Tarn	710	2350	.10	.04	13	41
Llyn Glaslyn	590	1950	.15	.06	19	61
Marchlyn Mawr	610	2000	.15	.06	15	48
Dubh Lochan	940	3100	.10	.04	11	36
Lochan Srath						
Dubh-Uisge	515	1700	.10	.04	6	18

Table 2 Statistics of some mountain corrie lakes.

Red Tarn, England's highest corrie lake. The trout are small; schelly also occur

'At one place Llyn Dulyn is 55 feet deep one yard from the shore!'
W. M. Condry, *The Snowdonia National Park*, 1966

A long trek, involving a steep climb, is usually required to reach these pools and so it is not surprising that such waters are rarely fished. However, the spectacular scenery, sparsity of human life, and the eagle, raven and red deer for company mean that the effort is always worthwhile, and besides trout (that might never have seen an artificial fly before) some corrie lochans also hold char which will sometimes take the fly on a warm summer evening.

From these smallest of natural trout waters there is a vast jump to the largest in the British Isles, Lough Neagh. With a surface area of 390 square kilometres (170 square miles) it is almost an inland sea but a shallow one, no depth point being more than 17 metres (56 feet). As in all natural lakes the shape, size and depth of Lough Neagh have been governed by its origin—a water-filled basin formed when the plug of an ancient volcano collapsed.

Whilst many of the other fisheries in Ireland are of the types found in the rest of the British Isles, Ireland also boasts a further sort of lake—the large, sometimes massive, limestone lake of the Irish Plain. Set in a vast depression in the undulating limestone countryside, and on the courses of large rivers, the shallow loughs, with their indented shorelines and scattered islands, provide some of the best brown trout fishing in the world. And not only are they superb trout fisheries, but they generally have good runs of salmon and sea trout, and many also hold huge heads of coarse fish such as pike and bream. Amongst the most famous and outstanding of these are Lough Mask (83 square kilometres, 32 square miles) and the incredible Lough Corrib (105 square kilometres, 65 square miles): names that make the stillwater trout angler's mouth water! To appreciate the quality of such waters is difficult unless you have fished them yourself, but there is one outstanding book which tells all, T. C. Kingsmill Moore's *A Man May Fish* (1979):

'Back at the hotel we weighed the fish, the six just exceeding thirteen pounds...It had been a day typical of Corrib in September when the fish run large but are not very numerous. We never got more than nine on a September day, but the average weight was always at least two pounds. From five to seven fish was normal, anything under this being disappointing, and anything over distinctly good. There was always a good chance of a four- or five-pounder.'

Man-made lakes In recent decades man has tampered with many natural lakes to turn them to his advantage. Dams have been constructed across outflow streams to raise lake levels so that the lakes can be used as bigger reservoirs for drinking water or hydro-electric power schemes. For instance, Manchester Corporation Water Board had the level of Haweswater in the Lake District raised by 29 metres, more than doubling its original depth of 28 metres and trebling its surface area. Loch More (on the river Thurso), Loch Tummel (on the river Tummel) and Loch Awe are amongst many that have been similarly affected in Scotland.

Of far greater significance has been the construction, mostly since about 1850, of large reservoirs to provide potable water for the growing urban populations of England. In Scotland and in most of Wales and Ireland there has always been ample water supplied directly from rivers or lakes, but this has not been the case in England. Water from some Cumbrian and Welsh lakes has been piped into the bigger conurbations of northern England and the Midlands to supplement local supplies, but these have been insufficient to meet the demands of the increasing population and industry of recent years. So, there has been an increase in the number of large reservoirs, many constructed since 1950, that has led to an explosion in the sport of stillwater angling. The most famous, and often the largest, of these lowland reservoirs have been formed in hollows in the the countryside: Draycote, Pitsford, Grafham and Rutland, the largest at about 10 square kilometres (four square miles). These lowland reservoirs are rarely long, narrow and deep (as are the larger glacial lakes), but (more like Loch Leven and the Irish limestone lakes) are wide and have bays, inlets and shallow lake beds which mirror the old farmland topography.

Rutland Water: a large lowland trout fishery where the water's productivity results in rapid growth of stock fish

Contrasting with these lowland reservoirs are reservoirs of the Pennine uplands. In these the upper reaches of streams and rivers have been dammed and often, due to the nature of the incised narrow valleys and steep slopes, the reservoirs resemble more the glaciated type of lake, being long, narrow and deep. Sometimes two

A Pennine reservoir formed by damming a steep-sided valley. The steeply shelving shore and large fluctuation in water level inhibit marginal food production and trout growth

or more dams have been built across one valley to produce a series of reservoirs, one above the other. For example, a dam across the Derwent Valley in Derbyshire resulted in a narrow, Y-shaped reservoir, Ladybower Reservoir. The arms of the 'Y' extend up the Woodlands (Ashop) Valley and the Derwent Valley. Then, in the Derwent Valley above Ladybower a second dam produced the higher Derwent Reservoir that extends into the Howden Moors. Not far away, in Longdendale, five reservoirs occur in series and, to the north of Bolton, three dams have resulted in three reservoirs, at different levels, on one stream. Two of the more recent upland reservoirs have been constructed by damming wider valleys—Cow Green in Upper Teesdale (3 square kilometres, 1.2 square miles) and Kielder Water in the North Tyne Valley (10 square kilometres, 3.9 square miles). They have less steeply shelving lake beds than the more typical upland reservoirs of the narrower steep-sided valleys.

Smaller man-made trout fisheries have developed throughout lowland Britain in recent years to provide for the demand for trout fishing and at the same time to provide a profit for the entrepreneur. Sometimes these are an off-shoot from commercial fish farms that were initially developed to provide trout for the fishmonger's slab. So it is quite possible to fish for trout in old disused gravel pits, millponds, flooded clay pits, 'flashes' caused by mining subsidence, the lakes of stately homes, dew ponds and even lengths of old canals.

Water flow   These, then, comprise the range of stillwaters that might contain trout, and immediately it should be remembered that certainly most and probably all of these are not really *still* waters. There is a slow, usually imperceptible, flow through them. Natural lakes often have several feeder streams which carry rain and snow-melt waters into them, and an outlet stream or river via which the water flows out. In such cases, therefore, the lake is really an extra-wide and deep length of river with a slow flow. It has been cal-culated, for instance, that it takes approximately one year for all the water of Windermere to flow through the outlet, the river Leven, and to be replaced by the feeder streams. The same principles apply to artificial stillwaters. In reservoirs the pumping of water out of the lake and into the drinking supply or through the turbines (in the case of H.E.P. reservoirs) is equivalent to the outlet river, and the feeder streams (in upland reservoirs) or pumping system from nearby rivers or boreholes (in pump-storage reservoirs) tops the level up.

The angler must therefore be aware of inlets and outlets where the 'stillwater' flow is at its greatest, just as the river angler looks with more expectation at the necks and tails of the bigger, slower river pools. The feeder streams may carry food for the trout into the lake. When they do so the trout will congregate close to the mouth of the stream and even enter the stream from the lake. Then, close to the outflow, the brisker current may draw food more quickly through a small concentrated area of the lake. Again, the fish may congregate, ready to intercept food items as they are sucked towards the outflow. In natural lakes these effects are greater following heavy rain; for example, I once caught 14 good brown trout in an afternoon from Windermere where Troutbeck, that was in spate, enters the lake. The same also applies to upland reservoirs. For instance, on Llyn Trawsfyndd I took a limit bag of rainbow trout in 30 minutes one July day just off the mouth of a feeder stream. Earlier I had fished along the lake shore for four hours without an offer.

On many natural lakes the bay around the outflow has frequently been profitable. For example, the exits of the river Leven from Windermere, close to Lakeside, and the river Crake from Coniston, close by High Nibthwaite, have yielded some large bags on spring days and summer evenings when only a short distance further into the lake I have struggled for an offer. Likewise, the artificial outflow from reservoirs has often been useful. In these the pumping of water is rarely constant in that water is drawn off to satisfy the needs of the purification plant and then pumping ceases. During pumping, which might last for a very short time, a quite distinct flow of water can be noticed towards the pumping tower. That this flow attracts the trout can be seen most clearly when there has been a small 'fall' of land insects which evokes a small spasmodic response from the trout over the majority of the reservoir surface. As the flow sucks the insects along the response is greater and, close to the pumping tower, larger numbers of fish break the surface. So, when in a position to benefit from a drift of natural food and the fish are feeding keenly (when fishing from the dam or bank or from a boat anchored or drifting near the outflow) the angler should be alert to what is happening.

Natural food production   Leaving aside the special cases of inflows and outflows, the questions often asked of any stillwater fishery are:

1.   how many trout are there?
2.   what are the size and quality of these trout?
3.   where are the trout?
4.   how should I try to catch them?

I am ignoring questions of the numbers and size of stock—fish that might *just* have been added to the water. Newly-stocked trout are a very special case. I am assuming that we are fishing, not for naîve fish that don't know what a natural fly or shrimp looks like, but for trout that are wild or behaving like wild trout (i.e. stock trout that have been in the lake some time). My four questions, therefore, can apply to the thousands of loughs, lochs, llyns and lakes where there has never been artificial stocking. They can also apply to waters that were stocked earlier in the season, or even to waters like Draycote and Rutland where the regular stocking simply 'tops up' the massive head of fish that are feeding and growing in the lake.

The answer to question 1 is: 'Sufficient, unless you are stupid enough to fish where there are no trout at all!'

The answer to question 2 is: 'That depends on the food available for the trout'.

The answer to question 3 is: 'The trout will be feeding where the food is'.

The answer to question 4 is: 'Ideally it depends on what the trout are feeding on'.

So, the clue to successful stillwater fishing is the trout's food, the natural food that is manufactured by the water itself.

The principle of all natural food production follows a clearly defined pathway:

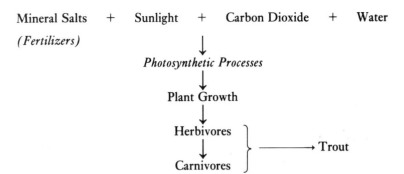

Mineral Salts   +   Sunlight   +   Carbon Dioxide   +   Water
(Fertilizers)
                            ↓
                  Photosynthetic Processes
                            ↓
                      Plant Growth
                            ↓
                      Herbivores ⎫
                            ↓   ⎬ ──────→ Trout
                      Carnivores ⎭

Sunlight, in terms of what reaches the earth through the year, is about constant, although some years are better than others. During the long, hot summers of 1983 and 1984 there was a better-than-average amount of sunlight in Britain, which meant increased photosynthesis and more plant growth. However, in 1985, when there was a dull summer with worse-than-average light intensities, less plant growth was recorded.

The amount of carbon dioxide in the air and dissolved in lake water also remains remarkably constant through the year. What do vary enormously, from one water to another, are the amounts of the various mineral salts dissolved in the lake water. In a lake with a low concentration of salts there will be little plant growth, whereas in one with a higher concentration there will be more plant growth. As all animals (including the trout) depend directly or indirectly on plant growth, lakes are said to have either a low productivity or a high productivity, although this is somewhat relative.

Freshwater biologists have two 'pegs' onto which they can hang productivity. At one extreme there are oligotrophic lakes (the word *oligotrophic* is derived from Greek and means, literally, 'little food', i.e. low productivity). Such waters have catchments of hard rock with little soil cover and, consequently, little agriculture (usually sheep grazing, grouse moor or deer 'forest'). There will also be few, if any, human habitations in the catchment. Rainfall percolates through the catchment drainage system into the lake and adds very little in the way of mineral salts. Many Scottish lochs on granite and gneiss bedrock, Pennine reservoirs on gritstone moorland, the lakes of northern and western Cumbria set below the crags of the hard Borrowdale volcanic series of rocks, and Welsh llyns amidst the mountains of Snowdonia fall into this category. Due to the low salt content of such lakes the population of plant plankton (phytoplankton) drifting in the surface layers of the open water is relatively low.

*A Hebridean lochan. Lochans are generally shallow so that light penetrates
to much of the lake bed. There are two sorts of lochan in the Hebrides. The
first, found in rocky and peaty hollows, are very acidic and low in mineral
salts. Their productivity, therefore, is small and trout, though abundant,
are small. The second type occur in the western "Machair" where
wind-blown shell sand makes the water slightly alkaline and high in salt
content. Productivity in these machair lochans is high and so the trout
grow quickly*

*A natural limestone tarn. A high pH and large amounts of dissolved
mineral salts result in huge fly hatches and fast trout growth*

In these oligotrophic lakes less light is absorbed by the plankton and thus light penetrates to a great depth. In the lake margins the sparsity of nutrient salts and the rocky shore, so characteristic of oligotrophic lakes, means that only small beds of rooted water plants such as water stonewort and quillwort can be supported.

The other extreme is the eutrophic or highly productive lake (*eutrophic* literally means 'good food'). Eutrophic lakes characteristically have a catchment area of softer rocks overlain with a thicker soil cover. There will often be a larger human population in the catchment and much more intensive agricultural farming (possibly dairy, possibly arable). Rainfall draining into the lake will have picked up large amounts of mineral salts from the soil and the feeder streams may carry salts from sewage works' outflows. Thus the amount of phytoplankton in the surface layers of the water will be greater than in oligotrophic lakes and consequently the water will appear to be cloudier and light will penetrate to shorter depths. Also, in the lake margins, where the softer rock and soil of the lake bank will tend to produce a silt lake shore, there will be lush growths of reed, water lilies and beds of *Potamogeton* weed and Canadian pond weed.

Many lowland lakes and reservoirs have eutrophic characteristics. The Irish limestone lakes of Connemara and Mayo, the reservoirs of the English Midlands and South (at Draycote, for instance, so great is the plant productivity that weed-cutters must be used to prevent the shallower water becoming overgrown), and some of the southern Cumbrian lakes are classic examples. However, in reality the oligotrophic and eutrophic categories are not clear cut and the two merge into one another in a middle 'grey' area.

The Cumbrian lakes

To reinforce this concept of productivity and to illustrate the variation in productivity from one lake to another I have chosen the Cumbrian lakes of northern England as an example. The reason for this choice is no other than that these waters have been intensively studied by biologists from the Freshwater Biological Association at Ferry House, Ambleside, for many decades. No other series of lakes anywhere in the world has received anything like this amount of study. They are also lakes that I have fished frequently and studied.

Table 3 provides data relating to productivity in a range of Cumbrian lakes. Wastwater, Ennerdale and Crummock are clearly oligotrophic; Esthwaite is definitely eutrophic. Coniston, Windermere and Bassenthwaite lie somewhere in the middle. The effect of

cultivation in the catchment areas on the amounts of mineral salts
and thus the productivity of plants (as measured indirectly by
cloudiness of the water and, directly, by the mass of phytoplankton)
is marked. The close correlation between plant productivity and
animal populations is also quite distinct. In this case the term
'animals' refers to bottom-dwelling invertebrates in the lake margins (i.e. possible trout food).

	% of catchment area cultivated	% of lake shore rocky to 10 metres	Trans-parency of water (Depth to which light penetrates in metres)	Production of phyto-plankton	Measure of animal population
Wastwater	5.2	73	9.0	1,100	194
Ennerdale	5.4	66	8.3	4,492	515
Crummock	8.0	47	8.0	5,218	847
Coniston	21.8	27	5.4	38,350	1,294
Windermere	29.4	28	5.5	136,596	2,815
Bassenthwaite	29.4	29	2.2	205,702	2,508
Esthwaite	45.4	12	3.1	336,466	5,987

(1) Phytoplankton productivity measured as mg dry weight per 1000 litres of
lake water
(2) Animal population measured as the number of animals collected in 100
minutes in a stony substrate at the lake margin

*Table 3 Indicators of the productivity of some Cumbrian lakes. (Data:
lecture by T.T. Macan, and T.T. Macan and E.B. Worthington,* Life in
Lakes and Rivers, *1972.)*

Incidentally, whilst it is unlikely that there are many waters more
oligotrophic than Wastwater in the British Isles, there are many
more eutrophic waters than Esthwaite. Numerous lowland reservoirs (e.g. Grafham and Draycote), set in the midst of rich farmland
and having a huge growth of plants, are more productive, as are the
rich alkaline lakes of Ireland.
    There is, however, a problem if eutrophication goes too far. Too
great an algal bloom and weed bed growth means that at night, in
periods of hot summer weather, the plants will remove so much
oxygen from the water by their respiratory processes that the water
will become depleted of oxygen and deaths of fish will occur. Over-
eutrophication has happened from time to time in several lowland

trout fisheries, sometimes with disastrous consequences. Fortunately, in the bigger lakes, this is less likely to occur.

Another interesting point worth making here is that very large natural lakes can often be considered as two separate waters. To take Windermere as an example, the North Basin of this lake, fed by streams draining high uncultivated mountains, is less productive than the South Basin which is set amid lower, softer countryside and benefits from the effects of salts added from the sewage works of Windermere town, Bowness and other small villages. The same features are seen in Loch Lomond.

Effects of shape and depth   Having ascertained that stillwaters vary in their productivity, the effects of shape and depth on the plants, animals and trout in the lake can now be examined.

Most stillwaters used as trout fisheries become *stratified* in summer—a feature that has important implications for the trout and for the angler.

During spring, as sunlight increases in both intensity and duration, the surface layer of the lake water absorbs the light energy. Some of it is used by phytoplankton in photosynthesis and the phytoplankton population increases to reach a maximum that depends, as already seen, on the quantity of mineral nutrients dissolved in the water. The greater the depth the light penetrates, the deeper that warm layer, but, of course, the more phytoplankton, the smaller the depth to which the light can penetrate.

As the summer proceeds and light intensity continues to increase, that warm surface layer becomes deeper. This productive zone is known as the epilimnion (meaning 'upper' or 'outer lake'). The deeper, dark zone of the lake, above the lake bed, never receives an input of light energy so it hardly warms up at all, rarely rising more than a few degrees centigrade above the winter low. The deep, dark cold layer is referred to as the hypolimnion (i.e. 'lower lake'). Between the warm light epilimnion and the cold dark hypolimnion is a zone of transition, the thermocline. When travelling down in the thermocline from the epilimnion temperature falls rapidly to that of the hypolimnion.

Generally speaking, stratification occurs from late May or early June through to September or early October, when sunlight is insufficient to maintain the high temperature of the epilimnion, and the high winds and cool rainfall of autumn combine to mix the lake water, thus breaking the stratification. Even in summer, a period of gales can temporarily mix the water, but when this happens the lake becomes stratified once more on the return of hot sunny weather.

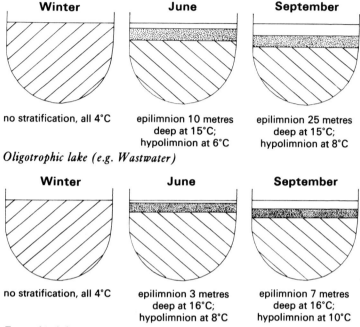

Winter	June	September
no stratification, all 4°C	epilimnion 10 metres deep at 15°C; hypolimnion at 6°C	epilimnion 25 metres deep at 15°C; hypolimnion at 8°C

Oligotrophic lake (e.g. Wastwater)

Winter	June	September
no stratification, all 4°C	epilimnion 3 metres deep at 16°C; hypolimnion at 8°C	epilimnion 7 metres deep at 16°C; hypolimnion at 10°C

Eutrophic lake (e.g. Esthwaite)

It is in the warm epilimnion that the huge productivity of phytoplankton occurs during summer and early autumn. Clouds of zooplankton, tiny crustaceans that include *Daphnia* and *Cyclops*, feed and grow on this phytoplankton. Some larger carnivorous invertebrates (e.g. phantom-fly larvae) feed on the zooplankton and the trout will feed on both zooplankton and carnivorous invertebrates. As the populations of these small drifting invertebrates increase, the more important they become as a food source for the trout. Thus it is in the more productive lakes, such as Esthwaite in Cumbria, Malham Tarn in the Pennines, the limestone lakes of Ireland and the reservoirs of the English lowlands, that during summer trout will seek out the high concentrations of *Daphnia* and will feed less in the lake margins. It is no accident that many anglers on some of the Cumbrian lakes regard angling from the bank a waste of time after early June, and on several Irish lakes they regard trout fishing as difficult once the mayfly season is over (i.e. late June), for this coincides with the peaking of the zooplankton populations.

Effect of wind   It has long been accepted that, when fishing from the lake shore, it is more profitable to fish into the breeze than fish with the breeze at one's back, even though casting may be a bit more difficult. Many writers have argued, with some justification, that this is because the fish will be lying off the windward shore, waiting for food to be drifted across to them. The artificial fly will therefore be cast over where the fish should be lying and will be brought back in the retrieve more naturally along the line of the drift.

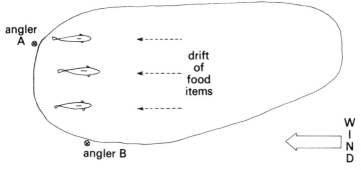

Angler at A casts into the wind and his flies drift back towards him and the waiting fish. Alternatively, if the wind is too strong the angler casts from B, across the wind, and allows the surface drift to carry his flies round to the fish

All this is true, but there is another factor that contributes to the wind-swept shore being the best—the effect of a wind on stratification.

The wind causes the epilimnion to drift, resulting in a much deeper epilimnion off the windward shore. The temporarily deeper epilimnion at this point will have a larger food supply (in terms of zooplankton and smaller animals feeding on the zooplankton) and here will be the trout. In the lake off the lee shore the epilimnion will be correspondingly shallow. Thus there will be less food off this shore and, consequently, fewer trout.

One summer's day in the North Bay of Windermere I encountered a classic example of epilimnion drift. The stiff wind was blowing directly across the lake towards the Low Wood–Bowness shore. I followed an erratic drift with difficulty, alternating spells of hard rowing into the waves and wind. As can be seen from the diagram on page 40 I caught fish only along the windward shore (three char and eight trout) and close to two small islands (three trout). Those fish taken close to the shore, in that tilted, deeper epilimnion zone, had stomachs packed with zooplankton.

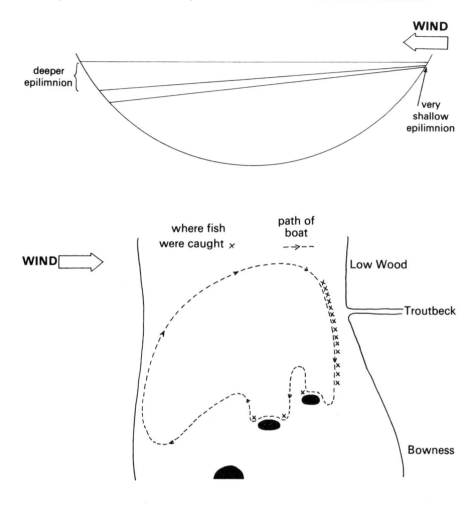

Migration of zooplankton One final point regarding zooplankton: P. Ullyott investigated the *Cyclops* and *Daphnia* populations of Windermere and found, in summer, that they followed a quite distinct vertical migration through the epilimnion. Over a typical 24-hour cycle the pattern is as follows:

around midnight—the population is concentrated in the top 5 metres;

at dawn (0400 hrs)—the majority are at a depth of 10–20 metres;

at midday—the majority of the zooplankton lie 30–40 metres deep (in the thermocline);

at dusk (2200 hrs)—they have migrated to 10 metres below the water surface;

at midnight—they are back in the top 5 metres.

Further investigation suggested that the zooplankton migrate vertically under the influence of varying light intensities; i.e. they attempt to remain in constant (low) light conditions and to do this must move into deeper (darker) water when the sunlight increases and back to shallower depths as sunlight decreases. It follows, therefore, that in clearer, more transparent, water the zooplankton (and trout if they are feeding on zooplankton) will move much deeper during the day, whereas in cloudier, more eutrophic, waters they will not migrate to as great a depth. All of this can have a great bearing on summer stillwater trout fishing.

First of all, most anglers are aware of the greater amount of surface activity of stillwater trout at night during hot midsummer weather, even though little in the way of food can be seen on or in the water. The answer seems to be that the zooplankton (and with them the trout) have arrived back at the surface.

Secondly, in mid-summer if we suspect that trout are taking food from the zooplankton then the depth at which they will be feeding will depend on the transparency of the water—the clearer the water, the deeper the fish will be and the more turbid the water, the shallower they will be. This is no real problem for a eutrophic lake such as Esthwaite, Draycote or Grafham. In these the trout are likely to be no more than 5–10 metres down at midday and a very fast-sinking line will reach them. However, in less eutrophic or oligotrophic lakes they might be 20 or more metres below the surface and out of range of the fly fisher's lures. Is it any wonder that the char fishers of Windermere use heavy leads and a series of spinners set at a range of depths to find out where the charr are feeding (see Chapter 10) or that on many Scottish lochs trolling a heavy lure is a popular and successful method of taking trout in mid-summer?

Thirdly, and most of us are only too aware of this, lake trout fishing is harder on hot, bright summer days than on cooler, dull days. It is not surprising really, if the trout are taking most of their food from the clouds of zooplankton! On a dull day the zooplankton will not move as deep to attain the appropriate dull light intensity that they seek, and neither will the trout. Thus the trout are more likely to encounter the angler's lure on dull days but not on bright days when they are at too great a depth.

Food sources in the hypolimnion   Whilst dealing with the deep open water zone it is probably timely to answer a question that you may have been wanting to ask! What about the hypolimnion and lake bed? Won't the trout find food there, despite the darkness, low temperatures and depth?

In oligotrophic lakes the trout may well move into the depths of the hypolimnion but food will be very scarce there. Due to the lack of light there are no plants and so there will be no real productivity. All that will arrive to provide food for animals will be dead planktonic organisms that have sunk to the bottom from the epilimnion, and accordingly animal life at these depths will be sparse. C. F. Humphries, for example, found midge larvae, pea mussels, phantom-fly larvae, aquatic worms and leeches in the darkest depths of Windermere. All these are animals that will feed on what rains down from above, but the densities Humphries found were exceedingly small.

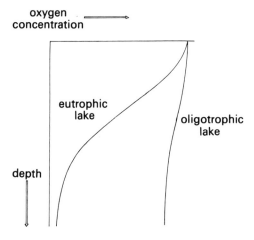

The graph, showing how oxygen dissolved in the lake water decreases with depth, illustrates the contrast between eutrophic and oligotrophic lakes. In the epilimnion the levels are similar in both types of lake, but in the hypolimnion the eutrophic lake is almost devoid of oxygen (and is inhospitable to trout). This is not the case in the oligotrophic lake where oxygen levels in the deepest parts are only fractionally lower than surface concentrations

In very eutrophic waters, where there is more productivity in the epilimnion, the amount of dead matter falling into the hypolimnion can be quite large. So much so that the effects of bacterial action on this organic matter may render the hypolimnion anaerobic (deficient of oxygen). In such circumstances the trout will be effectively excluded from the hypolimnion.

Again, there is a consequence for the angler. In obviously rich productive waters in summer weather the fish are unlikely to be lying on the bottom in very deep water. With an oxygen-deficient hypolimnion only eight metres or so beneath the surface, in July and August there seems no point in using the lead-core line to take the fly down to this depth. A sinker that takes the fly to the thermocline/epilimnion boundary seems far more sensible—and so it is!

One year I was fishing a small but very deep put-and-take fishery for the third time. On the first two visits the rainbows, certainly the larger ones, had sulked close to the bottom. A fast-sink line and a sinking time of 1 minute 45 seconds were needed to get the lure down to the fish. Anglers fishing floating or sink-tip lines had to be content with the smaller fish that were closer to the surface. However, on this third visit, in late July, things had changed. Prolonged hot bright weather had caused the water to become stratified and in the warm epilimnion there were masses of algae. By dangling a big white lure from the dam, to check for water visibility, I reckoned that the epilimnion was only about five metres deep and that the hypolimnion would be close to anaerobic. Yet no fish showed at the surface. I put on the slow-sinker and a small yellow lure. The fish were there, right enough, four metres down (sinking time 25 seconds). It took me an hour to work this out! In the next $2\frac{1}{2}$ hours I had 16 rainbows and kept my limit of four for 12 lb (5.5 kg). Then I went home. Only two other anglers, who had been experimenting like me, had fish. Most of the rest were using ultra-fast sinkers (that had worked so well only a few weeks before) that took their lures into the now inhospitable depths of the hypolimnion.

Lake contours Of course a lot of trout food (the majority in spring and late autumn) is taken from the shallower margins of the lake edge, from submerged reefs and from weed beds in shallower bays. Such zones depend, for their productivity, on sunlight reaching the lake bed so that algae and rooted water weeds can photosynthesise and provide food for invertebrates and smaller fish on which the trout prey. The two factors of light penetration and angle at which the lake bed shelves are important here.

In very eutrophic waters light penetration will be rarely more than three metres, possibly less. Therefore, rooted green plants and algae, together with their associated animal life, will be within the 0–3 metre depth contours. In oligotrophic lakes, where sufficient light can penetrate to 5 metres and more the water weeds (though sparser than in the eutrophic lake) will occur to greater depths. So, some knowledge of the underwater contours and a general idea of the lake's productivity will help to find the weed beds, trout foods and trout. At the same time it should not be forgotten that the shallower the water is the more light will reach the plant life; the more plant life there is the more animal life there will be and thus more trout food.

As long ago as 1934 H. P. Moon analysed this effect for Windermere where maximum light penetration is about 5.5 metres. He found that in the margin or littoral zone water depth (0–2 metres) there were the widest variety and highest densities (see table 4) of invertebrates (potential trout food). Beyond this margin, in the 'sub-littoral zone', where the water was deeper than 2 metres, there was less variety and the densities of invertebrates declined rapidly with depth.

Lake margins   There have been few similar studies since Moon's, due in the main to the difficulties of sampling in deep water. However, in those studies which have been undertaken the pattern has always been the same. It must be concluded, therefore, that the trout will take the bulk of their food from the shallow water. In Windermere this comprises all the areas where the water is up to 2 or 3 metres deep, but in more eutrophic lakes the effective depth is possibly less. Yet how often do we come across anglers wading out, through the productive margin, to cast into less productive water, and as they do so disturbing the trout that were (and ought to be) feeding close to the bank? How foolish!

The desire to wade seems to come from two mistaken beliefs:
1. That all the trout are out in the middle of the lake. This is *not* often true! And if it were, would wading really help? No! A boat would be the only answer.
2. That trout do not occur in very shallow water. *Not true!* I remember one evening, for example, on Entwistle Reservoir, when huge numbers of wild brownies and stocked rainbows were feeding in water no more than a foot (30 cm) deep.
I feel that wading ought to be banned on all stillwaters for there is rarely any good reason for it. It is unsporting in that it disturbs

	Littoral zone (0–2 m depth) %	Sublittoral zone (2 m plus depth) %
Several caddis larvae species	46	2
Several upwinged fly nymph species	6	19*
Two species of stonefly nymph	2	0
Alderfly larva	0	5
Midge (chironomid) larvae	15	30
Snails	23	6
Pea mussel	0	27
Shrimp	3	2
Aquatic worms	1	4
Leeches	1	4
Density of animals (individuals per square metre)	1300	883 at 3 metres 110 at 10 metres 30 at 13 metres

*these were *Caenis* (the tiny angler's curse)

Table 4 Density and variety of invertebrates at various depths in the margins of Windermere (after H.P. Moon). The importance of most larger invertebrates as trout foods is well known to all anglers. However, the nymphs of Caenis and the tiny larvae of the midges, which form a large part of the deeper water populations, are of little value to the trout as they live, hidden away, in burrows in the silt of the lake bed.

the fish and the sport of other anglers. It demonstrates a complete lack of understanding of trout behaviour.

The advantage of a boat when fishing the more productive shallows may not be obvious. How often do we hear, in spring, that the bank fishers are doing as well as or better than the boat anglers? The bank anglers certainly will do better if the boat anglers persist in casting over deep, unproductive or less productive water. However, a drift parallel to the bank, along the shallow contours, will enable a boat angler to cover far more of the productive water than can a bank angler. Similarly, wide shallow bays that have thick weedbeds can be thoroughly searched from a slow-drifting boat and, of course, should there be offshore shoals, islands or weedbeds these, too, will harbour large invertebrate populations and will be attractive to the feeding trout. The land-based angler cannot fish these.

It should also be remembered that the steeper the lake bed is the narrower the productive margin will be. In a steep-sided glacial lake or Pennine reservoir it might be only 5 or 10 metres wide, whereas in the shallow-shelving edge of an English Midlands reservoir or an Irish limestone lough the effective margin might be hundreds of metres wide. At the extreme, in a very shallow water body (such as some of the Hebridean lochans), the depth may be such that light can penetrate to the entire lake bed so that the water never stratifies and all the lake can be considered 'margin'.

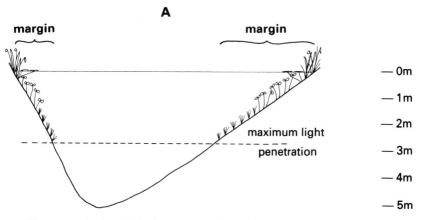

The steeper the lake bed, the narrower the productive margin

In this case the lake is too shallow for stratification and light penetrates all the bed of the lake. Such waters are often weed-choked by mid-summer

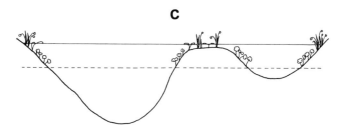

Lakes with offshore shoals and islands have a larger productive margin, but one that must be fished from a boat. Knowledge of underwater contours is essential if the angler is to find and exploit these likely 'hot-spots'

One final point whilst on the subject of productivity in the shallower margins of lakes. The majority of stillwater anglers in Britain fish reservoirs. In some of these reservoirs the water is not topped up from nearby rivers or bore-holes (as is the case with pump-storage reservoirs) and, consequently, during droughts when the feeder streams fail to bring in sufficient water, the level drops quickly. This may be such that what would normally be considered 'the productive littoral zones' are left high and dry. On some of the Pennine reservoirs that I know well (e.g. Stocks, Entwistle and Ladybower) this can be almost an annual occurrence so that no real marginal vegetation can develop and so there is never a large and diverse food supply available for the trout. These waters are also oligotrophic and therefore produce very small amounts of phytoplankton and, consequently, zooplankton on which the trout might feed. Such reservoirs are very hard on the fish, especially stocked rainbow trout (see Chapter 3) which have insufficient food to maintain their condition. They are also frustrating for the angler who is often wasting his time trying to match with his fly what the trout are feeding on.

Acid waters

In recent years a great deal of publicity has surrounded the apparently new problem of acidification of both rivers and lakes in parts of Britain. It has long been known that acid waters are less productive than neutral or slightly alkaline waters. Why this should be has been the subject of argument and investigation for years. The problem has been difficult to analyse because waters that are naturally acidic tend to have a low mineral salt level, so productivity of trout food and growth of the trout will obviously be low. However, some experimental work has demonstrated that, all other factors being equal, trout raised in slightly acidic conditions will respire and grow more slowly than trout raised in water that is alkaline, which indicates that acidity directly affects the trout. However, in areas where the lakes are already slightly acidic (for instance, some on the hard resistant rocks of Galloway) extra acid appears to have been added by 'acid rain'. Evidence exists that this unnaturally high acidity increases the solubility, in the water percolating through the catchment area, of poisonous metals (e.g. aluminium). Whether this is the case or not, such waters have suffered a decline of invertebrates and fish stocks, and remaining fish are reported as 'stunted' or 'malformed'. Some waters even lack fish altogether.

So far I have dealt with the aquatic environment as far as it will affect trout food supplies, the trout themselves and, consequently, the trout angler. This is quite reasonable, for the vast majority of trout food will come from animals that are either wholly aquatic (e.g. *Daphnia*, shrimps, corixids, small fish) or partially aquatic (e.g. sedges, upwinged flies, stoneflies, midges). However, many other food items may find their way onto the lake—daddy-long-legs from adjacent pastures, beetles from nearby woodland or moorland, moths from lakeside forests. Such will depend on the lake's surroundings. No matter how productive the water, if the fall of land-bred insects is large enough the trout will always take advantage of the bonus.

Whilst the stillwater angler ought to be conscious of what is going on beneath the water surface and should act accordingly for most of the trout season, he must also be aware of the possibility of trout being temporarily switched on to food that has originated away from the lake. Through the season the most successful angler is the one who is alert and prepared for any possibility.

3
The Fish

'How much does the planted takable fish add to the angler's sport? In a heavily fished water or one where indigenous trout are few it may make all the difference between some sport and none at all!'

W. Frost & M. Brown, *The Trout*, 1967

Two species of trout dominate the sport of stillwater trout fishing:
1. the brown trout, *Salmo trutta*, and
2. the rainbow trout, *Salmo gairdneri*.

Brown trout

The brown trout, Britain's native trout, has in past years been divided into a number of species, races and forms, although essentially they are all members of the one species. The sea trout is nothing more than a migratory brown trout that, like the salmon, leaves the river for the sea where it grows very rapidly before returning to the river to spawn. It must be remembered that all brown trout are, to some extent, migratory. Those in lakes migrate to feeder streams in late summer and autumn to spawn, returning to the lake when breeding is over in late winter and early spring. River trout move upstream to breed, sometimes passing through lakes on their journeys, and some river trout are almost sea trout in that they will move down into the river estuary to feed through the summer (these are usually referred to as 'slob trout', 'estuarine trout' or 'bull trout').

The greatest number of so-called 'varieties' of brown trout have been described from lakes where, over the centuries, inbreeding and adaptation through natural selection have resulted in trout that are said to be characteristic of each lake or series of similar lakes. The best known of these are probably the *ferox* or great lake trout, the gillaroo, and the Loch Leven trout. The *ferox* is really nothing more than a huge brownie, weighing usually 5 lb ($2\frac{1}{4}$ kg) or more, that normally lives in large, deep lochs or lakes and is presumed to be a 'cannibal' fish. The gillaroo, which occurs in some Irish loughs, is an incredibly beautiful, gaudy fish with yellow- and brown-patterned back and golden belly. The Loch Leven trout is a predominantly silver trout with black spots; it has been used by fish farms in the production of brown trout for stocking both rivers and lakes. **This strain is now found throughout Britain, sometimes**

Wild brownies averaging 6oz (170g), from an oligotrophic Scottish loch

A brace of two-pounders from a eutrophic limestone lake

hybridised with the local population. However, although these are regarded by some as distinct types, most lakes have a head of trout that is extremely variable. For instance, my son and I took a bag of 21 brown trout from one Hebridean loch in which no two fish were identical; one showed great similarity with the Irish gillaroo and two could have been described as Loch Leven fish. Similarly, in some of the unstocked Cumbrian lakes it is possible to catch, in one day, trout that range in colour from a dark steel-blue, through silver ('Loch Leven type'), an orange-brown colour with orange spots, to more of a river type of brownie with yellow belly, dark brown back and deep red spots. The same sort of variation can be found amongst trout from one particular lake in their meat colour, some having the red colour of fresh-run salmon, others a pure white flesh as found in cod and plaice. In such wild fish the red colour is presumed to be a result of a large amount of crustaceans (shrimps, *Daphnia*, etc.) in the diet which contain carotenes—orange-red pigments. So popular are such red-fleshed fish that some trout farmers supplement the diet of their stew-pond trout with carotenoids to produce this more pleasing and appetising appearance.

Natural stock   Some trout waters have never been stocked with brown trout and are dependent on natural reproductive output to replace those fish removed by anglers, other predators and disease. These comprise the overwhelming majority of Scottish, Cumbrian, Irish and upland Welsh waters. In others the natural population is supplemented by artificial stocking of brownies raised in fish farms. These include, for example, many Pennine reservoirs where the natural stock originated in the river or stream that was dammed during the reservoir construction. (One very interesting example is Stocks Reservoir, high in the Bowland Fells. Here the beautiful wild trout are a 'hybrid' between river brown trout and sea trout that were trapped when the dam across the river Hodder was completed in 1930.) Some of the smaller Cumbrian lakes and lowland Welsh llyns, and some smaller Scottish lochs where angling pressure is high due to the close proximity of the loch to the cities, have also received artificial stocking. Even that pinnacle of loch fishing, Loch Leven, has received stockings with its own strain from fish farms.

In all these waters the trout are merely supplements to the natural head of fish, although they are obviously very important for the angler and, of course, those that remain after the fishing season in which they were stocked will join the natural head by spawning in the feeder streams. There are also a lot of waters that have never, and would never, contain brown trout unless they were stocked and, due to the lack of suitable spawning grounds, will never have an established self-regenerating population. In such lakes the head of fish must be maintained by repeated stocking as anglers, other predators or disease reduce it.

Replenishment   The advantage of a water replenishing its own stocks is obvious. The natural recruitment is free and the fish are attuned from birth to the natural foods present in the water. Thus the fishing is, possibly, more interesting in that fly choice is often crucial for success. It can take stocked brown trout quite a while to become accustomed to wild foods so that they will naïvely snatch at any old fly or lure just after they have been put in the water. There is, however, a problem as far as some anglers and commercial fishery owners are concerned regarding the water stocking itself naturally. That problem is one of size and number of trout. In relatively unproductive oligotrophic lakes the indigenous wild brown trout tend to be small and nowadays, with the domination of the stillwater angling scene based largely on the lowland lakes of

England where a pounder is a small stockie, there is a tendency for many anglers to look down their noses at the small-fish waters. This is a pity, for the wild brown trout fight proportionally much harder than do their larger stock-farm brethren.

Table 5 gives examples of trout growth rates, which have been expressed in terms of length attained at the age of three years (from scale readings), from various waters throughout the British Isles, arranged in ascending order of productivity. In the barren waters of northern Scotland and the Scottish Western Isles, some of the lakes of Cumbria and gritstone moorland resevoirs in the Pennines (as shown by Entwistle) trout are very small at this age. In fact, they would not be takable as far as most angling clubs or fishery rules are concerned, which usually impose a 10- or 12-inch (25–30 cm) limit. However, in the more productive waters of lowland Scotland (Loch Leven), the rich limestone water of Malham Tarn and the famous limestone Irish loughs trout are at a takable size at three years of age. The longer trout need to reach takable size in a water, the fewer there will be, proportionally, to make that actual size because of natural annual losses. In unproductive waters a trout of 12 inches (30 cm) may be considered quite a rare specimen fish, whereas in productive lakes it would be nothing out of the ordinary.

	Inches	Centimetres
Entwistle Reservoir	5.9	14.8
Wastwater	6.1	15.2
Loch Urrahag	6.6	16.2
Loch Fadagoa	6.8	17.1
Loch Tay	6.9	17.3
Loch Lomond	7.9	19.8
Windermere	8.5	21.3
Loch Leven	11.1	27.5
Malham Tarn	11.4	28.5
Lough Derg	11.6	29.0
Lough Mask	11.7	29.3
Lough Corrib	11.9	29.7
Lough Sheelin	12.9	32.5
Lough Derravaragh	13.0	32.7

Table 5 Average length of wild brown trout at three years of age.

In trout farms where fish are fed on high protein food brown trout reach a standard 12 inches (30 cm) in around two years. If these are considered by anglers to be 'standard' fish, then I suppose

A stock brownie of 7½lb (3.4kg)

that wild trout in most waters will be considered small fry. With another year or two in the fish farm the brown trout can be stocked at weights which would, in waters relying on natural breeding output to supplement the stocks, be considered huge and possibly *ferox*. It is a sobering thought that, in one year, more brown trout of over 3 lb (1.4 kg) are taken from a few reservoirs of the English Midlands than from all the unstocked lakes of Cumbria and, possibly, Scottish lochs as well!

Rainbow trout

The rainbow trout, a native of the Sacramento river area of California, was first introduced into Britain in 1882. Besides its novelty value, from the start the rainbow trout had an advantage over the brownie for stocking purposes in that it showed a much more rapid growth, although it required a larger food supply. There was the problem, however, because it is primarily a river trout, of its strong migratory tendencies: many earlier attempts to stock with rainbows were frustrated by the fish finding lake outlets and departing.

Careful selection for faster and larger growth has paid off. Initially, in the 1880s, a $1\frac{1}{2}$ lb (0.65 kg) fish was a standard large fish and from a four-year-old female of this size 800–1200 eggs could be obtained to produce the next generation. Today the fish mature much earlier (at two years of age) and grow more quickly so that brood-fish (from which eggs and sperm are obtained) and the fish used to stock waters are much bigger. Thus from a large two-year-old female 5000 or more eggs can be obtained and, in almost half the time that it takes to raise brown trout to these sizes, rainbow trout reach 12 inches (30 cm) at about one year. At 18 months of age (when they are frequently employed for stocking many waters) they weigh up to $1\frac{1}{2}$ lb (0.68 kg) and reach up to 16 inches (40 cm) in length. Rainbow trout really are rapid converters of food into flesh. They are now one of the cheapest of fish on the fishmonger's slab. No wonder that they figure supreme as far as fish farms, fishery managers and many stillwater trout anglers are concerned.

Not surprisingly there have been problems in developing the stockie rainbow for angling purposes. One is that this fish will not breed in most British waters, certainly stillwaters. Hen fish that had overwintered in the reservoirs often became flaccid and egg-bound, and the cock fish developed their black courting-livery and grotesque shape which provided a sad spectacle for the successful angler. Efforts have been made to overcome this. Sterile hybrids, crosses between rainbow trout and American brook trout and known as 'cheetah trout', provided one answer, but a better solution has come more recently in the form of sterile 'triploid' rainbow trout. Stocking with these has been quite successful.

Incidentally, a 'triploid' is a fish that has an extra set of chromosomes. All animals normally have a double set of chromosomes in each body cell, and are therefore termed *diploid*. Man, for example, has two sets of 23 chromosomes (= 46). These chromosomes carry the genes that control growth and development of the body. When sperms and eggs are formed they contain a single set of chromosomes (referred to as *haploid*). The new individual obtains its diploid number of chromosomes as one set from its mother (in the egg) and one set from its father (in the sperm). To return to the example of man, sperm and egg each carry 23 chromosomes so that the offspring has the full diploid complement of 46. The manufacture of viable sperm and eggs, and the acquisition of sexual maturity, is a complicated process. If the cells in the body are not diploid then, save in very rare instances, the body cannot make sperms or eggs and can not become sexually mature.

A rainbow trout of 7lb 15oz (3.6kg). Rainbows are usually stocked at about 1½lb (680g). Growth of stocked rainbow trout depends heavily on the water's productivity

Thus, by producing rainbows with three sets of chromosomes (*triploids*) the fish-breeders have produced trout which are sterile and which cannot come into breeding condition.

So, the stocked rainbow trout is the bread and butter of the majority of reservoir and small fishery anglers and is the main stock in most other commercial trout fisheries, including lowland lochs, some Welsh llyns and smaller Irish loughs where wild brown trout might also occur. Many 'big fish' waters, such as Avington, receive rainbows (as well as other trout species) at weights well in excess of 10 lb (4 kg).

Char

Stocked brook trout (speckled char). Many put-and-take fisheries stock with brookies to provide variety in the anglers' bags. However, this is a species that is unlikely to oust the brown and rainbow trouts from being the stillwater anglers' main quarry

Other salmonids occur in some British stillwaters. The *speckled char* (or *American brook trout*), reared in fish farms, has become fairly popular as an alternative to the stocked brown and rainbow trout. Many anglers do not rate the brook trout at all highly as a sporting fish, likening its fighting ability to that of a bream or 'two-pound jam jar full of water'! Some might disagree, but the brook trout is also more expensive than the rainbow from the fish

farm. For these reasons it is unlikely that the brookie will oust the
rainbow and brownie as numbers one and two respectively for
stocking stillwaters.

Many glacial upland lakes have *char* or *whitefish* (schelly,
gwyniadd, vendace, powan). In some of these lakes these species
will, on occasion, rise to the fly, but they are more often taken by
bait-fishing or spinning. Also *grayling* occur in Llyn Tegid (Lake
Bala) and Gouthwaite Reservoir. Several lakes also have excellent
runs through them of *salmon* and *sea trout*, including Lochs Tay,
Ness and Maree and Loughs Corrib and Mask.

Water productivity and trout growth

As was explained earlier, in wild brown trout fisheries the head of
fish and size of fish are determined by the productivity of the water.

> 'If it is accepted that a stunted fish population is usually due to an
> insufficient food supply, there are certain implications which are not
> generally accepted by those who practise fishery management. The
> first is that, since any one body of water can obviously support a
> certain weight of fish and no more, the weight of each fish will
> depend on the total number of fish present. For example, if a pond
> can support 100 lb of fish, it may contain 400 fish weighing $\frac{1}{4}$ lb each,
> 100 fish weighing 1 lb each, or 25 4-pounders.'
>
> T. T. Macan & E. B. Worthington, *Life in Lakes and Rivers*.

However, merely killing half of the fish in a water where they are
tiny, stunted specimens will not solve the problem. The reproductive output will quickly replace those removed so that the same
population of tiny trout will ensue. Growth will not necessarily
result from the cull, even in the short term. An unproductive water
produces so little food that the benefits of a greater share for those
that remain immediately after the cull would be lost by the effort
they would have to make to collect that extra food. Experiments
have been carried out in smaller fisheries to attempt to increase
overall productivity of the water by adding fertilisers and lime. The
results of these have suggested that this would succeed in increasing, through the food web, the size of the trout. However, the
amounts of fertilisers that would have to be added to make a really
significant increase are prohibitively expensive.

> 'Academic research .. has shown that from 1000 lb of vegetation
> one should hope to obtain 100 lb of herbivores, 10 lb of primary

carnivores and 1 lb of secondary carnivores, which is what a fish is likely to be.'

Macan & Worthington, Life in Lakes and Rivers.

How much fertiliser is needed to increase the vegetation of a small tarn or reservoir by 1000 lb, and will the outcome of a lb increase in the fish stock make the expenditure worthwhile? I suggest not!

In all stillwaters, whether natural or stocked, both the angler and fishery owner want to see the fish grow, and growth comes from food. Except for those small fisheries where the manager supplements the natural food supply of the water with large daily helpings of trout pellets, food is a result of the water's productivity.

A proportion of the food that a trout takes will do no more than maintain its body weight and condition, and the amount of food needed to do just this depends on the temperature of the lake water. For instance, a trout living in water at 20°C (not unusual high summer conditions) will need, just to live, three times the amount of food than it does at 5°C. If this food is not available then in the short term the fish will quickly lose condition, and in the long term it will die. Keepers stocking oligotrophic waters with rainbow trout have often stumbled over this pitfall, especially in prolonged hot summers (e.g. 1976, 1984).

For three years Geoff Haslam, Peter and I fished a range of acidic unproductive Pennine reservoirs that had been stocked mostly with 12-inch (30 cm) rainbow trout which scaled around the pound mark. It was clear these waters were unproductive, not only from the extreme scarcity of freshwater plants and invertebrates (i.e. there was little trout food) but also from the fact that the wild brown trout rarely reached more than 8–10 inches (20–25 cm). The effect of this sparsity of food on the rainbow trout was incredible. They could not find enough food to maintain the condition at which they were stocked: they lost weight rapidly and within eight weeks of being stocked some scaled less than half their original weight and resembled thin caricatures of their former selves. For example:

12″ (30 cm) weighed	5 oz (60 g)
12″ (30 cm) „	6 oz (85 g)
14″ (35 cm) „	7 oz (165 g)
14″ (35 cm) „	12 oz (285 g)
16″ (40 cm) „	13 oz (310 g)
17″ (42.5 cm) „	1 lb 2 oz (430 g)

Stocking a stillwater. Most stock fish are removed within a few weeks of stocking. This means that angling will be very difficult after a while in waters where stocking occurs only once or twice during the season. It is not the case where stocking occurs weekly or daily

In a productive water such as Grafham or Draycote the last two would have scaled nearer the three-pound mark and would have been growing quickly. Altogether we caught 27 rainbow trout showing such sad condition over the three years. Of course it might be argued that this does not really matter in a stocked put-and-take trout fishery where probably 90% of the trout are caught within a few weeks of stocking, but one of the challenges of fishing is to try to entice the bigger fish or the more wily fish. To know that the fish will be the same size as when they were stocked, and that if one which has been in the lake for more than a few weeks is caught it will have deteriorated in quality, does not make for the thrill and expectation normally associated with angling.

When there *is* a surplus of food for the trout then growth will follow, for about 25% of the food taken by trout over and above that needed to maintain current size and condition is usually converted into growth (trout flesh). This is where the larger reservoirs of the English lowland and the big Irish alkaline loughs score heavily, as the following extracts indicate.

'Grafham grows 12-inch stock rainbows to $1\frac{1}{2}$ lb in just two months. In three months they are 2 lb and by the end of the season those 12-inch stockies become 3 lb bars of silver dynamite.'

'Draycote (April)
Nearly 12,000 stock fish have gone in since last season, but I'm thinking more about the 6,000 rainbows which were introduced last September. About 2,500 were caught before the end of the season, some probably failed to survive the winter, but there must be 3,000 or so left, and by now they must weigh 2 to $2\frac{1}{2}$ lb.'

Bob Church, *Reservoir Trout Fishing*, 1977

And of the wild brown trout in the large limestone loughs of Ireland it has been said:

'Lakes of this sub-type produce very fast-growing, thickset, silvery trout, the average size of which may be 2 lb or over. Trout of 4 lb or 5 lb and over will likely feature in any catch of half a dozen fish and 8 lb fish often come the way of the dry fly angler.'

E. J. Malone, *Irish Trout and Salmon Flies*, 1984

What a pity that such fisheries are so few!

4
Stillwater Flies:
Attractors and Deceivers

'It is somewhat difficult to decide to what extent the angler should be versed in the entomology of the loch, but I think that most will agree that a little knowledge at least of the subject is essential ... Some there are, as we are all aware, who profess to be content to fish with a cast of flies selected after some sort of plan, or even chosen at random by themselves perhaps, or, it may be, by some tackle dealer. It matters little to them what the flies are, and, they declare, the trout are no more particular.'

R. C. Bridgett, *Loch Fishing in Theory and Practice*, 1924

'As for me, I'm lazy. I started fishing thirty-five years ago with three size 14 pattern loch flies and have continued in the same style ever since. During the course of the season I rarely change either size or pattern and have no cause for complaint.'

Bruce Sandison, *The Trout Lochs of Scotland*, 1983

To the newcomer to stillwater trout fishing the numbers of lures, nymphs, wet flies and dry flies that exist must seem enormous and bewildering, and yet each year more and more new patterns, often involving newfangled materials, are added to the list. Some flies gain in popularity and then, after a year or so, seem to disappear almost as quickly as a different fad comes on the scene. This year it will be antron, next year fluorescent chenille, the year after glitter yarn, the year after sparkle yarn...*ad infinitum*. Marabous and Baby Dolls are replaced by Dog Nobblers and Frog Nobblers! What next?

Let's not beat around the bush. We go fishing to catch fish and when fly fishing it is our fly that does the catching. So Bruce Sandison has found three size 14 standard loch flies that will do nicely. Well and good. And there is, I believe, a gentleman who fishes Draycote regularly and catches his fair share of trout, and more besides, all on one fly, a yellow Dog Nobbler. Splendid. If the one-cast or one-fly man is happy with his sport then no one can complain, least of all him. However, there may be days when the one cast or one fly does not work, or there may be waters where it does not work. Alternative patterns must then be available. Besides, one of the greatest pleasures of being a fly fisher is the psychological satisfaction of having a lot of fly patterns, and of changing fly and tactics—possibly not to increase the catch rate, but just for a change or to boost morale when conditions are difficult.

Selective feeding

From my comments so far it may be implied that stillwater trout are by no means as selective or fastidious as are river or brook trout. There are some, however, who would encourage us to believe that stillwater trout are very selective and that anglers really need a wide range of artificial patterns to imitate accurately just about every invertebrate, amphibian and small fish that swims in our lochs, lakes and reservoirs, and every land-bred animal that might end up on the water.

In his classic book *Lake Flies and their Imitations*, C. F. Walker wrote:

'Discussing the question of selective feeding on the hypothesis that a trout contained more than 60 per cent of one type of food had been exercising the power of selection, he [K. R. Allen in 'Some observations on the Biology of Trout in Windermere'] found that out of 180 fish whose stomach contents had been examined, 65 per cent had selected one food animal and a further 6 per cent two food animals ...It is my firm belief that these selective feeders are much more common in lakes than is generally supposed, but as they may be presumed to be equally selective in the matter of artificials, they are not the ones caught by the average angler using the standard lake flies. Fortunately for him, there are plenty of trout with more catholic tastes...'

I am afraid that this paragraph contains so many false suppositions that it is the one flaw in Walker's otherwise excellent and interesting study.

Mr Walker says 'A trout which contains more than 60 per cent of one type of food had been exercising the power of selection', but why only 60 per cent? And need a fish that has a gut with one or two food species predominating be a selective feeder? If a trout encounters only one species of food during a bout of feeding, has the fish been selective if it took that one type of food? Surely not, for it had no choice. Similarly, if 61 per cent of the food species *seen* by Mr Allen's trout had been of one species and if 61 per cent of the food *taken* by those trout were of that same species, then Mr Allen would

*Spooning a trout is the surest way to find out what the fish are taking.
However, note that it does not necessarily mean the fish will take only an
imitation of their natural food. This trout was feeding on upwinged fly and
stonefly nymphs, and yet it took a March Brown*

have argued that such trout were being selective. This is, statistic-
ally, nonsense. Such an argument does not prove selective feeding.

Mr Walker also says: 'They may be presumed to be equally
selective in the matter of artificials, they are not the ones caught by
the average angler using the standard wet flies.' If this is true, then
the following instances will take some explaining:

(a) 42 brown trout taken from a Hebridean loch on Peter Ross,
Kingfisher Butcher and Blue Zulu had guts crammed with midge
pupae;

(b) 7 rainbow trout from a Pennine lake had guts crammed with
caddis larvae, but they took a Grouse and Claret;

(c) 3 rainbow trout from a large lowland reservoir that had guts
containing only corixids (lesser water boatmen) took a Woodcock
and Yellow;

(d) 9 brown trout had been feeding on freshwater shrimps from
a weedy margin of Ullswater but were taken on a small black wet fly
(Williams's Favourite);

(e) the willingness of rainbow trout to take a large black or white
lure in some lowland reservoirs, and wild brown trout in some
Cumbrian lakes, Scottish lochs and Irish loughs to take one of the
Butcher series when they are feeding on *Daphnia* in the epilimnion;

(f) and very many more similar instances!

These trout were selectively feeding, as far as the criterion Mr
Allen used was concerned, as quoted by Mr Walker. Their guts
each contained far in excess of 60% of one food item, but they were
not selective in choice of artificial fly. It ought to be pointed out, in
his defence, that Mr Walker admitted that he was not a stillwater
angler.

Considering the bulk of the food of stillwater trout is taken
beneath the water surface, in the littoral (or marginal) zone or from
the epilimnion, how selectively fastidious can we expect them to be?

The answer to this must be that if there is a superabundance of
several food species the fish might take one rather than another
species (i.e. be selective), but the selected food might not be the
most abundant in terms of number. Thus a trout nymphing in
weedbeds may select a corixid rather than an olive nymph should
the two appear in front of it simultaneously (i.e. it had a choice). Yet
how can we decide that the fish *preferred* the corixid, for it may
occupy only a small proportion of the food items in the trout's gut?
We can say that corixids *were* preferred or selected if the proportion
of corixids compared with other food items in the gut was greater
than the proportion in the trout's feeding area.

I have chosen this example deliberately, for it seems from comparing gut analyses with samples taken in the lakes, which I have carried out, that trout frequently go out of their way to take corixids. The guts of about 26% of trout that I have examined from the margins of Windermere, Coniston, Ullswater, some Scottish lochs and several Pennine reservoirs had corixids present, when sampling in the margins showed that this group of aquatic bugs was relatively scarce compared with other potential food species.

What I think encourages the trout to take corixids quite keenly are their erratic, jerky swimming behaviour, contrasting pattern of dark back and light underside, and the frequent visits that they must, of necessity, make to the surface to collect a bubble of fresh air. What also suggests that (some?) trout prefer corixids to many other organisms that might be in the lake margins is that one can take trout which have no corixids in their guts at all on a properly fished imitation. Certainly, if those trout were actively selecting the one or two species on which they had been feeding, as judged from gut analysis, then surely they would have ignored the imitation corixid?

Similarly, the trout (and char if they are present in the lake) that are feeding in summer in the epilimnion show a food preference. Gut analyses show that the fish usually feed on tiny crustaceans in the zooplankton. Are the fish 'selecting' zooplankton, and will they not accept a general fly or imitation of another food item? Or are they just mopping up what is a very large food supply that is readily available and would they, if other food were sufficiently abundant, turn to an alternative? I think they would and that is why they readily seize a lure (a large reservoir lure such as a Baby Doll, White or Black Marabou, or a more traditional lake fly such as a Peter Ross, Butcher or Teal and Green) that is fished through the clouds of zooplankton.

In *Reservoir Trout Fishing* (1977), Bob Church makes the following observation:

'Daphnia is a food item of the utmost importance—*the* most important in the case of Grafham rainbows. It cannot be imitated by the angler, but that does not matter, since we know that trout gorging daphnia are vulnerable to lures.'

The problem often is not what the trout are feeding on (or what food they are selecting) but whether they are finding *sufficient* food. This is certainly true of the oligotrophic lakes and, possibly, some relatively eutrophic lakes. Furthermore, because of the tendency of large stillwaters to stratify in summer even in eutrophic stillwaters the vast majority of food production is tiny zooplankton or a margin weedbed or stone substrata fauna that, though fairly diverse, occurs in relatively low density and in a relatively narrow zone of shallow water (see Chapter 2). Truly selective, fastidious feeding behaviour is thus most frequently encountered when large numbers of just one species appear in or on the water, switching trout from grubbing randomly about the lake margin or taking the blooms of zooplankton. However, such events are, alas, quite rare and often short-lived; for example:

large hatches of upwinged fly duns (e.g. mayfly, pond olive)
large hatches of sedges
midge pupae at the water surface prior to hatching
falls of land-bred flies (e.g. daddy-long-legs)
shoals of coarse fish fry in the margins.

When such events occur the angler who does not have adequate imitative flies will struggle.

Incidentally, when huge shoals of sticklebacks or fry are congregated in the shallows a lure (either a traditional one such as a Peter Ross, or one of the more modern lures such as the excellent Polystickle) is the logical imitation. Such lures have been termed 'attractors' in that they do not specifically imitate a particular food item, but these flies also 'deceive' the trout into taking them as small fish. It is when the trout are actually preying on small fish that the 'superior' angler, who would never stoop to using an 'attractor' and also insists that all his flies are 'deceivers', happily uses the former!

One of the greatest riddles in stillwater angling, especially in oligotrophic lakes, is that if food is not abundant or possibly even scarce, why don't the trout willingly grab any fur-and-feather concoction that is tied to the hook? I can take you to one Pennine reservoir which is full of stunted brown trout that are very difficult to catch. I can also take you to similar rainbow trout fisheries where, once the fish have been in the water for a couple of months and are losing condition due to the paucity of food, they are exceedingly difficult to attract to the fly. Why? These fish are starving to death, yet refusing apparently wholesome food!

A lot of anglers who frequent such sad fisheries are led to believe that the fish are feeding, but on what they know not. Possibly the trout are taking tiny midge pupae that are too small to imitate satisfactorily? The reasons for such anomalous behaviour seem to be that:

(a) the fish have been caught before;

(b) the fish do not recognise the artificial flies as potential food items because they have never (or rarely) met the sort of food represented;

(c) they have lost their appetites (this sounds rather foolish, but in many vertebrates e.g. salmon in the river, human prisoners-of-war, starvation leads to atrophy of the digestive system: it is likely that the pituitary gland, which is involved in stimulating the urge to feed, becomes suppressed by prolonged starvation);

(d) the fly or lure is at the wrong depth relative to the depth of the fish;

(e) the fly is presented unnaturally;

(f) the angler or his tackle have put the fish off;

(g) the fish are not prepared to look for food at that particular time of the day.

The latter four points, which apply to the best as well as to the worst waters, are considered in the next chapter.

River and lake trout feeding   In concluding this section it might be instructive to compare and contrast selectivity of feeding in river trout with lake trout.

One of the problems in stillwater angling is that anglers can rarely watch trout feeding and, at the same time, see the trout's food. In most rivers anglers are more fortunate: crystal clear water, small pools, fish that remain stationary on one lie for days, possibly weeks, are all most helpful. A fly flutters down the flow and the angler says 'Iron Blue Dun!'. The trout rises. The angler chooses his artificial and casts to the fish. If the pattern is not a good one then the fish will ignore it. If the pattern is acceptable then, barring accidents, the fish comes to the net.

We know that fish are often fastidious in rivers about both natural food and imitations—we can see it before our eyes. This is especially the case when they are taking duns, spinners and other flies from the water surface and to some extent when they are taking nymphs or pupae that are close to the surface and at the point of hatching. However, it is also known that the river trout are less selective when grubbing amongst the gravel of the riverbed or strands of water weed. There they will take a nymph, then a shrimp, then a hog-louse or whatever, but it must be remembered that the river is generally far more productive than the lake. The reason for this is that the steady water flow brings down the river a large regular supply of mineral nutrients to provide for massive growths of water weed, and organic detritus (e.g. leaf debris, cow dung, etc.)

to provide extra food resources for many species of invertebrates. The fish in the river, therefore, for much of the year have such a large food supply that they can afford to be selective, especially in the most productive time of the year (a time that happily coincides with the trout-fishing season). This is not the case in the lake, except possibly in the richest of trout lakes.

So, river trout very frequently become obsessed with a large hatch of fly at the surface (e.g. duns and sedges) and falls of dead and dying flies (e.g. spinners, hawthorn fly). It is also true of the lake trout *provided the hatch or fall is sufficiently large to encourage them to concentrate on it*. On this basis I would go along with the quotation from R. C. Bridgett given at the head of this chapter: the competent, all-round, stillwater angler must know something of the main lake flies and have imitations of these available should it prove necessary.

One hot summer day Geoff Haslam, my son Peter and I sat on the dam of a Pennine reservoir. The trout were taking black gnats that drifted across the rippled water surface by the breeze. We turned to appropriate dry flies and began to catch fish. A few yards along the dam another angler was fishing a lure on a sinking line, to no effect. Geoff landed his third trout.

'No good!' the lure-only man shouted to his wife, who was sunbathing on the mown grass of the dam top. 'The fish are taking dry flies today. Let's go home!'

And home they went.

The oft-quoted dictum of Francis Francis should be framed, like those texts beloved of an earlier and more God-fearing generation, and hung over the bed of every fly-fisherman in the land, so that it would never be forgotten.

'*The judicious and perfect application of dry, wet and mid-water fly-fishing stamps the fly-fisher with the hall-mark of efficiency. Generally anglers pin their faith to the entire practice of either one or the other plan, and argue dry versus wet, just as they do upstream versus down, when all are right at times and per contra all wrong at times.*'

Pay no attention, therefore, to the man who advocates either the dry or the wet fly to the exclusion of the other, but place your flies wherever you find the trout. If you don't, they won't see them, and you might as well pack up and go home.

C. F. Walker, *Lake Flies and their Imitations*, 1960

River trout are not very selective when they are feeding deep amongst weed or boulders and although some anglers have precise imitations of the invertebrates that may be found in these niches it has been demonstrated many times that such close imitation is not required. The same is true of the lake trout.

'I feel that the success of the pheasant tail [nymph] is indeed due to the fact that it might well, in the different sizes, be mistaken by fish, for one or another of at least a dozen nymphs, of various genus and species.'

Frank Sawyer, *Nymphs and the Trout*, 1970

'In my experience it is unnecessary to carry more than òne pattern of artificial nymph...wherever I have fished I have only found one necessary.'

Oliver Kite, *Nymph Fishing in Practice*, 1963

Correct use of the fly

The important point is to ensure that, whatever subsurface fly is being used, it is fished correctly. With large hatches or falls of fly at the surface of lakes being so relatively scarce compared with those on rivers, and consequently the bulk of stillwater trout foods being taken beneath the surface, the subsurface 'wet fly' (lure, nymph or standard wet fly) comprises the main armoury of the stillwater angler. This is why those who like to use just one method and are competent in that method can catch their fair share of fish the season through. It is also why Bruce Sandison 'has no cause for complaint' about his three size 14 loch flies.

Artificial stillwater trout flies

Many publications describe, clearly, the natural 'flies' that abound in British stillwaters. I would recommend four:

An Angler's Entomology by J. R. Harris (Collins, 1952) Alas, this book by an eminent Irish angler and professional freshwater biologist is now out of print. It deals with the natural history of the aquatic invertebrates, both river and lake, that are of interest to trout and angler; it is a most readable account. Also given are copious notes on how the fish respond to the various natural flies, how to identify the main species, distribution maps and some imitative fly-tyings.

Lake Flies and their Imitation by C. F. Walker (André Deutsch, 1960) Mr Walker, as I have stated earlier, was not a stillwater angler. In earlier years he had fished a great deal, mostly on flowing waters and especially the chalkstreams of southern England. What

Mr Walker did, with this book, was to encourage stillwater anglers to look more carefully at the natural foods of trout (as is the way of the river angler) and to attempt to imitate these foods with his artificial flies. Whilst I, and probably most other anglers who cast a fly onto stillwaters, do not agree with everything Mr Walker has written here, the book is nonetheless a classic.

Trout Flies of Stillwater by John Goddard (A & C Black, 1974, 4th ed.) This is a companion volume to his other books *Trout Fly Recognition* and *The Super Flies of Stillwater*. Certainly the most thorough treatise on the stillwater trout fly, the book contains detailed keys by which the various species can be identified and provides some background natural history of the main types. There is a long list of artificial flies with notes on how to fish them. The series of photographs of the commoner species are of great value.

A Guide to Freshwater Invertebrate Animals by T. T. Macan (Longman, 1959). A relatively inexpensive key, by the world's leading freshwater biologist, which deals with all the groups of invertebrates found in lakes and rivers. Look out for any book with T. T. Macan on the title page: it will be worth reading!

Should you want to delve a little deeper into collecting and identifying natural flies, then I would recommend that you contact: The Freshwater Biological Association, Ferry House, Ambleside, Cumbria. This organisation produces all the detailed scientific keys to freshwater animals and plants.

It is not my intention in this book to go into the life histories of lake invertebrates and how to identify them. The references I have reviewed above do this splendidly. What I will do here is suggest a list of artificial flies that are essential for the stillwater angler or that might, on occasion, be useful. I do this for two reasons. Firstly, as I intimated earlier, the number of published stillwater flies is now huge. In recent years I have tried a fair proportion of these—some appear better than others, some seem to be excellent, many are pretty useless. So I have produced a list of the excellent patterns, each one of which has a special role in stillwater trout fishing and is there for a purpose. Such a list is the core of my stillwater fly boxes, and I would happily fish any lake in Britain with the collection. It is produced bearing in mind my earlier thoughts on 'attractors and deceivers', and selective feeding amongst stillwater trout.

The second reason for the list is because, in the next chapter, we will be considering how to present the fly to the fish and how that is done depends, amongst other things, on the fly. I will also refer to the flies in the list in later chapters.

Before I give the list can I make two pleas? If you buy flies always make sure that the tying is correct and that the materials comprising each fly are of good quality. So often one finds that the dressing begins to unravel when tying the fly onto the leader or that after catching a trout the dressing falls apart. A good lure or wet fly should still be serviceable after taking a dozen trout, and a dry fly after half this many. Especially abysmal is the standard of hooks used by some commercial suppliers of flies. Their hooks are either so brittle that they snap or so soft that they easily bend. There are also hooks where the wire loop that forms the eye is incomplete, or where the barb is grotesquely huge and deep-cut, or where the point is much too long—all the signs of nasty hooks.

It is far better to learn to tie your own flies, not because home-tied flies are less expensive (often they are not for one always ties too many and finishes off giving a lot away!) but because you can have faith in their quality. The dressing will be as you want it and if you fancy a modification to a particular pattern then it is a simple matter to tie one up and give it a try. You can even devise your own patterns.

Here then is the list. I have relegated details of dressings to the Appendix.

Lures

I do not believe that reservoir trout are concerned about slight subtle features in the dressings of large lures. Colour, size and shape and, especially, the way the lure behaves in the water are important. For instance, there are several sorts of basically white lure and I think that really only one is necessary. It is worth, however, having some tied 'dog nobbler' fashion, with a great deal of weight at the head-end, to give an alternative type of action when being retrieved through the water (see Chapter 5). Most of my lures have in them, somewhere at least, a touch of orange or red. I feel that this is necessary because it seems that trout are particularly susceptible to lures (and standard lake flies) that have a splash of red in them. As Frank Riddell, in an excellent article on fish vision in the February 1980 issue of *Trout & Salmon*, put it '...the colour most visible to freshwater fish is in the red/orange region'. To give a variety of size I tie each lure in three sizes, 6, 8 and 10, using Partridge Bucktail hooks or Yorkshire Stronghold Streamer hooks. I have tried out one type of 'keel hook' where the point of the hook swims upper-most and reduces the risk of the hook attaching to underwater obstructions when fished close to the lake bed. These I liked because I lost far fewer lures, but I found the wire from which the hooks had been made too soft and springy.

My list has fourteen lures:
1. White lures:
(A) White Marabou (B) White Dog Nobbler
2. Black lures:
(A) Black Marabou (B) Black Dog Nobbler
3. Yellow lures:
(A) Yellow Marabou (B) Yellow Dog Nobbler
4. Green lures:
(A) Green Marabou (B) Green Dog Nobbler
5. Orange lure:
Whiskey Fly
6. Baby Dolls:
(A) Barbara Cartland (B) Candy Doll
7. Fish fry imitation:
Polystickle
8. Floating lures:
(A) Muddler Minnow (B) Floating Beetle

Standard lake/loch flies

There are many scores of flies that come under this general heading, most of them with a long tradition. Though some anglers have tried to explain the value of a number of them on the basis of imitation (e.g. Mallard and Claret represents the sepia dun, Black Pennell represents the Black Gnat, Woodcock and Yellow represents a sedge), it is rather tenuous, especially when one considers that they are often fished more quickly than these creatures can swim. Many loch flies are in series, usually depending upon the sort of bird from which the wing is taken: e.g. Grouse and —, Mallard and —, Woodcock and —. These are especially popular on the Scottish lochs and Irish loughs, not only for lake trout but also for sea trout and, in slightly larger sizes, even salmon. They have proved their worth in the stillwaters of England and Wales, too, especially for fishing from a drifting boat. Over the years I have tried just about every published fly of this sort and offer the following as a pretty reasonable representative collection.

These flies are usually fished in teams of three and sometimes even four (in Scotland). I find that three flies on one cast is sufficient and, in high winds, reduce the number to two. So, rather than simply giving a list of flies I have arranged them in a series of eight different 'casts'. I have also provided some notes as to where each cast seems most effective. Thus you can choose the cast most applicable to the region of Britain in which you are fishing.

As to sizes, there seems little advantage in fishing these flies in very small sizes, yet on the other hand if they are too large offers are fewer. So, I suggest that point-flies should be in sizes 8 or 10 and the middle dropper and bob-fly in sizes 10 or 12. I would also recommend Partridge De Sproat or Captain Hamilton Standard M/W wet fly hooks.

Cast	Point Fly	Middle Dropper	Bob Fly
1	Connemara Black	March Brown	Golden Olive Bumble
2	Kingfisher Butcher	Fiery Brown	Blue Zulu
3	Peter Ross	Mallard and Claret	Butcher
4	Bloody Butcher	Teal and Green	Zulu
5	Teal and Black	Silver March Brown	Kehe
6	Black Pennell	Woodcock and Yellow	Soldier Palmer
7	Cased Caddis	Williams's Favourite	Kehe
8	Peter Ross	Treacle Parkin	Straggly Spider

Notes:
Casts 1 and 2 are excellent in the loughs of Ireland and the lochs of the Scottish Islands. The dubbed fur bodies of five of these have 'buzz' and sparkle which gives the impression of life without specific imitation of one particular food form. The sixth, the Kingfisher Butcher, has an overall orange/gold colouration with a dark (mallard speculum slip) back and might be taken by the trout as a fish fry.

Cast 3 is a good all-round cast throughout the British Isles, from the lochs of northern Scotland to the rainbow trout fisheries of the English lowlands. It contains two flashing flies and one dull fly for contrast and is a cast that I use when trout are taking fry or when I have no clue as to what the trout are feeding on. It is, besides being a good cast for wild brownies, an excellent one for waters stocked with rainbows.

Cast 4 is essentially a good Scottish loch cast with a point fly that has plenty of flash and colour; a middle dropper fly that could, at a push, be regarded as a sedge imitation but, with the green seal's fur body, also glistens and glints; and the Zulu bob fly that makes a disturbance when dribbled across the water surface which, I believe, the fish take as a struggling insect that is trying to escape from the surface film.

Cast 5 is primarily a cast for the lochs of the Scottish islands, but will take trout elsewhere quite well. The Teal and Black and Silver March Brown are both attractors of contrasting style and tone whereas the Kehe, fished at the surface as the bob fly, once more represents a food form trying to escape from the hold of the surface film.

Cast 6 is a very good cast throughout mainland Britain, and is almost on a par with Cast 3. Frequently anglers fish the Black Pennell on the bob. However this entire cast fishes, in a wave, very close to or in the surface film. Thus I find that the Black Pennell fishes as well on the point, the brighter (possibly sedge-imitating) Woodcock and Yellow on the middle dropper and the extremely bushy, palmer-hackled Soldier Palmer on the surface. Fished as such this is an exciting cast to use.

Casts 7 and 8 are very good in the lakes of Cumbria and the Pennine reservoirs. The leaded Cased Caddis fished as point fly of Cast 7 takes the cast deep below the surface and can, if need be, be allowed to sink to great depth on a long leader. Fished slowly in this way the trout may take it for a caddis or, more generally, as 'something that may be good to eat'. At the same time the Williams's Favourite will represent a tiny black nymph or pupa and the Kehe, fished as bob fly once more in the surface film, a fly trying to escape from the water. This is an excellent cast when a range of depths is being sounded to find the fish.

In Cast 8 the Peter Ross, which the fish may take as a flashy attractor or a little fish, will work beneath the surface, but not as deep as a leaded fly. The Treacle Parkin, normally considered a grayling fly, and Straggly Spider both fish very close to the surface and both are meant to give a general insect-food impression. The Straggly Spider is placed on the top dropper because, with its long hackle and black seal's fur body, it has the 'buzz' so often necessary in the bob fly when fished properly in the surface film.

These casts of flies and the style of fishing that goes with them are quite delightful when it comes to experimentation. For example, when fishing a two-fly cast which one should you reject? Really it should be the middle dropper, but in some conditions (for example, when the flies must be sunk a little deeper) the top dropper or bob fly is the one to reject. You can also change them round for there is nothing sacrosanct about a particular three-fly cast. I bet that the

Connemara Black (point), Fiery Brown and Golden Olive Bumble (bob fly) is a superb cast on the Irish limestone loughs but for no deliberate reason I have failed to try it! These casts and flies are also subject to local and personal whim. I can imagine many Scotsmen saying, 'But where is the Grouse and Claret?'. But do the trout ever say, 'That fly is not tied with grouse, and there is no way that I am going to fall to a fly tied with bronze mallard!'

Imitative flies   These flies are best fished when it is certain, or almost so, that the trout are taking the natural which the artificial fly represents.

Chironomids (midges or buzzers)
Although some tiny midge larvae are free swimming and live amongst weed and detritus, most occur out of sight of the trout in mud tubes or burrows where they feed on tiny organic particles that they filter from the water or surrounding mud. When fully grown these larvae enter the resting pupal stage and, when ready to hatch into adults, leave the safety of their burrows and drift upwards to the water surface. This journey may take quite a long time, certainly many minutes in deeper water. Then, prior to hatching, the pupae often hang beneath the surface film. Both in the movement to the surface and during the final resting stage midge pupae are very vulnerable: trout take them keenly and in a big hatch to the exclusion of other forms of food. In those pupae that survive the exoskeleton (outer skin) splits and the adult midge emerges onto the lake surface. Its wings rapidly enlarge and dry, and the fly becomes airborne.

Both ascending and suspending midge pupae are ideally imitated by the lake angler. They are one type of natural food which can evoke a selective response from the trout in such a way that the angler must either use an imitation or 'go home fishless'. Midge

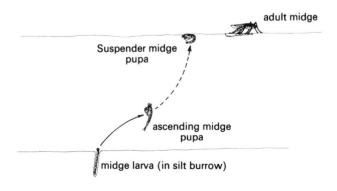

pupae vary widely in size and colour; these two features must be incorporated into the imitations.

Fly patterns:

1. Buzzer Pupa in sizes 10–16, in colours black, claret, olive, green and, if possible, red, yellow and brown.

2. Suspender Buzzer, in sizes and colour range as the previous fly.

Adult midges are amongst the most difficult natural flies to imitate for they are usually so tiny. A pattern may work one day but not another, even though the same species of midge is out and about!

Fly patterns:

1. Grey Duster, in sizes 14–18 dry fly. This is the best traditional dry fly midge imitation.

2. Floating Midge, in sizes 14–18 dry fly, in body colours black, green, olive, orange and grey.

Sedges (Caddis)

Most species of sedge larvae dwell in tubes made from tiny stones or bits of twig or leaf and they keep to the lake bed. Attempts to imitate caddis in this stage have been made, the best being Bob Carnill's Cased Caddis which I have included with the selection on standard lake wet flies earlier (it is usually fished randomly as point fly with two other wet flies on droppers). The mature larva pupates in its case and then, when hatching time comes, leaves the tube still as a pupa and floats up to the water surface where it hatches into the adult sedge. Trout are extremely fond of these pupae, both when ascending and resting beneath the surface.

Fly patterns:

1. Sedge Pupa, in sizes 10–12 (Yorkshire Sedge Hooks or Partridge Longshank Sedge Hooks), with body colours olive, orange and brown.

2. Suspender Sedge Pupa, in sizes and colour range as the previous fly.

There are very many species of sedge, some quite tiny, some huge. Consequently, there are a lot of dry adult sedge imitations, each to imitate one species or group of similar species of adult sedge. I do not believe that such a wide variety of artificials is necessary or desirable. For instance when sedges are on the water in numbers sufficient to really turn the fish on, then more than one species of sedge is likely to be out. Also the fact that sedges tend to hatch in the twilight, when subtle colours and shades begin to have less significance, reduces the need for a multiplicity of patterns. So, I would suggest only two basic patterns, each in a range of sizes.

Fly patterns:
1. Deer Hair Sedge, in sizes 8–12 dry fly.
2. Palmer-hackled Sedge, in sizes 8–12 dry fly.

Upwinged Flies (Mayflies or Dayflies)

The upwinged flies are far less important in lake fishing than they are in rivers. The *Caenis* or angler's curse is the most widespread and abundant, but it is so tiny and plentiful that a good hatch of this species can make angling virtually a waste of time. Hence the common name! At the other extreme is the true mayfly which occurs on many loughs of Ireland and a few lakes in England and southern Scotland. This is a huge fly and a hatch of these insects should be welcomed by the angler, because the fish feed keenly on the natural and often take a reasonable artificial with gay abandon.

In both these species the nymph burrows in the silt of the lake bed where the trout will not normally encounter it. Although both nymphs are taken, by trout, as they swim up to the water surface to hatch, there is no need to imitate them for the fish respond so well to the duns on the water surface that a dun imitation is far more effective.

Some lakes have good populations of sepia and claret duns, but again the nymphs of these are usually out of range of the trout, living as they do in deep crevices amongst boulders. Once more the dun (and spinner) are the stages to imitate, if need be. On upland lakes in northern and western Britain and in the Irish loughs occur some members of the *Ecdyonuridae*, a group of flies which includes the famous March brown (*not* a lake fly), the yellow May dun (known in Ireland as the yellow hawk), the dusky yellowstreak, the brown May dun (a species especially common in Ireland) and the autumn dun. The nymphs of this group, though undoubtedly taken by the trout, are of little value to the angler for they are 'stone crawlers'. In other words, these nymphs hold firmly all the time onto boulders (they cannot swim); any artificial fly that imitated such behaviour would be a frustrating one to fish! Again, the duns and spent spinners are of more interest.

Finally, there are three species of upwinged fly that inhabit some lakes where the nymph actively swims (in the river nymph angler's parlance, they are 'agile darters')—the pond olive, lake olive and the large summer dun. If these are present in the lake then they might be worth imitating when trout are feeding in the margins, but the dun and spinner stages of these three are far more important for the angler.

In this introduction to the upwinged flies I have referred to some species as being important. It is possibly overstating the case as far as many anglers are concerned, for they will rarely encounter a hatch of upwinged fly duns or a fall of spinners unless angling expeditions are made to the rockier waters of upland Wales, Scotland and northern England, or to the loughs of Ireland, where upwinged flies are relatively more abundant and of greater variety. In these waters the fish can become quite preoccupied with a hatch of duns or a fall of spinners and when this happens a good imitation is needed.

Fly patterns:

1. Sawyer's Pheasant Tail Nymph, sizes 14–16, probably the best pattern when trout are nymphing in the lake margins.

2. When fish are taking nymphs that are starting their journey to the surface the same pattern may suffice, but possibly a drifting unweighted pattern may be better. I suggest two:

A) Greenwell's Glory (Spider Variant), sizes 12–16 wet fly.

B) Olive Spider, sizes 12–16 wet fly.

Some of my friends and I have had a degree of success with these tied in 'suspender' fashion to imitate a nymph at the surface and on the point of hatching.

3. Mayfly Dun.

4. Mayfly Spinner.

5. Greenwell's Glory (Dry), to imitate duns of lake olive, pond olive, yellow may dun, dusky yellowstreak, in appropriate sizes (12–14).

6. Pheasant Tail Spinner, to imitate the spent spinners of the olives, claret, sepia and autumn duns, in sizes 12–16.

7. Large Summer Dun.

8. Yellow Spinner, to imitate spinners of the yellow may dun and dusky yellowstreak, in sizes 12–14.

9. Norris Sepia, to imitate the sepia and claret duns, sizes 12–14.

10. Paythorne Caenis, to attempt to represent the angler's curse! In sizes as small as 22–26.

Corixids

It is important that the artificial is weighted so that it sinks quickly.

Fly Pattern:

Corixa, size 12.

Shrimps

Shrimps feed amongst detritus and weed on the lake bed. Here is where the imitation should be fished. So, it must be heavily weighted to get down quickly to this depth.

Fly Pattern:

1. Lane's Shrimp, size 12.
2. Sawyer's Killer Bug, size 10–12.
Though the latter is less aesthetically pleasing to the angler, it is a superb pattern for use in the lake margins; the name 'Killer' is most apt. It could also be taken by the fish for a water hog-louse, a common inhabitant of weedbeds and boulder-strewn lake beds.

Snails
Snails are an important component of the diet of trout feeding in the shallower margins. However, there they are impossible to imitate realistically. In hot summer weather there is sometimes a mass movement of snails from the depths to the surface (possibly due to the deeper water becoming deoxygenated) where they glide, up-side-down, along the surface film. Many anglers have imitated snails and the one I give below was devised by Geoff Haslam and me—it is very easy to tie, and is extremely effective!

Fly Pattern:
Floating Snail

Land-bred Flies
These all appear from time to time on the water and when present in large numbers can result in the trout feeding selectively on them. One or two of each pattern, tucked in the corner of a dry fly box, may come in useful on occasion.

Fly Patterns:
1. Daddy-long-legs.
2. Black Gnat (for any black flies so tied in a range of sizes 10–14).
3. Wickham's Fancy (for dung and other brown flies, sizes 10–12).
4. Ants:
A) Red Ant.
B) Black Ant.
5. Green Caterpillar (for use when trees overhang the water).
6. Brown Moth (especially useful in summer evenings).

That completes my list—it is a long one, but every fly is there for a reason and some can be excluded if you fish only one water or one sort of water. For example, if I were just to fish the reservoirs of the English Midlands I would keep all the lures, retain just casts 3 and 6 of the standard wet flies, reduce the upwinged fly patterns to just two or three, and I would retain the rest. On the other hand, if I fished just the wild brown trout waters of Ireland or the Scottish Islands I would exclude all the lures, and keep most of the wet fly casts and all of the rest. However, as I said earlier, with all this collection I would feel confident on any trout water, anywhere in Britain.

5
Presenting the Fly to the Fish

'... when trout refuse your fly it is because they sense your presence from one or several fear-inducing phenomena. Not only are they at that moment refusing *your* fly but most probably they are refusing nearby natural foods as well...the fault lies with the angler and not with the fly. To paraphrase the song, 'It ain't what you fish it's the way that you fish it'.'

T. C. Ivens, *Still Water Fly-Fishing*, 1973

'This is all so elementary that I would be ashamed to mention it were it not for those fishermen who, year after year, pull tiny flies through the water at speeds which...can only be described as fantastic. The fish must regard such phenomena with the same startled surprise that we would experience if we saw the postman zoom up the lane at 90 m.p.h. on his push bike.'

Hugh Falkus, *Sea Trout Fishing*, 1975

1. The approach

During the 1960s and 1970s, when the sport of reservoir trout fishing was mushrooming in popularity in the lowlands of England, great emphasis was put on distance in the cast. Strong, powerful rods were invented that took heavy weight-forward or shooting-head lines. These, used in conjunction with the 'double-haul' style of casting, enabled competent anglers to throw a line thirty-five, forty and sometimes forty-five metres. This was quite revolutionary, for in the earlier lake styles shorter casts were made from a drifting boat, or from the bank, to trout feeding very close inshore, in the lake margins. Then, to give an even greater amount of apparent distance, the new style of reservoir angler started the trend of wading to thigh depth to increase the amount of deep water covered by a cast from the bank, the supposition being that trout would not be in shallower water.

Both of these tactics (casting for distance and deep wading) are sometimes, possibly often, tactics that help the angler fail to catch trout. I will not deal with casting techniques in this book: so many others have described the mechanics of casting that it would be a waste of space repeating them here. However, it seems that in the minds of many anglers the attempt to gain distance completely overrides consideration of the fish and I must point this out—few other books have. Several false-casts flash the line to and fro in the air over the trout. Can the fish see the line as it bats to and fro? Most anglers never give it a thought! Yet the angling press has published a lot of correspondence over the years about the *pros* and *cons* of dark, dull line colour compared with bright, pale colours, and of the effects on fish of the false-cast, especially with pale lines. I know that the controversy still rages over pale versus dark floating fly lines but the experiences and views of great stillwater trout anglers must be taken as evidence, and if Peter McKenzie-Philps and the late Richard Walker came out on the side of dark lines then one must listen. Observations like the following have even more bearing on the case for dark fly lines.

A couple of years ago I was leaning over a wall by Ladybower Reservoir watching, with my polaroids, a shoal of rainbow trout cruising just beneath the water surface and about fifteen metres from the bank. They approached an angler who did not see them (he was too low at the water's edge, nor was he wearing polaroids). He began to go through the casting procedure—five false-casts with a white shooting-head floater. As the line flashed in the air over the fish for a third time the convoy stopped and then scattered. By the time the angler completed his cast he was fishing in fishless water.

I have made similar observations on, for example, Bank House Fishery near Lancaster, where trout showed signs of anxiety when I made repeated false-casts with a white line over them but they did not when I used my normal brown or green floating fly lines. False-casts with light-coloured lines, can make trout very nervous and a nervous trout is not a taking trout. Hugh Falkus made the following comment about false-casting in *Sea Trout Fishing* (1975): 'False casting is the curse of fly-fishing. Most of it is quite unnecessary. The trouble is that it becomes a habit, practised by anglers who, intent on distance, seem to forget they are trying to catch a fish.'

So, use a dark line (either dark green or brown) and reduce the number of false-casts to a minimum and you will increase your catch rate. Also learn to cast properly! We all have to false-cast to some extent when fishing stillwaters from the bank, but the need for more than a couple of false-casts is usually due to poor technique, i.e. the line speed is not great enough to shoot sufficient line to complete the cast, and this is due to bad timing linked to incorrect use of the rod and body.

Line speed, then, is.the critical factor in reducing the number of false-casts. Too slow a line speed also results in the line splashing the water on the forward false-cast (thereby frightening the trout even more) and dropping on the back-cast so that bits of the countryside become attached to the fly or the point of the hook is broken against stones. Should any of these defects rear their ugly heads, it might be advisable to see a casting instructor.

Some anglers will suggest that I am overstating the case against the false-cast. I am not! When we need to cast a long way then the false-cast is a necessary evil. The same is not true of deep wading by bank anglers. This is an unnecessary evil in 99.9% of cases, for, as I explained in Chapter 2, deep wading merely pushes trout that ought to be feeding in the shallow margins further from the shore and makes them more wary. I know that some poor casters, who whip the water to froth with their awful casting and who splash their way through the shallows in thigh boots, do catch fish, but, I think, most of the fish they take are the silly new stockies who imagine that the splashing signals the arrival of a supply of trout pellets!

So, as in all angling, remember that even though you might not be able to see the fish you are trying to catch, they might be able to see you or, through your clumsiness, be made aware of your presence. Also remember that no matter how the fly is eventually presented, if you have scared the fish earlier you are not likely to catch them. Therefore, when approaching the water do so quietly, with no stamping around or splashing at the water's edge. If fishing from a boat do not go heavy-footed and heavy-handed. The trout's lateral line is sensitive to even the slightest of underwater vibrations and when fishing from a boat don't stand up, not only for reasons of safety, but also because an angler who is standing up will be far more conspicuous to the fish than one who is sitting down. The closer the fish come to you, the easier they are to catch.

There now remain the most important aspects of presentation of the fly – speed of retrieve, depth the flies should be fished, and other factors that might affect the effectiveness of the fly as an attractor or deceiver of fish.

2. Speed of retrieve of the flies

Flies should represent living animals on which the trout feed or would be prepared to feed. Thus we should look at the fly or flies on the leader, ask ourselves what they represent, and fish them at the appropriate speed. So, how fast do natural trout prey swim?

The answer to this important question is much slower than most of us imagine. It is a question that is less important in waters that have just been stocked with trout from the fish farm. For instance, I have fished a static dry fly (when sedges were on the water) over newly-stocked rainbow trout and failed to catch, but then, when I have pulled the fly across the water at ridiculously fast speeds I have caught fish. Similarly, I once watched the reaction to an artificial nymph of a large bucketful of stocked brown trout which had been recently poured into the pool. This fly, too, was ignored unless I pulled it very quickly back through the water. So, when there are new stock fish about you can catch them easily by attracting them by fast, absurdly fast, movements of the fly.

Unfortunately, this predilection of uneducated stockies for the rapid lure has deceived many anglers, who fish the modern put-and-take fisheries, into relying heavily on such a technique in all their fishing. They depend on a big lure, usually on a sinking line, stripped back quickly, or on a team of wet flies jerked through the water at speeds that must make real nymphs marvel! Anglers who use this technique catch a lot of trout, especially rainbows, but where there are no stockies or the stockies that remain have become familiar with natural foods, and possibly fallen for the fast lure once and been returned to fight another day, the high-speed lure- and nymph-stripping mode of presentation is less successful. It is especially so in productive waters where natural food is relatively abundant and in oligotrophic lakes when there is a reasonable hatch or large fall of natural flies. On such waters, including some of the clear Scottish lochs and lakes of northern England, I have seen, several times, wild brown trout ignore or turn away to avoid a ludicrously fast-fished wet fly or lure.

For those of you who, having read the book so far, think that I am anti-rainbow, anti-lure and anti-stockie, may I point out that the rainbow trout has enabled me to fish for big trout at a fairly small cost. I use lures a lot in reservoirs and lakes that have rainbow trout and without stocking we would have fewer waters holding trout and, in many waters, fewer trout. However, catching huge numbers of stockies can *never* be equated with top-quality fishing. 'Stockie-bashing' requires little skill, and for the more experienced angler there is certainly no challenge. I think the old adage, that there are three stages through which anglers pass, applies:

'1. When they want to catch the greatest possible number of fish;

2. When they want to catch the largest fish;

3. When they want to catch the most difficult fish and are less concerned with numbers or size.'

E. R. Hewitt, *A Trout and Salmon Fisherman for Seventy-five Years*, 1948

Speed of natural food

The speed of natural trout foods has been studied very little. Some timings I carried out of minnows in the shallow margins suggested a top speed of possibly 3 or 4 kilometres per hour (around 2 m.p.h.), but that was for very, very short distances. On another occasion I timed a tiny brown trout which a larger rainbow trout kept pursuing through shallow water on a straight line parallel to the bank. (The brownie would dart into a crevice in the stone bed of the lake just before it was caught, but would then re-emerge only to be chased back from whence it came!) Over 8 metres the little trout probably reached a maximum speed of about 6 kilometres per hour (about 4 m.p.h.) These, then, are the sorts of speed at which the fish-imitating lures should be fished:

a big lure (e.g. Baby Doll, Polystickle)—24–45 seconds to fish a 20-metre retrieve

a smaller flashy wet fly (e.g. Butcher, Peter Ross)—45–90 seconds to fish a 20-metre retrieve.

These suggested timings include times when the lure is not being retrieved. No fish swims continuously in straight lines and at a constant speed. There are stops; a little fish behaving naturally jerks forward a few inches, then halts. It may change direction. Ideally, the lure of a fish-imitating wet fly should, once it has been cast in and allowed to sink to the required depth, be brought back with little tweaks or short pulls on the line—possibly two or three centimetres, possibly ten to fifteen centimetres at a time—and with pauses in between, just as a little fish would stop after each small darting progression. Sometimes it also pays dividends to change the lure's direction slightly by swinging the rod over during the retrieve. Incidentally, such slow speeds are those of a team of attractor wet flies fished loch-style from a boat during a drift, or when cast, again from a boat, and allowed to move as the line bellies round as the boat moves downwind (see Chapter 8).

There are two further tricks with the bigger flies that often help to convince the trout that what it is chasing really is a little fish which is trying to escape. As the lure reaches the angler (on the bank), it is worth fishing the cast right out to the rod tip for, as it is brought up towards the surface in the water's edge, the fly is behaving like minnows and sticklebacks when being pursued by a bigger fish. They try to jump out of the water! A lure that also looks as though it is trying such an escape route is behaving naturally. In fact, I have caught two rainbow trout on lures and four wild brownies on attractor lake flies as they actually left the water.

It is also worth increasing the speed of retrieve considerably *over the last few metres*. A pursuing trout will often make a grab when this is done. Certainly the acceleration seems to suggest to the trout that its quarry is making a final effort to escape in the lake edge and so it had better act, fast!

I remember once, on Draycote, trout after trout following my lure right into the bank and taking literally at my feet as I speeded up the lure and as it rose towards the surface. Incidentally, the same trout would not follow the lure in if it was fished so quickly *throughout* the retrieve. On many occasions, when fishing in company almost invariably it has been the *slower* retriever of the lure who has been successful and when other anglers have copied his retrieve rate all have been rewarded with success.

The horizontal movement of smaller food species is much slower than I have described for small fish. Even the most active of invertebrates (corixids, damsel-fly nymphs and freshwater shrimps) rarely move at speeds of a metre per minute for more than a few seconds at a time. Such would involve a 20-minute retrieve for a 30-metre cast!

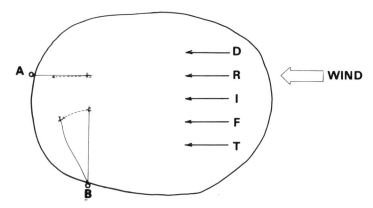

Angler at A casts into the wind and allows the flies to drift back to him by simply collecting the slack line that develops. Angler at B casts across the wind and drift and allows the flies to come round slowly with the drift

For animals in the surface film (nymphs and pupae that are waiting to hatch or those that have hatched, and insects that have fallen or been drifted by the wind onto the surface) movement can be more rapid due to drifting of the water surface. This drift may be caused by the breeze or by the effects of streams entering or leaving the lake (water pumps in the case of reservoirs). Only two casting angles are possible for the bank angler to give a realistic behaviour of drifting insects: into the wind so that the flies are brought back to the angler who simply gathers the slack line to keep in touch with the flies, or across the wind and the flies are allowed to drift round with no line retrieve (see diagram on p. 86).

If the flies are cast downwind then they will be retrieved through the water unnaturally against the drift of the natural food. The boat angler can drift with the wind and either cast downwind loch-style, or across the wind and allow the flies to drift with the boat.

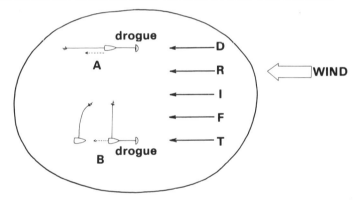

Angler in boat A casts downwind and by using the drift of the boat (slowed down by a drogue), together with correct line retrieve, his flies fish naturally with the drift. Angler in boat B casts across the drift and allows the boat and flies to drift with little or no line retrieve. Again, the boat's drifting speed is slowed by a drogue

In the case of streams entering or leaving the lake the small insect-imitating flies should be presented as in river fishing, so that they float down the flow with no drag. On rivers this is best done by casting up and across the stream. Similarly, when fishing imitative flies at or just below the surface close to inflows and outflows of lakes the flies are cast 'upstream' and allowed to drift naturally (see diagram on p. 88).

When the trout are feeding deep, in the lake margins, then a different style is called for involving deeply-fished, ideally weighted

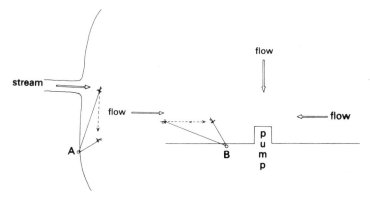

Fishing at inflows and outflows. In both cases the anglers (A and B) cast up into the flow and allow their flies to drift naturally along it

flies such as Lane's Shrimp, Corixa, the Killer Bug and Sawyer's Pheasant Tail Nymph. Once more, however, the movement of the naturals will be extremely slow, relative to the typical stillwater angler's retrieve rates. In fact, what movements the natural creatures at this level have, namely short, jerky ones, often in a vertical direction just above the lake bed or amongst weed, are ideally what the angler should try to impart to his imitations. By far the best way to do this is by allowing the fly to follow a very deep drift in conjunction with occasional small rises in the water. The latter is achieved by the angler raising the rod tip quickly, for just

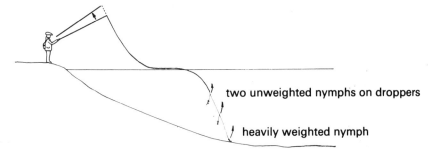

Fishing deep still margins. The angler casts and allows the weighted nymph (or shrimp, bug, etc.) to sink, carrying with it the (optional) unweighted flies. The line is kept tight by drawing in the slack with the non-casting (usually left) hand. Very occasionally the rod is raised, causing the nymphs to jerk upwards for a few centimetres. In this way the margin is thoroughly searched with flies that act in the same way as the naturals. A major factor leading to success is discerning the offer

a few centimetres. The nymph will then rise jerkily a little in a most realistic way. (This was the essential feature of the 'induced take' described by Sawyer and Kite in their books on nymph fishing.) In the deeper water one or two extra flies can be attached to the leader on droppers to provide alternative flies for the fish.

However, whereas trout that take a lure, subsurface wet fly and dry fly produce good positive offers that are (usually) hooked with ease, the very slow-moving, deeply-fished nymph is seized and rejected quickly and quietly, often with the angler being unaware of what has happened far beneath the surface. The clue when fishing this style is to have a good indicator of an offer—a well-greased floating fly-line tip and leader butt—and to watch it like a hawk. A dipping, tweak, jerk, or any other anomalous slight movement is then responded to *immediately*. Trout reject these flies so quickly that a moment's hesitation and, too late, all will be lost. To appreciate the effectiveness of this deep technique, but also the importance of discerning and reacting quickly to the subtle signs of an offer, I would recommend fly fishers to read the following classic works on the subject: Frank Sawyer's *Nymphs and the Trout* and Oliver Kite's *Nymph Fishing in Practice*. I would also suggest that, if you have not tried this technique, it is worth going to a heavily-stocked trout fishery where you can experiment to your heart's content.

3. Depth

It is clear from what I have just said that not only must the flies move at speeds that render them acceptable imitations of natural foods, but they must also be at the right depth—the depth at which the natural foods would normally be found. For example, no trout would expect a shrimp, which normally inhabits the weedbeds and algae-covered boulders, to be swimming quickly through the surface of the epilimnion.

There is another side to the issue of depth and that is the location of the fish. If the trout are feeding in the surface layer of the lake, then a fly that is being fished much deeper than this will be ineffective. Likewise, if the fish are feeding deep in the epilimnion, or grubbing around the lake bed in the margins, then they may be reluctant to rise by many feet to intercept an artificial fly fished at or close to the surface.

So, logically, we ought to look at our range of flies and lures and ask ourselves: 'At what depth would trout expect to find the natural organisms which these flies represent?' and, 'At what depth should I expect the fish to be feeding today?'

I have divided the natural foods of lake trout into seven categories (see Table 6). Whilst there will be some overlap between different categories it is probably as well to keep them separate as far as depth is concerned, for if trout are preoccupied with feeding at one depth (e.g. on pupae at the water surface) they will often ignore the same food at a greater depth (e.g. pupae beginning their journey to the surface from the lake bed).

Category A Small fish, such as minnows, sticklebacks, stunted rudd or roach, will be present in most lakes throughout the year and the trout will move into the shallower water to take them. This seems especially so in the early mornings or late evenings of late spring, when the fish shoal prior to spawning, and in late summer when huge shoals of fry might be present in the shallower bays.

Sometimes the bigger trout will make raiding sorties from the depths into water, which is little more than a few inches deep, to take a tiny fish. One brown trout that just reached the two-pound mark, which I eventually caught on a Bloody Butcher in Parsonage Reservoir, actually splashed its way through clumps of rushes at the water's edge—later the water proved to be only ten centimetres deep where the trout was taking sticklebacks. In this cast the floating line was essential so that the wet flies did not become snagged on the bottom. On other occasions a sinking line was preferable: for example, where the fish were feeding in a few feet of water.

Category B Freshwater shrimps, corixids and nymphs and many insect larvae live in weedbeds or amongst boulders of the lake bed. It is essential, if the artificial fly is to represent these adequately, that the fly gets down to that depth quickly, and is fished very slowly and properly. Many anglers attempt to achieve depth with sinking lines. This is a mistake. The sinker will keep on sinking even though the flies have reached the effective depth and so, to prevent snagging on the bottom, the flies must be fished too quickly. It is far better to use a floating line, well-greased, and a leader that is a bit longer than the depth of the water. For point fly use a weighted nymph, shrimp, corixid or bug. Unweighted flies can be fished a little higher in the water on droppers. If depth is correct, the point fly will *occasionally* collect bits of weed, etc. from the lake bed. If it snags up on every cast, then the leader is a little too long and should be shortened a fraction.

The advantage of this method, besides being less arduous than most others (!), is that you are assured that depth is correct and the flies are behaving like the naturals. This is not possible with a

Table 6

Category	Food	Depth Zone	How best to achieve depth	Flies
A	Small fish	Close to lake bed; amongst weed in margins, shallow bays; amongst shoals and islands	Floating or sinking line as necessary, plus appropriate sinking time	Unweighted lure or attractor wet flies
B	Shrimps, corixids, nymphs, larvae, hog-louse	—ditto—	Floating line with leader slightly longer than the water depth	Weighted shrimp, nymph, corixid with unweighted flies on droppers
C	Nymphs and pupae rising to surface to hatch	Drifting and slowly rising to the surface	Floating line with long leader so that flies fish mid-water	Combination of weighted and unweighted nymphs/pupae; some standard fly casts
D	Nymphs and pupae at surface; floating snails	Beneath surface film	Floating line and suitable fly patterns	Either: unweighted nymphs/pupae, or: suspender nymphs/pupae, or: combination with dry fly
E	Hatched duns, midges, sedges, land-flies	Standing proud on surface film	Floating line and leader	Dry fly
F	Spent spinners and other dead and dying flies	Lying flat on surface film or drifting in surface	Floating line and leader	Dry fly or wet fly
G	Zooplankton and associated animals	Variable depth in epilimnion and thermocline	Line density appropriate to depth of trout	Lure or attractor lake flies

sinking line and, as I explained earlier, the tip of the fly-line and greased leader butt provides a very good indicator of even the most subtle of offers.

Such a method of fishing for lake trout should be one of the bank angler's main armaments throughout the year or should be used by the boat angler who is anchored up in a shallow bay or close to a large weedbed.

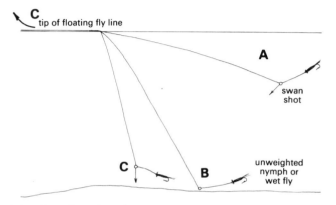

The ledgered nymph: an alternative system

A. *Following the cast, the swan shot sinks quickly and carries the nymph with it.*

B. *The shot holds the bottom and the nymph holds on or close to the bottom, moving slowly in the current.*

C. *Short lengths of line are occasionally pulled in, causing the swan shot to lift and then fall. This movement is mirrored by movement of the nymph.*

This is a variation on the theme used by some anglers to catch stocked trout: 'the ledgered trout pellet fly'. In that case an imitation trout pellet, made of brown deer hair spun on a big hook and trimmed to pellet-shape, is used instead of a nymph. Some anglers even use this method to fish a real trout pellet on a hook! The latter is, of course, against fishery rules if the water is 'fly only'. Some fisheries do not allow the use of any 'ledgered' or static fly

Category C From May to the end of September there *may* be hatches of sedges, midges, etc. and such hatches will be preceded by a movement of pupae and nymphs from the lake bed to the surface. (Note: the mature nymphs of stoneflies and some upwinged flies crawl from the lake and thus are of little value to anglers.) As most 'hatches' occur in the afternoon or evening (afternoon in spring and autumn; later evening in high summer), this initial movement commences some time prior to the hatch. In late spring the trout may become preoccupied with nymphs and pupae that are drifting very slowly upwards from the lake margins, but which are still at quite a depth. Also, as the pupae drift upwards, currents may carry them away from the shallower water, where they developed, and into the main body of the lake.

As the main direction of movement of such potential food items is upwards, with a secondary lateral drift, a sinking fly-line is not suitable because that would carry the artificials downwards (i.e. in the wrong direction) unless the retrieve was unnaturally fast. So, a floating fly-line with a team of weighted or unweighted pupal or larval imitations, or small sparsely-dressed wet flies (e.g. standard wet fly casts 7 or 8, or even some flies of the northern river wet fly style such as Snipe and Purple, Olive Bloa, Orange Partridge and Waterhen Bloa), seem ideal. They should be fished very slowly.

Category D Such nymphs and pupae included in Category C eventually settle beneath the surface film prior to the emergence

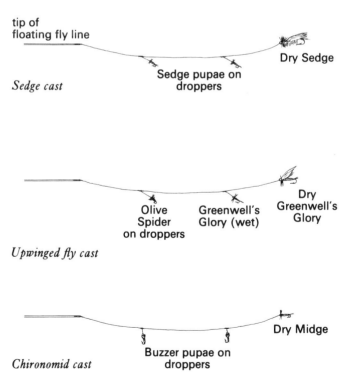

onto the surface as adults. Fish taking them at this stage do so with dimpling of the surface, or with a rise that breaks the surface as they porpoise along, scooping up defenceless, inert, resting creatures.

Many anglers fish the same style as they would for Category C (which is not unreasonable, for there is an overlap between the two). However, there are two better ways of coping with fish taking nymphs or pupae at the water surface, they form a system that keeps the artificial flies bobbing up and down at the surface, like the naturals do. The first is to use a combination of dry fly and nymph, the dry fly acting as a bite indicator as well as being a legitimate lure (later there will be flies on the surface as the natural nymphs and pupae hatch).

An appropriate cast is made up, depending on what is known or thought to be at the surface. The flies are cast into or across the breeze and allowed to drift. If the dry fly disappears suddenly, then it indicates that one of the subsurface flies has been taken. Sometimes the dry fly comes hurtling across the surface, dragged by a fish that has taken one of the wet flies. Once I had a brown trout that scooped up one of the nymphs and then the dry fly before I could react. This is a most relaxing (but keep your eye on that dry fly!) and interesting way of fishing.

Alternatively, you can use a team of 'Suspenders' which float perfectly in the surface film. These were one of the great inventions of John Goddard, as Suspender Buzzers, to imitate midge pupae on the point of hatching. In his book *Trout Flies of Stillwater* Goddard describes how the Suspender was devised and gives details of the tying. The idea is that a conventional nymph or pupa is tied up and included in the dressing is a small piece of ethafoam, rolled into a ball, enclosed in a piece of lady's tights material and tied in at the head. This is the way that Geoff Haslam and I tied ours until, by chance, we were discussing Suspenders with Gerald Forsyth, the well-known Bolton fly-dresser and angler. 'What you want is some of these...' he commented, as he pulled a huge white bucket from his car boot. It was full of tiny polypropylene (I think) white spheres, which varied in size, and were, Gerald told us, used in cavity wall insulation. He gave us a boxful. So we now use those instead of the less satisfactory ethofoam and can choose a sphere appropriate to the size of the nymph.

The idea is that the foam sphere keeps the nymph floating with its head in the surface film and body and tail held vertically below; much in the way that a mature nymph or pupa hangs prior to emergence. Whereas Goddard used the idea primarily for buzzer

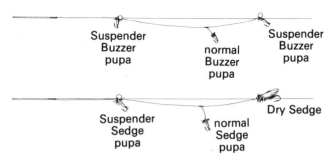

Suspender Buzzer pupa   normal Buzzer pupa   Suspender Buzzer pupa

Suspender Sedge pupa   normal Sedge pupa   Dry Sedge

imitations, we tie a wide range of small deceiver or imitative wet flies (e.g. Spider Greenwell's Glory, Olive Spider, Sedge Pupa and even northern wet flies such as the Waterhen Bloa and Williams's Favourite) in this style as well as buzzers.

They are effective for both wild brownies and stocked fish and are much more relaxing to use than standard patterns in that they need no retrieve and therefore less casting. What is even more important is that they match the behaviour of the natural flies much better.

Once more, a dry fly can be used as a 'bite indicator', but as Suspenders fish high in the surface film this can be dispensed with and another Suspender (possibly of a different colour) tied to the leader-point. When these floating nymphs are taken there is usually a noticeable swirl, indicating that the angler should tighten immediately. Incidentally, it will be noticed from the diagram above, that I usually tie a plain wet fly as middle fly on the leader. This is to sink the nylon (see page 96).

Category E Sedge, midge, and upwinged fly hatches offer more in hope than in reality on most days on most waters. For this reason, when hatches are sparse I usually stick to the Category D method with nymphs/pupae plus dry fly to hedge my bets. If the hatch is a big one, then it is simpler to stick with just one dry fly on the leader. The same also applies when there is a big fall of land insects (e.g. daddy-long-legs, hawthorn fly). However, there is a problem when fishing at the surface, especially in calm water or a slight ripple: Floating Nylon Syndrome.

Floating Nylon Syndrome (F.N.S.)   At this point I ought to refer to the problem that confronts the angler when he fishes any type of fly at the surface. Nylon is superbly inexpensive, tough, strong, reliable and rot-proof, but it has one drawback. It quickly attracts grease, from the fingers or from the traces of oil found in all waters, and then it floats. You can degrease it quite easily with

sinkant (see Chapter 6) but in what seems no time at all it begins to
float again. It is no real problem when used with a sinking line or
weighted fly—they drag it down—but when used with surface or
lightweight subsurface flies the floating leader point glints in the
sun, causes a furrow on the water surface and definitely puts the fish
off. I have frequently watched trout come to my dry fly or nymphs
hanging from the surface film and turn away at the last moment
—a good indicator of F.N.S.! If the nylon is sunk on the next cast,
the fish will often come again and take the fly.

So, when fishing at or close to the surface always coat the nylon
with sinkant at the start of fishing, whenever the nylon has been
handled (e.g. after changing the fly or landing a fish) or at the first
signs of the nylon beginning to float. It is also worth sticking a plain

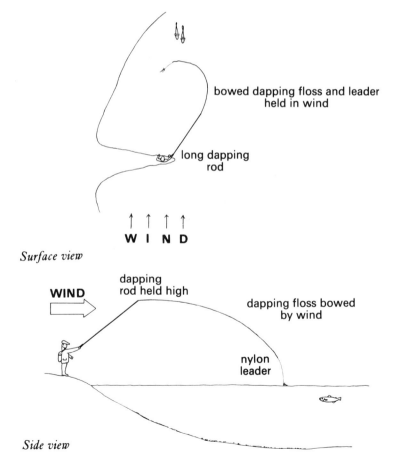

bowed dapping floss and leader
held in wind

long dapping
rod

↑   ↑   ↑   ↑
W I N D

Surface view

WIND

dapping
rod held high

dapping floss bowed
by wind

nylon
leader

Side view

wet fly or nymph on a dropper to pull the nylon beneath the surface (see Categories D and E).

Sinking tapered leaders are now available on the market, the most recent being a braided type that includes fine strands of wire to weight it. These could be the best solution to F.N.S. (F.N.S. can make the difference between a good bag and none at all) but they are rather expensive.

Alternatively, you can dap the dry fly so that only the fly touches the water, fly-line and nylon leader being airborne. Although dapping is traditionally carried out from a drifting boat, it can also be done from the bank, say, from a promontory which the wind sweeps across (see diagram on page 96).

Much used on Irish loughs and Scottish lochs, dapping is becoming increasingly popular on the lowland reservoirs of England. It makes an interesting change from the other styles of fishing the fly which require repeated casting, is an effective way of presenting a floating fly to a trout, and the take is superbly exciting (see Chapter 8, p.145).

Dapping is frequently carried out with natural flies. In Ireland, for example, the mayfly is often used and in Scotland and northern England the daddy-long-legs is preferred. These can be impaled on lightweight, long shank, mayfly hooks (about sizes 10–12) by threading the insect's thorax onto the hook. When dapping the daddy-long-legs two insects are sometimes used on the one hook to increase the size of the 'bait'. Alternatively, special dapping bait hooks can be bought, with a spring-clip that attaches the fly to the hook. Of course, if the fishery rules stipulate 'artificial fly only', fishing the natural fly is not allowed. Then a bushy dry fly, such as a Palmer-hackled Sedge, Daddy-long-legs or Brown Moth, or the artificial mayfly patterns, should be used.

Category F Although this would seem to be dry fly fishing, as is Category E, in this case the fly lies waterlogged *in* the surface film. Just as on some occasions the trout will select only flies riding proud on the surface, sometimes they will accept only flies that are lying flat and waterlogged at the surface. Examples which I have encountered are falls of spent spinners and some land-bred insects that have been blown onto the water and are drifting across the lake. When the fish appear to be so pernickety then an unoiled dry fly, or a dry fly with most of the hackle clipped away, or a suitable wet fly with the leader carefully greased, is often the answer.

Category G As was outlined in Chapters 2 and 4 a lot of trout food may come, in summer, from the epilimnion in the form of zooplankton and, as Bob Church showed, trout taking zooplankton will take a lure readily. However, the zooplankton can occur at various depths depending on light intensity, something that varies according to time of the day, brightness of the day and water clarity. In the very early morning or late evening, or on a dull, overcast day when there is a chop on the water, a floating or slow-sink line might be effective. But in the full sunlight of a hot summer day the zooplankton and trout may be quite deep and a fast-sinking or lead-core line will be essential. It is necessary to discover the correct depth, because all evidence suggests that the fish feeding at one depth are not often prepared to move up or down by any significant amount to take a lure or a big wet fly.

To work out depth an appropriate fly-line can be chosen (bright day and clear water: lead-core or ultra-fast sinker; dull day and cloudy water: floater or slow sinker). Then, by timing, the line and lure can be allowed to sink to known depths and trials be made until the correct depth is discovered. The same method applies when the fly fisher is after those large brown trout (of the *Ferox* type) that

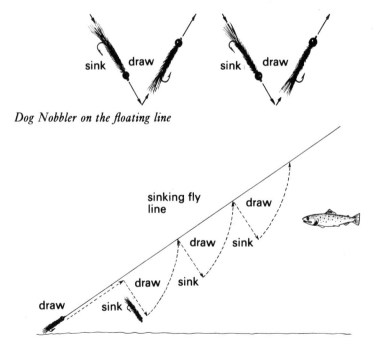

Dog Nobbler on the floating line

Dog Nobbler on the sinking line

spend much of the day deep in the epilimnion or the thermocline. The big lure fished at the correct depth (usually very deep in this case) is effective for large trout in waters as diverse as Loch Ness and Loch Morar, and Draycote and Rutland Water.

In recent years some new types of lure have developed, most notably the Dog Nobbler, in which the head of the lure is heavily weighted. These should be fished on a floating line so that with a quick stop-and-start retrieve the lure behaves in an exaggerated sink-and-draw manner.

Many anglers fish these heavy-headed lures on a sinking line, often with a uniformly fast retrieve which defeats the whole object of having the extra weight concentrated in the head of the lure. However, when fished properly on a sunk line (cast, line and lure allowed to sink to depth, retrieved with a metre's quick draw followed by a few seconds of time for the lure to sink, and so on) these lures are excellent when the fish are deep but the exact depth is not known. By their rises and falls they cover a range of depths, thereby increasing the chance of the correct depth being found.

Note: These and other gaudy lures have received a lot of criticism, alas, from many circles as being unsporting, fishmongering implements. 'Glorified spinning!' is a common moan. It is true that, sadly, many anglers pin their entire hopes on such techniques, and that they catch their fair share of fish, but the good all-round angler should be prepared and capable of using any legitimate technique when necessary in his quest to catch fish. Unless these big lures and fast-sinking lines were used some of the biggest and best trout would never be caught.

The case of the Muddler Minnow and the Floating Beetle   There are two anomalous, yet incredibly exciting and fascinating, ways of stillwater fly fishing: using the Muddler Minnow and the Floating Beetle. In some ways they are so similar in that both are fished at the surface on a floating line, and whilst reasons have been sought for the success of each, it does take a big stretch of the imagination to accept them. The Muddler, for example, was invented in the U.S.A. to imitate a small, large-headed fish, but it has been described as imitating a dry sedge skittering across the water surface. However, no sedge ploughs its way so powerfully as does a Muddler when fished to best effect. Similarly, the Floating Beetle (and its many derivatives) which seems to have its origin in the reservoirs of north-west England, though the Americans have similar tiny floating lures known as 'Poppers', is described as a land

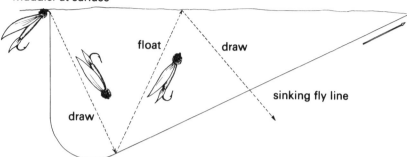

Muddler at surface

float

draw

draw

sinking fly line

beetle struggling on the water surface, or a skittering sedge, or even a daddy-long-legs. But none of these bobble at such jerky speeds as does the Beetle when fished properly. Yet both these floating lures are extremely effective, and not only for rainbow trout but also for wild brown trout, suggesting that it is not just stupid naîvety on the part of the fish that makes them so effective.

The Muddler is at its best from late May to the end of the season (September) in a fair old 'chop'. Cast across or down the waves and retrieved fairly quickly so that it cuts through the wave crests and ploughs a furrow in the wave troughs (how many aquatic creatures can do this?), the trout grab the lure violently. So much so, that it would be folly to use less than a $4\frac{1}{2}$ kg (10 lb) B.S. leader. Less conventionally, the Muddler can be used on a sinking line when it behaves as a sort of inverse version of the Dog Nobbler (see diagram). The lure is cast and the line is allowed to sink to the required depth. When line is retrieved (in one long pull) the lure is dragged under the surface. When the retrieve ceases, the lure floats upwards and hangs from the surface with deer-hair head in the surface film.

The Beetle, in its various forms (see Appendix) is cast onto the water and is retrieved with rapid bursts of short 'tweaky' pulls interspersed with periods when it lies stationary and also with periods of tiny, smooth little draws. The trout find such erratic movements irresistible. They may circle beneath the lure once or twice but when they grab they do so with a positive thump. Again, it is essential to use very strong nylon. There are some anglers in the north-west of England (especially in the Bolton area) who use nothing but these 'Beetles' and they rarely fail to catch. Whereas the Muddler needs a fair wave to be really effective, the Floating Beetle is as good in a flat calm as it is in a ripple or a wave.

6
Tackle for
Stillwater Fly Fishing

'Fly rods are like women: they won't play if they're maltreated! All rods can catch fish: their success depends on the hand that uses them. But there are rods and rods!...A faultless rod is one of the best trump-cards a fisherman has for attaining his goal.
The proper use of a rod's action depends on the line and the fisherman's hand.
It [the leader] is as important as the rod and the line and must be minutely balanced to complete uniform continuity...'

Charles Ritz, *A Fly Fisher's Life*, 1959

'First, let your rod be light, and very gentle; I take the best to be two pieces: and let not your line exceed (especially for three or four links next to the hook), I say, not exceed three or four hairs at the most, though you may fish a little stronger above, in the upper part of your line; but if you can attain to angle with one hair, you will have more rises, and catch more fish.'

Izaak Walton, *The Compleat Angler* (5th ed.), 1976

Most angling books start with a section on tackle and then proceed to consider fish, flies, etc. and how to fish. This seems illogical. An angler needs to know what sort of fly he is going to fish, how far he will have to cast and, especially important, how deep and how fast he will be fishing the flies. Then, and only then, can he choose appropriate tackle. Thus I have postponed a discussion of tackle to this apparently late but more logical stage. Fishing tackle must be able to propel a fly or team of flies, that may vary in size from a tiny size 16 or 18 dry fly or nymph up to a heavy size 6 lure, at times a long distance and at others only a few yards. It must do this as delicately as possible. The tackle must also present the fly quickly at a wide range of depths within the lake. Then an offer must be easily registered and the hook set effectively in the jaw of the trout. Finally, the fish, which may vary from a tiny wild brownie of a Scottish lochan to a massive rainbow of a put-and-take fishery of the English lowlands, must be played out and landed. This all demands a great deal and there is no substitute for the best items of tackle available.

There are plenty of bargains, but cheap items are generally expensive in the long run for sooner or later they let you down and must be replaced. Go to a good, well-known tackle dealer who has a reputation to maintain, ideally to a tackle dealer who is, himself, a fly fisher of note. He should be prepared to give you plenty of time and advice whilst you make your choice. Find someone like Pete Hemmings (of Angus Stuart's, Grantown-on-Spey) who happily takes purchasers of tackle down to the water so that they can test what they are buying. There are many of this calibre if you seek them out. Beware of spivs who want to take your cash and see you leaving the shop quickly. As Arthur Ransome said, in *Rod and Line* (1980):

> 'No one cares a hang whether his grocer takes sugar in his tea or whether he takes tea at all. But the pleasure of a visit to a tackle-shop depends a great deal upon the knowledge that at the week-end the tackle dealer will be fishing like his customer. All the great tackle dealers were good fishermen...Bad tackle dealers, who are not fishermen, take their chance and lose their customers.'

So buy the best, look after it (I have a friend who broke the top length of his salmon fly rod by using it to poke a jackdaw's nest out of the chimney) and have all your fishing tackle insured for the full replacement cost.

Tackling up! Consistent success demands the best tackle

Rods

Without beating about the bush I will say this: buy rods made of carbon fibre or boron fibre. Whilst there is possibly still a place for built-cane on rivers and streams, such rods are unnecessarily heavy for long continuous use on stillwaters where the angler is often casting more or less non-stop throughout the day. The other common rod material, fibre-glass, is now obsolete as far as fly rods are concerned, though effective enough for bait and spinning rods. Carbon and boron rods are so light that they can be used all day without the angler suffering from fatigue or muscle twinges. They are powerful, so that long casts can be made effortlessly. They are also versatile in that they allow for a wider range of lines to be used with them compared with the other older rod materials which have a narrow line tolerance. The only (very slight) criticism that I have of carbon fibre is that its stiffness deadens the movements of a hooked fish so that there is not the feel of playing the fish as there is, for example, with cane or fibre-glass rods.

As for length of rods for stillwater trout fly fishing:

'It really comes down to nothing more than a personal preference; there is no *right* length for a fly rod.'

Alan Pearson, *An Introduction to Reservoir Trout Fishing*, 1984

I cannot agree with the implication of the quotation. Carbon and boron rods are so light that one ought to take advantage of this and use as long a rod as is convenient. A good length means that the line on the backcast is automatically lifted high, thus reducing the possibility of hitting obstructions to the rear, such as high banks, dam walls and tall vegetation. The angler has more control over the way the flies fish through the water, certainly from a boat and also at close quarters when fishing from the bank. A long length also confers greater control over a fish that is being played out, for you can more easily keep the line out of the water, thereby preventing it being 'drowned', and you can play out and net the fish in deeper water with the longer rod. You can cast the same distance with balanced tackle using a rod of eight feet or a couple of metres, but casting for distance is only one function of the rod.

So, I would recommend rod lengths of at least nine feet six inches (2.85 metres), preferably ten feet (3 metres), and eleven feet (3.3 metres) if possible. Unless you are content to fish just one style all the time, then I would suggest different rods to suit different styles.

Sunk line fishing from bank or boat A powerful rod is needed that can handle a very heavy line for when the fish are very deep and when heavy, big lures are being used. In such circumstances a little delicacy can be sacrificed in favour of power. The types of rod to use are:

Bruce and Walker 10′ Carbon Reservoir Rod with WF 8–9S or SH 9S;

Bob Church 10′ Trevor Houseby Dog Nobbler with WF 8–9S or SH 9–10S;

Bob Church 10′ Boron with WF 8–9S or SH 9–10S.

Floating line fishing from bank or boat The floating line is used when the fish are feeding at or very close to the surface or in fairly shallow water (up to 10′ or 3 metres) where a long leader used in conjunction with the floating line can take a weighted fly to the bottom. In these circumstances it is imperative that the cast disturbs the water surface, and the fish, as little as possible. Thus it is essential to use rods that take as light a line as is practical and on this basis I would suggest that the best for the job are of the following types:

Hardy 11′ Carbon Deluxe Stillwater with DT6F or WF7F.

Bob Church 11½′ Boron with DT6F or WF7F.

Bruce and Walker 11′ 3″ Century X/L with DT4F or WF5F.

Remember, a long rod will do what a short rod will do, but not *vice versa*.

Dapping rods Dapping, though traditionally a sport practised on the Irish loughs and Scottish lochs, is gaining in popularity. It is now possible to purchase cheap telescopic glass rods which are ideal for this purpose. For example, the Shakespeare 17′ Telescopic O Series allows a very long line to be fished in the lightest of breezes. Alternatively, there is no reason why a long carbon fibre salmon fly rod should not be used if it is available (one 15′ in length is suitable).

Note on home-made rods. The cost of fishing rods can be greatly reduced by making or having made for you rods from the components of blank, handle, reel-fitting, rings, etc. The most important point is finding the perfect blank, something that only a good tackle dealer can advise on, but the advantage of such rods, besides cost, is that they are made just for you. Thus you can have your own favourite type of handle fitted. You can also put on the best rod rings and reel-fitting. The rod should finish up just as *you* want it to.

There are a few pitfalls in the 'roll-your-own' rod, the most important of these being that it is not too difficult to make an awful mess if you don't know exactly what you are doing, and if the materials are at all defective (especially the rod blank) there is little

chance of a replacement or refund of cash once you have started to
build. It has been argued that 'roll-your-own' rods command a very
low second-hand price. That to me is irrelevant. How many of us
buy any rod with a view to selling it?

For those who may be interested in pursuing the idea of making
their own rods I would recommend that the following firms be
contacted:

Hopkins & Holloway Ltd, Brickyard Lane, Studley, Warks.

John Norris, Dept A, 21 Victoria Road, Penrith, Cumbria.

McHardys, South Henry Street, Carlisle, Cumbria.

Fibatube Blanks, Alnwick, Northumberland.

Lines

Many books deal at great length with the terminology of fly lines,
backing lines, knots, etc. and such matters will not be repeated here,
but rod and line go together in presenting the fly to the fish so let
me recommend the following.

Floater This is essential and is preferable in brown or green. I use
the brown Yorkshire Fly Line but the firm supplying them
(McKenzie-Philps Ltd) is, alas, no more. An alternative is the green
Cortland Floater. If only white lines are available, then dye them by
putting them into *hand-warm* brown Dylon dye and leave overnight. The following morning dry the line and coat with a plasticiser (e.g. Permagrease or Permaplas).

I do not use shooting-heads (though others do so quite successfully) or heavier lines when fishing the floater. If the fish are fairly
close to the surface, then I am prepared to sacrifice some distance
for delicacy. So, I stick to the weight-forward line where distance
is required, or a double-taper line for close-up work (e.g. when fish
are very close to the bank, in small fisheries, or when fishing from
a boat).

Sinkers Two of the biggest (and best) manufacturers of fly lines
offer a range of seven (Cortland) and five (Scientific Anglers) different sinking lines. No one but the wealthy could afford such a
range, considering that each line would need a separate reel or
reel-spool. However, for the practical angler more than one sinker
is required. Firstly, a slow sinker that will fish the lure or wet fly just
below the surface: for this I would recommend the Cortland Inter-
mediate or Slow Sinker, or the Scientific Wetcel I.

At the other extreme are the essential lines that will take a lure
quickly down through the water when the fish are feeding deep in
the epilimnion in summer or close to the lake bed in early spring.

Cortland produce two weights of Kerboom Lead Core Line for this purpose, though some writers have argued against lead-cored lines on grounds of safety. Scientific Anglers produce an alternative, the Wetcel Hi-Speed Hi-D Supafast Sinking Line. One of these is essential. They will take the lure down through the water at about a foot a second: no other sinking line can match that!

In between these two there is some advantage in having an ordinary fast sinking line (e.g. Cortland Fast Sinker or Wetcel II) for use in water that is not very deep (say, 10' or 3 metres) and where one of the ultra-fast sinking lines would constantly snag the lake bed. It is good for you when you need to fish fairly deep, yet with control.

To sum up: use a floater of about DT6F (Double Taper Size 6 Floater) and WF7F (Weight Forward Size 7 Floater), or a slow sinker of about WF7S (Weight Forward Size 7 Sinker), with the longer lighter rod when fishing close to the surface; use a fast sinker of about WF8S or SH9S (Shooting Head Size 9 Sinker), or an ultra-fast sinker of about WF8S or SH9S, with the slightly shorter, more powerful rod when fishing deep. The actual line specifications (AFTM number) will, of course, depend on the rods being used.

Some might say, 'But where is the sink-tip line?' Sink-tip lines are not needed by the stillwater angler. It is far better to use the slow sinker, a much more versatile line and one that, on stillwaters, is easier to handle than the sink-tip.

Dapping Line (or Blow Line) If you plan to go a-dapping for trout, then you will need some dapping floss, a light floss line that is easily picked up and held in the lightest of breezes. This is extremely inexpensive compared with normal fly lines; any make will do nicely.

Reels

If I could afford it I would have all my fly lines on Hardy Perfect $3\frac{5}{8}''$. Unfortunately, I cannot! There are, however, many good quality second division reels available of which I would recommend:

Shakespeare Beaulite $3\frac{1}{2}''$ wide.

J. W. Young 1500 Series $3\frac{1}{2}''$ wide.

I do not like geared reels for fly fishing, for I find that playing a big fish from the reel is much more difficult with such models. It seems that the gears, which are so useful for retrieving slack line quickly, make it much harder when reeling against heavier weights. However, I have several geared reels that I use on occasion, the best being:

Shakespeare Speedex $3\frac{1}{2}''$ wide.

All the above will take the lines recommended together with enough backing. I use 25 lb (11.4 kg) breaking strain monofilament; there seems little point in paying a lot of money for special braided backing line though many anglers do. With shooting heads flat monofilament (e.g. Cortland's Cobra) is preferable to conventional round monofilament.

At least two reels will be needed, for most anglers will want to change from floating to sinking line during the day, especially those fishing stocked waters, and will set up two rods at the start. Other lines can conveniently be carried on spare spools which are considerably cheaper than full reels.

Tackle maintenance

The three items of tackle, rods, lines and reels, are expensive and well repay time spent on regular maintenance. Too often anglers neglect this, so may I suggest some basic rules of tackle servicing:

1. Always wipe down the rods after use with a damp cloth, paying special attention to the rod rings. Check rod rings for wear or chipping and replace them immediately where necessary.

2. Always clean out the internal 'works' of the fly reel after use. Bits of grit can quickly damage reel bearings and reel spindles. Oil the moving parts regularly. I reckon that my reels need a light re-oiling about once in every six fishing days (60 hours of use).

3. A well-maintained fly line will last at least twice as long as one that is neglected. So:

(a) Floating lines—after about every ten days' use wash thoroughly in luke warm water to which has been added a few drops of mild liquid detergent. Rinse thoroughly and wipe dry. Then re-coat with a line dressing agent (e.g. Permagrease or Permaplas). I have a Yorkshire DT6F that is now five years old and has been used for at least 300 days' fishing. It has several more seasons left in it. My previous DT6F was not looked after as this one has been; it lasted me just two seasons.

(b) Sinking lines—wash regularly as above and treat with a line plasticiser. Sinking lines frequently become stiff and wiry so that they kink and form annoying tangles. Regular applications of plasticiser reduce this, and when sinking lines have not been used for a few weeks it is worth giving them a good stretching before starting to fish.

4. Store tackle so that it cannot be easily damaged. When not in use rods should be hung up, in their bags. Reels should be stored in

boxes or reel cases in a drawer or cupboard. It takes only a slight knock to crack the wall of a carbon fibre rod or to buckle the gate of a reel. When you are going fishing keep the rods in strong plastic tubes on the journey in the car and don't force a fishing bag, containing the reels, into a small corner of an over-filled car boot. 5. Remember that modern rods, lines and reels are precision instruments. Treat them as such and they will never, ever let you down.

Leaders   Relatively short level leaders of about nine feet (2.7 metres) of nylon monofilament will suffice with the sinking lines. These should be of a breaking strain appropriate to the size of fish that are likely to be encountered, to the size of lure being used and to the depth at which the lure will be fished (the deeper, the stronger). I would suggest the following as a general guide:

		Leader breaking strain	
Lure size	Fly line	lb	kg
Tandem hook lures	Ultra-fast sink	12	5.5
	Slow sink	8	3.6
Size 6–8 long shank	Ultra-fast sink	12	5.5
	Slow sink	8	3.6
Size 10–12 long shank	Ultra-fast sink	10	4.5
	Slow sink	8	3.6
Size 6–8 standard length	Ultra-fast sink	10	4.5
	Slow sink	8	3.6
Size 10–12 standard	Ultra-fast sink	8	3.6
length	Slow sink	6	2.7

Alternatively, a bought, no-knot, tapered leader butt can be permanently attached to the fly line and then a three feet (about one metre) point tied to this butt of nylon of the appropriate breaking strain.

When fishing close to the surface, or when fishing deeper with leaded nymphs or shrimps on the floating line, a tapered leader is essential to reduce the risk of tangles and to allow a better turn over of the leader during the cast. Most anglers make up their own tapered leaders from lengths of different strengths of nylon, but these must be tied with care. I have experimented with home-made tapered leaders and suggest the formulae on page 109.

Measurements given of the various strengths of nylon making up a leader are knot-to-knot lengths. Thus in the preparation of a leader allowance must be made for losses that occur in the tying process.

It is easily possible to vary the above formulae to give different

Breaking strain of Length of leader nylon					
lb	kg	9′	(2.7 m)	12′	(3.6 m)
30	13.6	-	-	48″	120 cm
26	11.8	48″	120 cm	24″	60 cm
19	8.6	15″	38 cm	12″	30 cm
14	6.4	9″	23 cm	12″	30 cm
10	4.5	9″	23 cm	12″	30 cm
8	3.6	9″	23 cm	12″	30 cm
6	2.7	18″	46 cm	24″	60 cm

leader lengths or leaders with different strengths of points. To vary length simply increase or decrease, as appropriate, the length of each link in the leader. I have given the details for the two leader lengths that I find most useful. If a point of, say, 4 lb (1.8 kg) B.S. is needed, reduce the length of the 6 lb (2.7 kg) link to 9″ (23 cm) and tie a 4 lb point to this. If an 8 lb (3.6 kg) point is needed, then have the 8 lb length as 18 or 21″ (46 or 53 cm) as appropriate and increase the first heavy length (the 26 or 30 lb 'butt') by 9″ (23 cm).

On the floating line especially it is not unusual to use two or three flies. One or two of them will be tied onto droppers which should be attached to the leader as follows:

9′ (2.7 metre) leader—
Top dropper tied in at the end of the 19 lb (8.6 kg) length.
Bottom dropper tied in at the base of the 6 lb (2.7 kg) point.
If only one dropper is being used, then it is best attached on the short 10 lb (4.5 kg) link, 36″ (90 cm) from the point fly.

12′ (3.6 metre) leader—
Top dropper tied in at the end of the 26 lb (11.8 kg) link.
Bottom dropper tied in at the end of the 10 lb (4.5 kg) link.
If only one dropper is being used, then the top dropper is left out.

The length of droppers should be about 6″ (15 cm), and new ones should be tied when the old ones become much shorter than this consequent to changing flies. The strength of the droppers should be identical to that of the leader point. As to knots, this is a matter of personal preference. I use a five-turn water knot.

The most important point as regards leader strength is to make doubly certain that it is sufficient to hold *any* fish that may be encountered in the lake you are going to fish. To fish too fine so that you risk breakage should a particularly large trout grab the fly is unsporting: no good angler is prepared to allow a trout to suffer by carrying a hook and trailing length of nylon in its mouth. Of course there must be *some* compromise when using tiny hooks, especially close to or at the surface, for the behaviour of the fly is impaired if too stout a nylon is used. Also, the finer nylon reduces the debilitating effects of 'Floating Leader Syndrome' (see pp.95–98).

To reduce the risks of leader breakage you could incorporate a short length of elastic 'Shock Gum' into the butt of the tapered leader. The idea is that when a fish takes a lure with an explosive bang (a take that may ordinarily result in breakage) some of the force is taken up by the Shock Gum stretching rather than the less elastic nylon leader snapping. I have tried this relatively new innovation and found that it is a good insurance against breakage either on the strike or during playing the fish.

There is a new development in leader design that is worth the stillwater angler considering. The fishing tackle industry has been supplying plain nylon leaders for many years and lots of anglers use them. Recently special floating- and sinking-leader butts have been developed which are attached to the fly line and the angler simply attaches a point (and droppers if necessary) of monofilament nylon using a needle knot. These butts stay in place for at least one season, thus reducing the need for carefully tied-up leaders or the repeated expense of purchasing ordinary nylon tapered leaders. I have used the floating and sinking braided butt leaders introduced by Bob Church and Sue Burgess: they are excellent. They 'turn over' much better than home-made knotted leaders and are far more durable than bought no-knot tapered nylon leaders. It only remains for the angler to renew the monofilament point and droppers when it is considered necessary. The one thing to be careful of is the method of attachment of the braided leader butt to the fly-line. With some are provided plastic-tube collars. The fly-line is slipped into the end of the hollow leader butt and secured by one of these collars. Unfortunately, after several hours' fishing these stiff collars wear through the plastic covering of the fly-line. I have found it better to slip the end half inch (or centimetre) of the fly-line into the end of the hollow braided leader and coat with Superglue. Then, when the Superglue is dry, I coat the joint with two thin coats of fly-tying varnish. This seals the joint from water.

Note: Many writers advocate the use of Superglue for connecting backing line and leaders to the fly-line. However, in time *all* Superglues appear to be weakened by repeated contact with water. So, check such joints regularly.

Miscellaneous extras It is likely that no two anglers take exactly identical sets of tackle down to the water. There are some items that we all consider, or ought to consider, essential.

1. *A landing-net* This should be as large as possible, with a long net handle. I use a folding net with a telescopic handle which is especially convenient when there is a lot of walking to do. The mesh ought always to be of the soft, unknotted type so that any fish that has to be netted before being returned is not damaged by hard knots.

Note: Never handle a fish with bare hands if you want to return it alive to the water. Either release it by shaking it from the hook gently (barbless hooks help here), or hold it in the wet net bag. The skin of a trout is a sensitive structure, containing masses of nerve endings, especially along the lateral line, and is easily damaged. Thus a fish that has been handled may die soon after release or, following infection by *Saprolegnia* fungi, some days later even though the angler could see nothing wrong when he released it. It is for this reason that many stocked fisheries (such as Draycote and Grafham) insist that every captured trout must be killed, and the angler stops fishing when he has taken his bag limit. Others (e.g. Stocks Reservoir) insist on the use of barbless hooks once a limit bag has been caught. A few private put-and-take waters have a rule prohibiting the use of any barbed hook. This is so that fish which are to be returned to the lake need not be handled at all.

2. *A Priest* No angler should venture forth unless he has a priest. To attempt to kill trout by hitting them with blunt objects found on the lake shore puts the sport of trout fishing into disrepute and anyone who allows trout to die slowly by flapping to and fro on the bank or in the bottom of the boat should be prosecuted under the 1981 Countryside Act for causing the fish unnecessary suffering.

3. *Sinkants and Flotants* To degrease nylon so that it will not float is essential if Floating Line Syndrome is to be avoided. Before starting to fish and at the first sign of F.L.S. appearing a sinkant should be coated on the leader. Though it may seem a niggling little job, this can make the difference between catching a trout and not catching one. Make your own sinkant by mixing Fuller's Earth powder (obtainable from most chemists) with washing-up detergent to a smooth creamy consistency.

When fishing with a floating line it pays to have the tip of the fly line and the butt of the leader well greased so that they float high on the water and act as a good indicator of an offer should a fish take the nymph or whatever. Some anglers use one of the mucelins; I prefer Permagrease which also contains a fly line plasticiser. Thus the line flotant also acts as a conditioner to the part of the fly line that does most work, namely the last few metres.

A liquid flotant is needed for dry flies, the one invented by the late Dick Walker (Permaflote) being the best.

A useful tip: treat all your dry flies with flotant at home and let them dry before putting them into the dry fly box. They will then have a good coating of flotant on every hackle and tail fibre. They will float all day long. This is not the case when the fly is dunked into the flotant just before use, for a lot of the liquid flotant is lost during casting. Then, when you have caught a fish on a dry fly, remove that fly from the leader and tie on a fresh one. When you return home give all the dry flies that you have used a wash in luke warm water. Let them dry and then re-treat with flotant. If you do this, your dry flies will last much longer and they will always float.

4. *Spare Nylon* One of the commonest arguments amongst anglers is over the merits and demerits of different brands of nylon. Personally, I prefer Maxima in the heavier breaking strains (5 lb, 2.27 kg) and either Kroic or Platil in the lighter lines. Tom Saville supplies a very good stiff nylon called Tynex which I have used recently and found excellent. Nylon must be stored out of the light as it is weakened by ultra-violet light waves. Keep it, in the fishing bag, in a black polythene bag or box or in a spool dispenser, and at the end of the season burn any nylon of less than 10 lb (4.5 kg) B.S. Storing nylon is a false economy. It is far better to purchase new stocks for the new season than risk losing a fish on nylon that has deteriorated.

We all have tangles or wind knots that appear by magic in the leader from time to time, so we all have nylon to discard when fishing. However, never leave any nylon on the lake bank; even nylon that has been cut into tiny lengths. Put waste nylon into your bag and burn it when you get back home. Don't put lengths of nylon into the dustbin for it may end up scattered about the local rubbish tip and countryside.

This is important. Every year thousands of waterside creatures die due to discarded bits of fishing tackle. Each death brings the sport of angling into disrepute and gives more armour to the anti-fishing lobby. Besides (and of far more significance), what would a river bank or lake shore be like without the water birds, amphibians and mammals?

Every piece of discarded tackle brings the possibility of bans being imposed. Consider the lead shot/mute swan problem! We will not be able to use lead shot through much of Britain because of deaths of swans that were attributable to discarded lead shot. Do we want to see the use of hooks and nylon similarly banned or restricted?

Every angler ought to go home after a day's fishing leaving nothing at the water's edge but footprints.

5. *Scissors and Artery Forceps* I put these together because it is possible to buy special scissors and forceps usefully combined into one. Whilst the uses of the former need no mention here, the latter is essential where a hook is difficult to extract from a trout that must be returned to the water. Note my point made earlier about the careful handling of trout. If a hook is so badly embedded that the fish bleeds then dispatch that fish quickly. Artery forceps can also be used to flatten the barb of the hook when one wishes or, because of fishery rules, when one has to fish with a barbless fly.

6. *Marrow Spoon* On any fishing trip it is useful to find out what the trout are feeding on as soon as possible. To 'spoon' out the trout as one catches them is a good policy. G. E. M. Skues, the great chalkstream angler, devised the use of an old marrow scoop or spoon for this purpose and today you can buy special spoons for the job. I use old plastic thermometer tubes for the purpose; they are free and work just as well. Get an old, hard plastic tube about one centimetre in diameter and cut as shown in the diagram below.

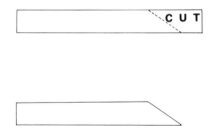

The scoop is pushed into the mouth of the dead trout and deep into its stomach. It is then turned around and then slowly extracted, bringing with it the remains of the trout's recent meal. These can be examined by floating them into a small plastic bowl or saucer containing a little lake water (see diagram on p. 114).

7. The following are non-essential items carried by many anglers, but they are all useful.

(a) *Fishing bag*—to store spare tackle and food.

(b) *Creel or bass*—to keep the catch fresh; it is far better than the modern plastic bag.

(c) *Spare leaders* carried on *cast carriers*—useful when you are going

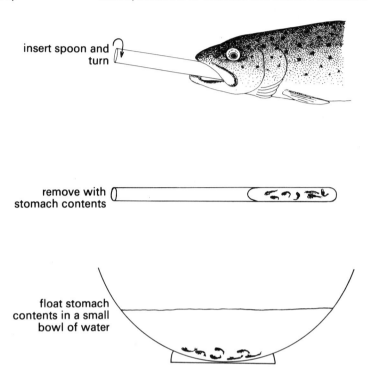

insert spoon and turn

remove with stomach contents

float stomach contents in a small bowl of water

through a spell of tangling up cast after cast. Having spare leaders tied up at home is certainly more convenient than tying them hurriedly at the lake edge.

(c) *Anti-midge lotions*—essential in the highlands of Britain where particularly obnoxious biting midges await the angler. The best, by far, is Jungle Formula Mijex.

The rest of the tackle is entirely a matter of personal preference. I always carry a torch, just in case I am tempted to stay late for the sedge hatch, and a compass and map if I am out in the wilds. Clothing and footwear depend on location and day. I am happy afloat on Draycote or Ullswater in summer with shirt-sleeves, but out in the hills I always carry a pullover and waterproof and wind-proof coat, even on the hottest days, in case the weather turns foul. I also consider polaroid sunglasses as indispensable when fishing in daylight hours.

7
Fly Fishing
from the Bank

'I have a slight preference for bank-fishing even though I accept that
the advantage lies with the boat angler.'
   Geoffrey Bucknall, *Modern Techniques of Stillwater
Fly-Fishing*, 1980

'...there are really two schools of bank fisherman. There are those
who prefer to select a spot where trout are known to feed ... On the
other hand you have the 'roaming' type of bank fisherman who
prefers to explore the more distant and less fished parts of the
water ... During a day's fishing this chap will cover several miles of
shore line ...'
   Jim Calver, *Bank Fishing for Reservoir Trout*, 1979

To be a successful bank angler it is essential to know exactly where
the fish are, or are likely to be, and it is often *not* the banks closest
to the car park or fishing lodge! It always strikes me as incredible
that, on the larger lakes, most trout anglers invariably congregate at
the most accessible points under the misapprehension that if the
trout are not there now, sooner or later they will arrive.
   Only recently (a very cold early season day) my son and I arrived
at a large northern trout fishery. Over a hundred rods had signed in
and from the car park we could see most of them, scattered at
regular intervals like herons along the shores of the nearer bay. We
watched for a few minutes to see if any were catching. They were
not. So we followed the path, over a little hill, which led us to the
upper reaches of the lake. Then, in the distance, where two feeder
streams enter the lake and join to form a big channel, we spied three
fishermen. Ten minutes later we joined them at our chosen spot. To
cut a long story short I can summarise the day by saying that over
200 anglers fished this lake and just eight caught fish: the five of us
who had tramped to that far corner and another three who had,
likewise, sought fish feeding at the entrances of feeder streams. Of
course we all *knew* that there would be a lot of fish there, but why
did not at least some of the others eventually arrive at the same or

similar spots, having slowly and methodically fished their way along the shore? Idleness? Lack of thought?

Someone who fishes a lake for the first time is at a disadvantage over the regular, for he has to find the fish whereas the regular can, often, go straight to them (hence the validity of the two approaches to bank fishing mentioned by Jim Calver in the quotation at the head of the chapter).

A newcomer must seek out the fish if he is to have the best chance of success. So he will carry the minimum of tackle, having decided the general tactics, and slowly fish his way around the lake, making a few casts every few yards. If a particular area catches his eye, such as a peninsula or an offshore weedbed, then he might spend a few minutes there and fish it more thoroughly. By such a slow progression our first-time visitor should eventually find one of the better fishing areas and catch some trout.

For the regular visitor to the lake this is not necessary. As I described earlier, he can go exactly to where the fish will be lying, without using a trial and error system. He might know of two; there will be others to try.

New territory   Sooner or later we all visit lakes that we have never fished before. We do so with feelings of anticipation, but unless we can find the hot-spots or are very lucky, then our bags will remain light and our hearts grow heavy!

Imagine that you are going to a lake that you have not fished before. How do you find the trout?

There are a few points to be made before you arrive at the water. Because you will be fishing from the bank, you will be fishing the lake margins. You will be looking for trout that are mainly feeding at random on whatever food they can glean from the lake bed or more selectively on mature nymphs and pupae that are rising to the surface to hatch into adult flies. If you are lucky you might find fish feeding on adult flies if there is a large enough hatch, or there may be a fall of land-bred flies that are being drifted across the lake by the wind and ripple to the side you are fishing. If you can find a feeder-stream that is bringing food items into the lake, you might expect quite a concentration of trout to be lying in wait in or just off the stream mouth.

Time of year is important when fishing from the banks of most lakes. In spring the deeper water that may be mostly out of casting range will be unproductive and you can expect the fish to look to the shallower margins for all their food. However, at this time of the year there are relatively few sparse hatches of fly (mostly a few midges) so that the fish will be deep and unseen. Remembering that the highest density of invertebrates occur in water up to 10–15 feet (3–4 metres) deep this is the sort of depth you should be looking for. You should search for areas where the lake bed shelves gradually, giving a broader band of margin feeding for the trout, rather than for areas where the shore plummets to vast depths where the natural foods will be in a very narrow zone and thus more scarce or, in eutrophic lakes (where the hypolimnion becomes devoid of oxygen in summer), virtually non-existent.

As in every rule that one tries to formulate in angling there are exceptions. The exception here is newly-stocked trout, especially rainbows, which commonly patrol the deep water off reservoir dams in large shoals until they have learned that twice-daily helpings of trout pellets are not going to be provided and that they must seek natural foods.

If you were visiting the lake later in the year, there would be a bloom of plankton in the epilimnion. Where this is huge, as in eutrophic lakes, the trout might leave the margins and turn almost exclusively to this food supply. In big lakes they will then be mostly out of reach of the bank angler and the boat angler will have the upper hand, but a large movement of pupae or nymphs to the surface to hatch, or a hatch of flies on the surface, or a fall of land flies, may attract the fish. Such occurrences tend to happen in the early morning or late afternoon and evening of summer. So, if you fail to score through a hot, bright day, you can look forward to the final few hours up to darkness as being the time to fish with real confidence. Where you are allowed, in the dog days of high summer, it is worth planning a fishing session to start in the early afternoon and continue well into darkness. That is when the big sedge, midge and upwinged fly hatches tend to occur in the margins. It is also when the trout will congregate in the margins and when you can (or should) catch them easily.

Night fishing

In *Freshwater Fishing* (1975) Fred Buller and Hugh Falkus say the following:

> 'From our observations we have noticed that, like river brown trout, reservoir brown trout continue to feed after dark, whereas reservoir rainbows do not. It would be more strictly true to say that we and our friends have continued to catch brown trout well after dark, whereas we have not succeeded in catching a single rainbow in the same circumstances.'

This I find quite amazing, for I and many of my friends frequently catch rainbows as well as brown trout in the darkest of summer nights when there are good hatches of sedges or midges. The two Brians (Hoggarth and Wells), both outstanding trout anglers, regard night as being the logical time in high summer to be catching both brown and rainbow trout. In the stifling heat of the 1975, '76, '83 and '84 summers, when not a fish stirred through the day in many of the lakes I fished, fly activity resulted in good trout fishing (including rainbows) into the night. This was not just twilight, but through to one o'clock in the morning and beyond.

For example, on one occasion my creel was still empty at sunset. It had been an almost unbearably hot still day. Not an insect had stirred, or a fish broken the flat, mirror-like water surface. Then, in the last light a few sedges and clouds of midges appeared over the margin of the small bay. A few fish broke the surface out in the lake. Gradually activity increased, trout moving closer and closer so that eventually they were in casting range. In the gloom I tied on a cast with a Deerhair Sedge (point fly), and a green Sedge Pupa and a black Buzzer Pupa on the droppers. I coated the leader with sinkant, thoroughly wet the two wet flies with saliva so that they would sink immediately, and made my way to a stone spit that commanded a view over the entrance to the bay. It was 11.15 p.m. and the light had gone. Fishing by touch (it is incredible how the senses function so acutely at night when there is little to distract them from the job in hand) I hooked eleven fish and landed eight—five rainbows and three brown trout—in the period up to 1.30 a.m., all in complete darkness. Of course the fishery rules allowed me to continue to this early hour.

Closure of fisheries at night Unfortunately, on most rainbow trout waters the angler may not fish at so late a time; and this is possibly the reason for the comment made by Fred Buller and Hugh Falkus. The smaller put-and-take fisheries frequently have very strict fishing hours, sometimes rather like a shift system. On some of these the last shift ends abruptly as early as eight o'clock in the evening (i.e. well before dusk in mid-summer). On the larger reservoirs the rule is usually for fishing from sunrise to one hour after sunset. I cannot find a more exasperating regulation, for it means that anglers must pack up and leave the water just as the evening hatch is getting under way. Thus the pleasures of fishing the imitative dry fly or surface-hatching nymphs and pupae to feeding fish are discouraged.

Fishery managers will argue that they must close their waters through the night to prevent rules being broken by unseen anglers using bait on fly-only waters or taking more than their bag limits. Such an excuse does not bear close scrutiny. I have seen evidence of bait being used on many of our more famous fly-only reservoir fisheries in broad daylight. On very few waters are bags and cars checked to make sure that anglers are not taking more than their limits; and when checks are made a minority is always found to have stolen a few extra despite daylight.

Safety is another excuse to close the water at night, but if it is safe enough to fish the natural lakes of upland Britain in the dark why should it be less safe to fish artificial lowland lakes (especially from the bank)?

Fishery owners aim, of course, to make a profit and would argue that they would have to employ staff to cover night fishing and thus their costs would rise. However, most private fisheries are guarded through the night to prevent poaching. Such nightwatchmen are already paid for by the fishery owner. (Incidentally, to allow *bona fide* anglers to fish at night would greatly reduce the risk of poaching, and night anglers could be charged for the privilege.) On the other hand, many Water Authority reservoir ticket waters are not thoroughly bailiffed during the day so why the bodies controlling these waters should be concerned about having staff there at night puzzles me.

There is another possible argument for closing a fishery overnight and that is 'to give the water a rest'. Resting the water is a fallacy! The water is rested when the fish cease feeding and refuse to take the angler's flies. The time *not* to rest the water is when the trout are feeding keenly. In bright hot summer weather this means from late afternoon through well into the darkness.

Location of trout

To go back to the discussion on where the fish are likely to be, there is a reasonably well-established pattern:

1. *Spring and late autumn*—when water temperatures are very low and the lake is not stratified. Trout are concentrated in the margins, especially in bays and inlets, and around the entrances of feeder streams or close to outflows (including pumping towers of reservoirs). When it is very cold, trout will be lying close to the lake bed but will be reluctant to feed.

2. *Summer and autumn*—when surface temperatures are higher and the lake is stratified. Trout may spread throughout the lake, often

away from the margins and mostly out of reach of the bank angler. If there is a fall of land insects during the day the trout will turn to them, and if there is a hatch of aquatic flies in the evening the trout will feed on them. You must find areas where flies will be more concentrated or areas of margin where hatches are greatest. In this respect the effect of wind must be noted, for the wind (and wave) will drift natural foods in the water surface into the windward margin.

3. *Put-and-take fisheries*—for at least a few days after stocking the shoals of trout, especially rainbows, may patrol deeper water (e.g. off the dams, deeper channels). Later hunger will cause them to spread out more through the lake and the appropriate pattern 1 or 2 (above) will apply.

I have included a couple of sketch maps, the sort that you might draw when describing the best fishing areas to a friend who is going to make his first visit to that water.

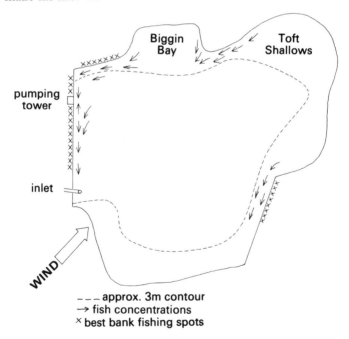

- - - approx. 3m contour
→ fish concentrations
× best bank fishing spots

Draycote Water is a well-known English lowland reservoir. Much of the shallower water is out of reach of the bank angler (e.g. Toft Shallows and Biggin Bay) and these are superb boat angling areas. The best areas for the bank angler are the dam close to the inlet and outlet, and the margins that are exposed to the wind

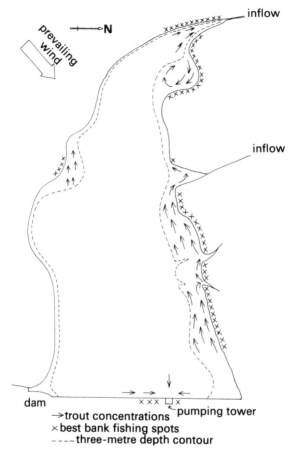

Entwistle Reservoir is a typical Pennine reservoir with wild brownies and stocked rainbows. Notice the importance of the inflows and the wide shallow margin on the north (windward) shore. The dam close to the pumping tower is especially productive when water is being drawn off the reservoir

At this point I ought to say a little about the tinier fisheries, both natural and put-and-take stocked waters. In these finding the fish is not difficult. It is a simple matter to fish quickly around these pools; and with fairly long casts most of the water will be covered by the flies. There is not the feeling, as one sometimes gets on the bigger lakes when the fish are not breaking the surface, of the trout possibly being out of range. These little pools are the sort of water that are good for the novice, who can concentrate on the choice and presentation of the flies without having to find the trout.

The other advantage of the novice serving something of an apprenticeship on the smaller waters is that he will learn the art of reading the water as the trout still tend to congregate in hot-spots even in these pools. He can thus acquire the expertise necessary to read the bigger lakes.

A very important point to think about when you go to any lake for the first time is what sorts and sizes of fish you will find there. If the fishery has been stocked, then you should know the likely size of the average trout. It may be that you are going to fish a 'big trout water', stocked with brown trout and brook trout over 3 lb (1 kg) and rainbows over 10 lb (4 kg) weight. You may, therefore, require heavier tackle than you would need when fishing a loch full of small wild brownies.

It is also worthwhile knowing how long it has been since the lake was stocked. In waters that rely on stocking to maintain the head of fish, generally the longer the time since stocking, the more difficult will be the fishing (i.e. the more wary and attuned to natural foods the fish will be that are left). Also, in a water that is heavily fished, the bulk of the stock fish are usually taken soon after stocking.

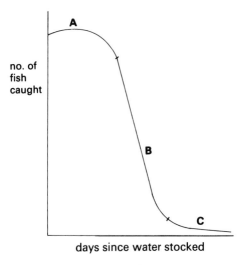

days since water stocked

In A the fishing is easy; there are a lot of uneducated trout that will grab almost any lure. In B the fishing is becoming increasingly more difficult as, with every day that passes, fewer of the new stockies remain and those that do become a little more 'educated' and harder to catch. In C very few stockies remain and those that do are usually extremely wary; only a lucky or good angler will catch them

Thus, if it has been some time since the last stocking there may be very few left (see diagram on page 122).

On the other hand, when fishing a naturally stocked water you also ought to know the size and numbers of fish you are likely to find. Sometimes this information can be gleaned from guide books or articles in the fishing press. Local tackle dealers can be a mine of information, as can be the offices of estates that own the waters. Of course, you can also gain an idea of the probable size and numbers of fish by looking objectively at the lake and its surroundings. Unproductive lakes, set high in the mountains, it will be remembered, will have tiny trout whereas those of the lowlands, set in the midst of farmland, have larger fish.

Only an idiot goes to fish *any* water without knowing what he is likely to catch, and a word of warning: it is essential to check details afresh each year. I have a couple of friends who spent a full day fishing on a small loch that was absolutely fishless due to a pollution incident the previous winter.

Method   The last point to consider before you arrive at the fishery is how you are going to catch the fish. In this chapter we are just dealing with fly fishing, but in many natural waters you could employ spinning or bait (see pp. 174–80).

The vast majority of anglers, when visiting a lake stocked with rainbow trout, think immediately of lure-fishing, usually with a sinking line. And why not? It is a method that probably catches more rainbow trout than any other. Indeed, it is one that I invariably try when confronted with a new water which contains rainbows. When used with a little thought it usually produces a bag of fish, but as I explained in Chapter 5 depth of the lure and speed of retrieve are of paramount importance, especially when the trout have been in the lake for more than a few weeks. So, when lure fishing it is worthwhile, having found a likely hot-spot, varying depth and retrieve rate by some form of measurement. Then, when the optimal depth and speed have been found (by catching a fish), they can be repeated fairly accurately.

This can be explained, as follows. Cast your normal length of line and count as the lure sinks: 'One...two...three...and so on.' By doing a series of retrieves at, say, 10, 20, 30, 45 and 60 seconds sinking times you know that all depths have been carefully fished. Incidentally, I am assuming here that at 60 seconds the lure is close to the bottom and occasionally snags the lake bed. If you catch a fish or have an offer following a particular sinking time, you have discovered the depth of the fish and, what is more important, you can put your lure again at that depth precisely. You will not be bringing the lure back high above or far below the trout. This assumes, of course, that the trout are not prepared to move up or down through the water to any considerable extent to take your lure. Often they are not; sometimes, happily, they are.

Varying depths   Even if you catch at one depth it may be worthwhile trying others. For instance, if you have had a couple of trout on a lure that was allowed to sink for 30 seconds and which you know was not very close to the lake bed, try going much deeper. Time it: you may lose the lure or it may come back with weed attached. How long did it take? 75 seconds? Then retrieve the lure after 70 seconds and you know you will be deep enough. At these depths some of the bigger trout can be found, possibly from previous years' stockings. These are trout that are reluctant to rise to the fly or trout that are possibly 'ferox' in habits.

Example: Draycote at the end of April, fishing the corner of the main dam. Four rainbows came to the net after a 15-second sinking time. They were around the $1\frac{1}{2}$ lb mark and obviously recent stockies. The line was then allowed to sink deeper (for 75 seconds) and a lure was lost due to snagging on the lake bed. Further casts at this depth resulted in a rainbow of $4\frac{1}{2}$ lb and a brown trout of 3 lb. Two more were needed for the bag limit. Fishing continued at the greater depth and three more lures were lost on the bottom. In frustration a return was made to the 15-second depth. A fish was lost, and then one taken: again, a smaller rainbow of just over a pound. The day ended, therefore, with five smaller trout taken close to the surface and two larger ones taken close to the bottom.

Incidentally, when fishing the margins an ordinary fast sink or slow sinking line is the one to use, depending upon water depth. Unless the lake bed shelves extremely steeply an ultra-fast sinker, such as a lead-cored line, will have to be brought back too quickly otherwise it will continue sinking to the lake bed and become 'hung up'. Where the water is fairly deep (e.g. off a dam wall or in a particularly deep gully) an ordinary fast sinker will do; in most lake margins where the water is only a few metres deep a slow sinker is far more effective. It can be allowed to sink to the appropriate depth and retrieved very slowly without the weight of the line continuing to take the lure quickly down to the lake bed. The slow sinker is especially advantageous whilst the deeply-fished lure is being brought into the side through very shallow water. Then the lead-cored line and fast sinker will often result in snagging and loss of the lure—the slow sinker will snag much less. To prevent this problem, those anglers who do use lines that sink too quickly for the depth of water they are fishing often roll-cast the line when it is still several metres from the bank, in an attempt to prevent snagging in the shallows and at the same time start the next cast. It is a mistake for, as I pointed out in Chapter 5 (pp. 85–6), sometimes the trout will follow a lure right to the side before taking at the last minute. It is essential, therefore, to ensure that the cast is properly fished out and that the type of sinking line that is used allows this to be done.

Retrieve rate   Occasionally one hears of anglers who, having fished for some time unsuccessfully, suddenly catch a trout 'on the drop'. By this they mean that the lure (or wet fly) was taken as they allowed the line and lure to sink. Possibly this suggests that they were previously fishing too deeply, but more likely it is because they were fishing too quickly. A sinking lure on a sinking line does not sink vertically. It moves slowly back towards the angler as it sinks (see diagram on p. 126). So, when a fish takes 'on the drop' after you have been fishing for a little while, it may not be just the depth that was wrong before but also your retrieve rate (i.e. it was too fast).

For example, I was fishing Loch Roinevat with a team of wet flies on a floating line. Nothing had moved at the surface. I let the flies sink for ten seconds or so, so that the Bloody Butcher was well down when I started the retrieve—a slow jerky, tweaking retrieve. After about thirty unproductive casts a trout took just after the flies hit the water. The Blue Zulu on the top dropper had scored. I reckoned depth was probably reasonable, for the bushy Blue Zulu would still be close to the surface even after ten seconds' sinking time. Had my retrieve been too quick? I then fished with no real retrieve, allowing the flies to drift in the ripple and simply keeping the line tight by pulling in any slack that developed. The result? Seven trout in about twenty casts! Certainly, earlier I *had* been fishing too quickly.

The same applied when Peter and I were fishing together on one of our northern reservoirs that was stocked with rainbows. A humiliating example, for Peter was only 13 years of age at the time! We started off fishing side-by-side. Peter lost one fish. He then moved around to the top of the reservoir. I saw Jack, the bailiff, watching him.

'Fish!' he shouted. He landed it and dropped it into his creel. The score was one-nil. I began to fish hard. 'Fish!' the lad cried. He added that to the creel. Two-nil to Peter. I fished even harder.

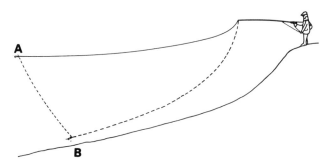

The angler casts and the lure lands on the water at A. He then allows the lure and line to sink before starting the retrieve. During the sinking time the lure will, in fact, move very slowly from A to B: both vertically and horizontally through the water

'Fish!' he proclaimed in a loud adolescent grating din that broke the stillness of the placid water. Three-nil to Peter. I cast as far as I could and retrieved the line with gusto. Peter arrived with Jack. Both were smiling.

'There's a lot of fish up there,' said the juvenile novice to me, his angling mentor. 'Go and have a do for them!' With great humility I followed his advice. He sat where I had been, talking with Jack. I cast and cast and cast, retrieved and retrieved and retrieved my lures. Then I saw Peter lengthening line. The score was still three-nil. I worked even harder.

'Fish!' the little devil screeched. And with his first cast he pulled out a good rainbow exactly where I had been fishing for over an hour for nought. Four-nil to Peter! What was I doing wrong?

The evening had a happy ending, I am pleased to report! I saw sense. I was dragging my lures back too quickly, so I slowed down considerably, to a slow almost imperceptible tweak and took three rainbows in three casts!

As depth of sunk lures and wet flies must be correct, so too must be retrieve rate, and the way to do this again is to count, each number marking a pull or tweak of standard length of the line:

a fast retrieve—'one, two, three, four, five . . .'

a slow retrieve—'onnne . . .twoooo . . .thrree . . .'

a very slow retrieve—no real retrieve at all; just keep the line tight and let the natural drift of the water do the rest.

New stock fish often fall for the quicker retrieve and a slow or very slow retrieve often attracts the bigger, older trout. Also, the colder the water, the slower the flashy lures or wet flies should be recovered. The reason for this has its basis in a biological law. For every 10°C rise in temperature a cold-blooded animal (e.g. a trout) automatically doubles its energy production. Thus in water at 5°C (early spring) the trout's ability to react to a lure and accelerate to take it is only half the rate that it will be at 15°C (late spring).

When you have arrived by the lake and, if necessary, obtained your permits to fish and checked the rules it's a good idea, if possible, to glance at the recent returns which are sometimes displayed in the fishing lodge. If there is a fishery warden on hand you might also ask his advice about the best fishing spots. You can then look at the map. Ticket waters often provide a map which might have depth contours. Alternatively, you could use the 1 : 50000 Ordnance Survey maps which give soundings in 10-metre intervals. Next you should look at the lake and the topography of the surrounding countryside. Look for what should be the most productive margins, for bays and promontories between bays, for where there might be weedbeds that afford the trout good feeding, and for inflows and outflows.

You should determine the direction of the wind, too, for this will affect the drift of potential trout foods within the surface layers of the water, pushing them to the better bank onto which the wind is blowing, and, in summer, tilting the thermocline and attracting a concentration of trout closer to the windward shore.

You can, therefore, gain clues as to likely hot-spots in the new water and these you can now fish thoroughly with lure or standard wet fly. If you are lucky, you may see the fish moving or feeding at the surface. Then you can fish more confidently with your lures and wet flies or, if you suspect that there is a hatch, turn to imitative flies.

The right approach   You are now ready to fish! So how do you start? Which set of tackle should you use? What fly?

Such questions are best answered by experience, since there is never a precise, correct set of answers. You may recall Bruce Sandison's remark that he rarely uses anything other than one cast of three size 14 wet flies for loch trout. Many anglers, when fishing fisheries that hold rainbow trout, invariably grab the sinking line, tie on a big lure and start from there. I know a few who always begin with the Floating Beetle. In the north of England many anglers put up the floating line and a cast of three tiny spider-type wet flies, no matter what the water, and others always begin with the nymph. All are successful some of the time and unsuccessful some of the time.

Over the years I have visited well over two hundred 'new' waters
of all types where I have been restricted to fishing from the bank.
Some of them I have re-visited; a few are old friends that I fish
several times each year. Let me describe how I attack a water for the
first time, having worked out where the hot-spots are likely to be
(because of the wide range of stillwater trout fisheries, I will
describe my approach in a variety of waters).

Small put-and-take fisheries   Fisheries where there is a
heavy stocking of rainbow trout and, possibly, American brook
trout and brown trout. There is little problem working out hot-
spots, for the size of the water often means that the fish will arrive
sooner or later in front of me, if they are not there already. I try,
however, to find deeper water, from a dam if possible, or a casting
platform that projects out into the pool, or the steeper bank where
it is likely that the lake bed shelves steeply. I bear in mind that in
many of these pools the amount of stock fish is so huge that the
water can provide insufficient food for the trout to feed fastidiously
and I know that the bulk of the fish may not have been long in the
lake.

Lure fishing   I set up two rods. On one goes a floating line with a
12′ (3.6 m) leader onto which I tie a size 12 Leaded Shrimp, Corixa
or Killer Bug at the point and two biggish (size 10 or 12) unweighted Sedge or Buzzer Pupae on droppers. On the other rod I put a
sinking line—a slow sinker if the water seems to be fairly shallow,
but a fast sinker if I am on the dam where the water may be more
than about 10m deep. Onto the leader I will tie either a Black or
White Marabou. This will be used first.

I check the time. How long am I going to be fishing? There will
be little point in rushing around the water, so if I don't catch it will
be a matter of changing fly or technique and persevering. If there
is a 'shift' system (say, of eight hours) I will decide that after half an
hour with no success will come the first change.

Out goes the lure. I count to five and slowly retrieve it. I do this
for about ten casts. I make another ten casts, but this time allowing
a sinking time of ten seconds. Then I make a series of casts with
longer sinking times. Thus, over the first fifteen minutes or so I
make a series of exploratory casts, fished at a range of depths from
just below the surface to deep down, close to the lake bed. In the
latter case I may lose the odd lure: well and good—at least I know
that I have fished deeply enough! Afterwards the whole process is
repeated, but this time with a different lure. If I started with a

White Marabou, then I now use the Black Marabou or *vice versa*.
Floating line   If lure fishing proves fruitless after the allotted time,
then the sinking line is reeled in and the rod laid aside. Out comes
the lighter floating line with the nymphs. The leader butt and last
few metres of the fly line are given a coat of Permagrease, and the
nymphs are wetted with saliva. Then the cast is made. Whilst the
nymphs sink I do nothing other than gather any slack in the fly line.
The nymphs are brought back very slowly with little sink-and-draw
movements by raising the rod tip a few centimetres and then lower-
ing it so that the nymphs lift and fall in the water. There is no real
retrieve, but slack line is brought in as it develops. It takes a long
time to fish out the cast, so it is less physically demanding than lure
fishing with its more frequent casting, but I must concentrate on
the floating tip of the fly line or, when closer, the leader butt. Any
jerk, twitch, dipping or other unexpected slight movement of these
is responded to by an immediate and quick flick of the rod tip.

Once I know that I have thoroughly fished the water around me
with these nymphs, and they have failed to catch, then I may change
patterns. For instance, I may try Carnill's Cased Caddis on the
point, a bigger Sedge Pupa on the top dropper and my Straggly
Black Spider on the middle dropper, and may continue fishing
these very slowly. If they remain unproductive after, say half an
hour, then it is time for another change. The sinking line comes
back into use once more, but now with another lure. I may try a
Barbara Cartland or a Candy Doll, again fished over a wide range
of depths. Once I feel that these have been given a fair try I will turn
to a Dog Nobbler, again on the sinking line, but retrieved more
quickly with long pulls on the line alternating with periods when
the lure is allowed to sink. If that fails, I will go to the other extreme:
a Muddler Minnow also on the sinking line. This lure is fished as
close to the lake bed as possible, with long pulls on the line (which
causes the Muddler to swim downwards) followed by extended
pauses during which the Muddler rises and then stays suspended
like a helium-filled balloon over the lake bed.

And so the day proceeds—ringing the changes, varying the
techniques, perservering—with no alteration of location unless I am
feeling desperate! That is the aim until a fish is caught, after which
the successful method is retained until, not having caught again for
a while, I feel that it is time for another change.

So far I have been fishing deep below the surface. This assumes
that there are no fish showing at the surface. If there are, however,
then the floating line comes into action and appropriate flies are

chosen. Initially, on small, heavily fished and heavily stocked waters, at the sign of fish at the surface I turn to my combination of dry fly with nymphs or pupae on droppers—possibly a big Deerhair Sedge with a wet spider Greenwell's Glory and Sedge Pupa on the droppers. If these fail and I think that the fish are definitely interested in something at the surface, but I don't know what, I try a dry Hawthorn Fly on the point and two tiny Buzzer Pupae on the droppers. Alternatively, a bright lure, such as a Whiskey Fly, brought back fairly fast just beneath the surface may do the trick; or even a yellow Dog Nobbler, again fished fairly quickly, sink-and-draw on the floating line.

Should a fish come to the net then it will be spooned. Trout of heavily stocked, smaller fisheries, alas, rarely have much in the way of natural foods in their guts, but on a few occasions I have come across fish in pools which have been greatly attracted to insects, usually midge pupae, that are moving close to the surface. Quite honestly, however, in the tiny stocked waters natural foods can often be ignored.

Floating Beetle   There is another technique that is really well worth trying should trout be moving close to the surface—the Floating Beetle. Fishing should be an interesting and exciting sport. Varying flies and techniques and solving the problem of how to catch the fish makes fishing these little waters interesting. Excitement is when a big rainbow takes the dry fly with a swirl, when a big brownie hits the lure hard, or when a tightening of the line following the detection of a subtle offer to a nymph is followed with an explosive rush of the hooked fish. When using the Floating Beetle there is the excitement of the dry fly together with the added thrill of the trout hitting the lure violently, so much so that the rod can almost be wrenched from your hand!

All these methods, when used properly, catch me some fish on these small pools. Once I have caught a few on one fly or method I usually change over to another, even if it is less successful. These waters give the angler the best chance of experimenting as well as often catching a lot of trout. Why keep catching trout after trout on one method? The bag limit is all you can take home. Why not try a new technique?

Larger fisheries stocked with rainbow trout   Such waters may also contain stocked brookies and brownies and, especially in upland Britain, a head of wild brown trout.

In these lakes finding the hot-spots is half the battle, for it is impossible to fish the entire shoreline, nor is it possible to cast across most of the water as is the case with little pools. When I am out for the day I usually identify three, four or more hot-spots that I will try during my stay at the lake.

One rod or two? A difficult problem, I find, especially if I might have to cover a lot of ground whilst I am actually fishing; a rod left behind as I slowly progress along the bank, casting as I go, means that I have to retrieve it at regular intervals. It is not much of a problem, though, if the likely hot-spots are very discrete and cover only very small areas as opposed to long lengths of shore.

Rod and sinking line   Generally, therefore, I will use just one rod if a lot of walking is involved. In early spring or late autumn, when the water is cold and the fish are likely to be deep, I will usually take the rod with the sinking line, considering that a range of lures will be my best chance of catching some fish. However, I usually put a reel with a floating line in the bag, just in case, but I rarely change over. Alternatively, from mid-spring and during the summer if I am going to take only one rod it will be the one that has the floating line (but I always carry an appropriate sinker in the bag). Then I can fish a wide range of lures, nymphs, wet flies and dry flies on or close to the surface yet, if these all fail, I can change the floater for the sinker and go deeper with the lure. Where little walking may be expected I will always take both rods.

Range of lures and flies   Where the likely best areas are discrete (e.g. promontories, the entrances of feeder streams, small bays) I will try a wide range of lures and flies at a variety of depths at each place. In the course of a long day I may visit four or five such points on the water. One thing I will not do is spend the day at one place, even if I catch some fish there. It is more challenging to identify, say, five points around the lake where I reckon on being able to catch trout and to see if I am correct. I will try to stay at least one hour at each. Should I catch a couple of fish in the first and fail elsewhere, I can always go back to where I was successful earlier on.

However, where there is to be much walking and fishing as I go (i.e. where the hot-spots are not clearly defined) then one lure (e.g. a Marabou) or a team of wet flies (e.g. Cast 3) will be used and I will progress slowly along the shore in search of the trout. A cast is made, a pace is taken and the flies are retrieved at an appropriate depth and speed. This is followed by another cast, then a pace and the retrieve, and so on. Should some feature take my eye that was not revealed by the map, such as a weed bed or area of deeper water surrounded by shallows, I will concentrate on this for some time and try a wider range of flies and techniques. Similarly, should a fish move at the water surface then I will stay there for a while. It is foolish to ignore areas where you see fish, and at the same time fishing step-and-cast along a shore is tiring. To be able to settle down once you have found some fish is more relaxing, and you can concentrate on offering the fish that you can see feeding the full repertoire of flies.

Spooning   On these bigger waters I spoon every fish that I catch *immediately*. If the stomach is empty or contains *Daphnia*, I will fish hard with lure or a team of standard lake flies. If it contains a collection of items obviously grubbed from the bottom or amongst weed, such as shrimps, *Corixa* or immature nymphs, then I will turn to a weighted imitation of one of these on the point of a long leader, with a couple of other unweighted patterns on droppers; it will be fished on the floating line. If the gut contains mature nymphs or pupae that were obviously taken close to the surface appropriate patterns will be used, and if it contains wind-blown land insects, such as beetles, then out will come the Floating Beetle.

If I am very lucky, or in the late evening of summer, there may be plenty of insects on the water and there can be no doubt what the trout are feeding on. Then come the delights of offering the dry fly to fish that can be seen taking these naturals. It is a simple matter of choosing a good imitation. Similarly, if trout are moving close inshore and minnows or sticklebacks are jumping from the water as they try to escape from the trout, then a good lure (the Polystickle is my favourite for this purpose) should catch some trout.

The essence of catching trout is really trial and error, per-severance and, at the same time, observation. You must find the trout, work out what they are feeding on and choose appropriate flies and technique.

Incidentally, in late spring, summer and early autumn I always spend lunchtime at the hottest spot and tie on a Deerhair sedge and two nymphs (on droppers). These I cast out and then I sit down, put the rod down, and have lunch. The dry fly and nymphs drift around and, when they reach the bank, I stand up and recast. A splash, and I lift the rod in case a trout has taken one of the flies. Stocked trout will often take these flies and hook themselves! I first discovered this when my son and I were fishing our way around a largish lake. I sat down for a rest, tied on the team of flies and cast it out. Peter continued fishing his lure. He hooked a good fish and, leaving my rod, I strode along to net it for him. We admired his trout and chatted for a while. Then I returned to my rod. The floating fly line was extended into the reservoir in the opposite direction to the ripple-drift! Why? I lifted up the rod and pulled in the slack line. At the end was a two-pound rainbow, firmly hooked in the scissors, on the Deerhair Sedge.

Since then Peter, Geoff Haslam and I have spent many happy days sitting back in the sun chatting as our flies have fished around in this manner. In recent years the three of us have caught a lot of trout by this lazy, but sociable, effective method!

Small lakes holding wild brown trout   These little waters are delightful to fish, even though the trout are usually not huge. I normally fish around them because it takes only a few hours, making several casts from one position before moving to a new position further along the bank. Sometimes, however, after a quick glance at the water and an eye to the breeze, I will concentrate on what I consider to be the likeliest best place.

In such waters I find that I rarely use (or need) the sinking line; and the larger lures appear to be less effective for wild brownies than they are for stockies. I start with an appropriate cast of two or three standard lake flies on the floating line and retrieve them very slowly or let them just drift around with the wave. If trout are showing at the surface then I will stick to these same wet flies unless there is a hatch, in which case I will use suitable imitative flies. Once more, every trout that I kill is spooned so that I can find out what it has been feeding on. Then, if I wish, I can choose an appropriate imitative pattern.

Unless the lake is heavily fished the wild brownies of these little pools are exceedingly obliging. Even when they are feeding keenly on a natural fly that is moving beneath or on the surface they will often fall for some of the standard wet flies which bear no resemblance to what they are actually taking.

Large lakes holding wild brown trout   In these waters more than in any other the angler who is based on the bank must find the places where the fish are likely to be concentrated. They can certainly be the most difficult of waters to fish from the bank with a fly. What is especially frustrating is that the larger fish tend to occur in some parts of the lake and not in others. So, one needs to accumulate experience at finding not just hot-spots, but those hot-spots that are likely to hold the bigger fish. It is also frustrating for the bank angler that the larger trout tend to occur, through the day, out of reach, for instance amongst offshore islands and skerries.

They may come inshore in the evening should there be a hatch or fall of fly, but often they won't! To be catching trout after trout, all in the six to eight inch (15–20 cm) category, whilst big fish wallow in the surface far out, is one of the worst frustrations of trout fishing on natural wild trout lakes. That is why, on the largest and best natural trout lakes, such as some of the Irish loughs and Scottish lochs, most anglers fish from a boat.

It is worth mentioning that wild brownies do not roam around in shoals as do stock fish. Apart from just before the breeding season, when they congregate close to the feeder streams in which many spawn, they tend to be independent of one another. Sticking to one spot, therefore, is not very productive. My motto for this type of water is 'Cast and Move'. I take the minimum of tackle, including just the one rod with a floating line, and aim to cover as much of the potentially best parts of the margins as possible.

If there is little sign of fish moving at the surface, I will choose a suitable standard lake three-fly cast and explore the water carefully. Where possible I cast at an angle to the wind (which should be blowing onto or across the shore I am fishing) and retrieve the flies very slowly, keeping the bob-fly moving in the surface film. In lightly fished waters (and most of this type usually are) the trout will often lie close to the bank in the most productive part of the lake margin. To avoid disturbing them I try to keep a few metres away from the water and fish each cast right out to the side. It is quite exciting to have a trout taking the fly as it leaves the water right under the rod tip!

Should there be a big hatch or fall of fly then I turn to imitative fly patterns (sometimes dry fly alone, sometimes dry fly on the point and nymphs on the droppers). This may be considered to be something of a personal whim, for the trout will still take the attractor lake flies just as keenly, but I find that fishing the imitative dry fly and nymph is a little more satisfying and is much easier, there being less casting.

To get the best out of these large, natural waters one needs to know the water fairly well or have carried out some thorough research before setting out. And for me they are best fished from a boat, which leads me to the next Chapter.

Postscript   Alas, it seems that very few anglers keep diaries or proper diaries. This is a pity. By recording details of locality, date and weather (including wind strength and direction, fish caught, successful flies and depth and rate of retrieve, any hatches, etc., the results of spooning the fish and hot-spots) one can accumulate on paper a lot of experience that is otherwise hidden in the subconscious or lost for ever. A reading through of a season's or several seasons' records can reveal lots of interesting patterns that yielded success. Indeed, this book contains a digest of my diaries, summarising many hundreds of days fishing and thousands of trout caught. If you have never kept this sort of diary, can I urge you to do so.

To make your diary more entertaining jot down who you were fishing with, the trout that other anglers caught, and on what they were caught. If you came across anything of interest, write it down (e.g. broods of ducklings, a fishing osprey, capsized boat, who fell in, etc.). Carry a camera and stick in your diary photographs of the larger fish, memorable bags and the lakes you fished. Not only will you have a diary from which you can construct your own ideas and theories, but in later years you will be able to bore the grandchildren and look back with nostalgia at days long since gone!

8
Fly Fishing from Boats

'All the Corrib boatmen were good. They knew the lake as a landow-
ner knows his own demesne. But Jamesie knew it as a blind man
knows the home he lives in, with absolute certainty.'
                    T. C. Kingsmill Moore, *A Man May Fish*, 1979

'Terry Thomas once asked me in a television interview what was the
real secret of catching a lot of fish, and without hesitation I replied
'boat handling'.
                         Bob Church, *Reservoir Trout Fishing*, 1977

For the bank angler there is always the nagging feeling, especially
when fish are not breaking the water surface close to the shore, that
the trout are just out of range! So, he concentrates on casting as long
a line as he possibly can and, alas, wades as deep as he can to gain
that extra yardage towards the middle of the lake. Thus on his first
day afloat our novice boat angler, who has previously been limited
to fishing from the bank, has a feeling of relief. At last he has the
whole water at his command. The trout will definitely be covered
by his flies.

What does our novice do? He rows or chugs out to the middle
—the part of the lake that, in his subconscious, he wanted to reach
when he was fishing from the bank. He ships the oars or switches
off the engine, reaches for the rod and proceeds to cast a line *just as
if he was still on the bank*. Then he notices that something is wrong
for, as he lets the line and/or flies sink beneath the surface, he finds
that the belly of the line is moving beneath the boat and up the lake!
After a couple of abortive casts he realises that it is not the line that
is moving but the boat, and that rapidly he is drifting with the
breeze across the lake and overtaking his fly line and flies. He reels
in the line, moves the boat back to where he started and slings the
anchor overboard. If the anchor is a good one (and often it won't
be!) the boat stays secure and he happily casts away, going through
the full repertoire of fly lines and flies from his stationary floating
platform. If he is lucky he might catch a fish or two, but often he

won't. This is because he is fishing in the same way he would a bank hot-spot. At the end of the day he returns to the shore to discover that the bank anglers have generally done as well as most of the boat anglers, possibly better and certainly better than him. He also notices that one or two boat anglers have had an outstanding day and caught their bag limits and more besides.

He spends a few minutes passing the time of day with one of the fishery staff or one of the more successful boat anglers. He mentions the drift problem and is told to buy a drogue. So, on his next trip he is prepared: he will be able to slow the drifting boat.

With the new drogue in attendance our novice sails to the lee end of the lake, slings in the drogue and more slowly drifts the length of the lake, casting as he goes. This he repeats all day and, to his delight, finds that his catch rate has improved a little over his previous effort, but it is still no better than it was when he was restricted to the bank. When he returns to the fishing lodge he finds that his bag is still far less than some of the others who were out in the boats and, to his surprise, many bank anglers.

On the next visit he is more cunning. As before he sails to the top of the lake and begins to drift, fishing as he goes. However, he notices that some of the boats seem quite close to the bank, even though from the shore they appear a long way out, and that the anglers in these boats are catching fish regularly. He copies them as best he can, again making straight drifts down the wind, but now closer to the shallow margins. This time he is luckier! He returns to the fishing lodge to find that his bag is comparable with those of the other boat anglers and better than the majority of bank anglers. He feels that he has found the solution.

To some extent he has, certainly as far as stocked reservoir trout fisheries are concerned, but he is missing one important point. He has not given any thought to where the fish will be, how deep they will be, and the best way of presenting his flies to those fish from a moving platform. He is basing his plan of campaign on an irrational, blind assumption that the trout occur evenly spaced, whether singly or in shoals, across the whole lake and that straight line drifts across the lake will cover them. On many reservoirs, stocked with rainbow trout that patrol much larger areas of lake than do brown trout, he will be successful to some extent. But on some reservoirs and the large natural brown trout waters of Ireland, Scotland, north-west England and Wales he will find life exceedingly arduous.

At the head of this chapter are two quotes from a couple of great and contrasting boat fishermen. Re-read them. What made Jamesie so special as a Lough Corrib boatman was not just that he knew his way about Corrib, but that he knew precisely where the trout were in Corrib and could row Kingsmill Moore there with certainty. Put this with Bob Church's comment, that the secret of success is boat handling, and we have the crux of this chapter: successful trout fishing from a boat depends on knowing exactly where the fish will be, and in manoeuvring the boat in these areas so that the fly or flies can be fished properly.

There is, in essence, no real difference between successful bank and boat fishing, for in both the water must be read and hot-spots identified. The advantages of the boat is that the angler can drift slowly through the likely best areas in relative comfort, that more of the potentially better areas can be fished more conveniently, without the need for walking around the lake encumbered with tackle, and, especially important, that some hot-spots will be available to the boat angler which cannot be reached from the shore.

There is another advantage of boat angling. Many of the best-known bank hot-spots on the more popular lakes become crowded. Anglers mark their 'peg' with a landing net stuck in the lake bed and they never move. So often it is impossible for an angler who arrives late or is slowly working his way around the lake taking full advantage of these better areas. With a boat this problem is removed. Take the dam corner at Draycote, for example, where anglers sometimes fish shoulder-to-shoulder: with a boat one can drift around the area without hindrance.

At this juncture I must make the following points:

Manners

The boat angler has freedom that the bank angler does not have. So, when fishing a lake from a boat:

1. Never approach the bank anglers closer than at least 100 metres, i.e. at least double their maximum casting range. To do so is unsporting, for it interferes with their angling.
2. Never bring the boat ashore where bank anglers are fishing, unless, of course, they are fishing from the mooring jetties. Again, it is unsporting.
3. Never cut into the drift of another boat. If a boat is following the drift that you want to follow, then head upwind and follow it at a safe and reasonable distance.
4. If you are anchored in a potentially promising position and a boat is following a drift that will bring it very close to you, be reasonable.

Up-anchor, move away and let it drift through unhindered. You can always go back to your chosen spot once it has passed. Of course, if you have the lake to yourself you may do as you please, but where other anglers are sharing the water with you, be it on the bank or in other boats, treat them with consideration.

The first job for the boat angler is to work out where the fish are concentrated. Except in eutrophic lakes where they may feed, in summer, amidst the blooms of plankton, it will be where the lake invertebrates or small fish are most concentrated and that will be in shallower water. This will include the lake margins and bays (areas important for bank anglers, too), off-shore shoals and the margins and reefs around groups of islands (areas where the bank anglers cannot reach). These latter areas are especially important trout-holding places in the bigger lochs of Scotland and the loughs of Ireland. Sometimes they are not visible from a casual glance over the lake, nor do many Ordnance Survey maps show them. Advice must be sought from local anglers or a gillie. For instance, an angler setting afloat on Lochs Maree, Lomond, Tay and Ness or Loughs Corrib or Sheelin might have to spend many days simply making

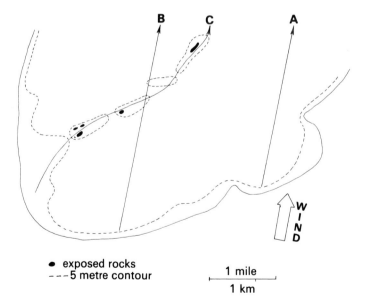

• exposed rocks
– – –5 metre contour

1 mile
1 km

Straight drift A would be in relatively fishless water. Straight drift B would cross the middle of one good shoal and cut the corner of another; it would be better than A. Controlled drift C would cover fish for virtually the entire time

transects across the lake in search of these productive areas where a little advice may save all that wasted time.

Consider the example on p. 139: part of a large lough that produces a lot of big trout.

What we need in this practical situation is to be following the line of drift C. But how? Firstly, we can achieve this with a gillie who, knowing the water, manoeuvres the boat on its irregular route using the oars. A gillie who can do this is worth his weight in gold.

Many anglers, however, cannot afford a gillie or there may be none available. In that case, unless they are prepared to share the rowing duties on a shift system (and why not?), some gadgetry is needed. There are several possible systems:

—anchor plus drift, interspersed with rowing for position
—drogue, possibly with a rudder
—leeboard

An electronic depth sounder could be used with these so that the boat can be kept, as much as possible, over the productive shallower water.

Fishing at anchor

There are times when a boat can be usefully anchored in a position adjacent to an area that is likely to be very productive (e.g. just off a dam wall towards which the wind is blowing, or at the entrance to a large weed-girt bay), areas not easily covered from the bank. Alas, the boats that one hires on some lakes have hopeless anchors. Some are nothing more than lumps of concrete or bricks; others are the sort of mudweight that works well enough on the Norfolk Broads but is useless on a rocky or sandy lake bed. Some boats that I have hired actually had no anchor at all! If you are thinking of buying your own boat, buy a good anchor that will hold the bottom in all

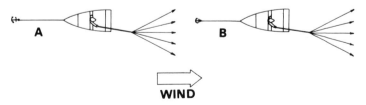

Angler anchors at A and thoroughly fishes the immediate area downwind. He then raises the anchor, allows the boat to drift forwards and lowers the anchor at B. He fishes that area thoroughly. Slowly, therefore, he fishes along a line of drift

weathers, but has a hinge system that will release it even when apparently snagged. Also, if you do a great deal of lake fishing from hired boats, it may be worthwhile buying a good anchor and taking it wherever you go fishing.

Of course, when fished at anchor, the boat is just a floating casting platform. However, it is a method that can be used to produce the slowest of all possible drift. As the boat, on a drift, approaches a good fishing area the anchor is slowly and carefully lowered and the boat stops. Several casts are made downwind and across the wind, searching the water thoroughly. Then the anchor is raised a little, the boat is allowed to drift forwards a short distance, and the anchor is re-lowered. The next section of water is then fished thoroughly, and so on. Should a large concentration of fish be encountered the boat can be held on station until activity ceases (provided, of course, that no other angler wants to drift through the lie). For the novice to boat angling this is the easiest way of effectively fishing a controlled drift.

Holding the boat in position is particularly effective when the angler is trying to catch trout that are lying deep, on a lead-cored

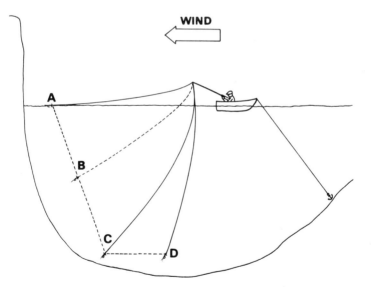

The angler casts to A and the line and lure sink to B. Then as the line continues to sink it pulls the lure horizontally through the water (B to C to D). The angler does nothing in this period. Offers mostly come in the later stage (C to D). When the lure is at D the line is retrieved and recast with, if thought necessary, a change in position of the boat

line. When the boat is drifting this line may not reach the required depth without being overtaken by the boat and, as I pointed out in Chapter 7, these lines frequently get hung up during the deep retrieve on the lake bed as they are drawn into the bank by the shore-based angler. So, the ultra-fast sinker is cast from the an-chored boat and allowed to sink. As it does so the lure also moves in a horizontal direction, back towards the angler until eventually it lies beneath the boat. During this time the angler has done nothing, but it is during the later stages of the movement that the deeply lying trout usually take the lure (see diagram on p. 141).

The drogue

A drogue is simply an underwater parachute that trails in the water behind the boat, slowing down the rate of drift. You can buy one from fishing tackle dealers or you can make your own out of strong rot-proof nylon cloth obtainable from ships' chandlers or yachting suppliers. Ideally, it should be at least 4' (1.2 m) square, with a hole about 3" (7.5 cm) in diameter in the middle.

The greater the amount of line paid out, between drogue and boat, the deeper will be the drogue and the slower will be the drift.

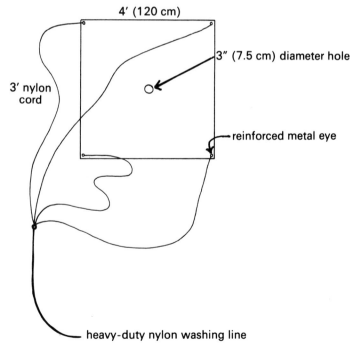

4' (120 cm)

3" (7.5 cm) diameter hole

3' nylon cord

reinforced metal eye

heavy-duty nylon washing line

With the drogue alone the drift will be in a straight line downwind. This is fine if the lake is of a fairly uniform depth and of even fish-holding capacity, or if you are drifting along a straight margin. However, it will not be enough if the boat needs to change direction to stay within an irregular productive zone of the sort shown earlier. This is where the rudder comes in useful.

The rudder

The rudder allows slight changes in the direction of a drift to be made quickly and easily. Bob Church (in his book *Reservoir Trout Fishing*) gave details of the construction of an all-metal rudder. I have a wooden one designed and made for me by a friend who is a keen woodworker. There are several important features of a good rudder. Firstly, the blade should be a reasonable size, ideally about 18″ × 12″ (45 × 30 cm).

The second essential is that the rudder can be locked in one position, and that the lock can be quickly undone, the rudder position changed to alter the direction of drift, and relocked. Thus the rudder can be used to keep the drift along an irregular line that follows the more productive water. If someone has to keep hold of the rudder handle, he cannot fish and might be better employed using oars to control the drift as do the Irish and Scottish gillies. It

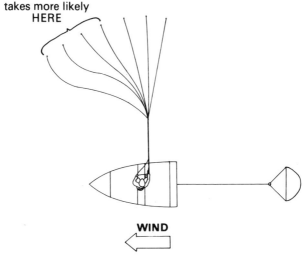

The angler casts square across the wind and line of drift and allows the flies to fish round with no real retrieve. Takes usually come in the latter stage of the cast

is the combination of wind effects on the drift, modified by subtle changes in the rudder position, that confers the incredible advantage of the anglers in the boat being able to concentrate their efforts on fishing hard in the best water, without having to reel in and row or motor back into position as the wind drifts them unchecked off the fishing grounds.

The third essential is that the rudder can be quickly attached and removed from the boat. If you only fish waters where you can take your own boat, the rudder can be built into the boat. However, where you might be fishing one week on an English reservoir, then be heading across the Irish Sea to the loughs of Mayo, and be renting boats wherever you go, the rudder must go with you. It must be detachable, yet firm when attached. For this purpose there is nothing to beat a big G-clamp, but make sure that the fishery or boat owner is happy for you to use the rudder and, when preparing the trip, that the boat will take a rudder: some of the skiffs hired out on the Cumbrian lakes will not.

The full range of fly techniques can be used with the drift controlled by drogue and rudder, but more often a team of standard lake flies fished on the floating line or, possibly, a lure on one of the sinking lines or the floating line is preferable. In both cases the flies are best fished at right angles to the line of drift and the angler simply keeps everything fairly tight by taking in any slack line that develops. The flies move round on the bellying line, accelerating as they do so. Then is the best chance of attracting and hooking a fish.

If two anglers are sharing the boat, they each have opposite sides.

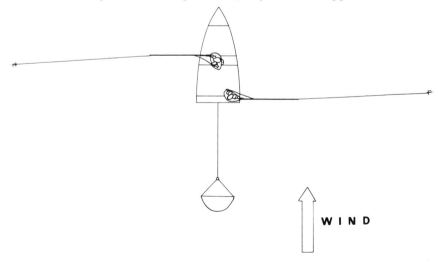

WIND

The angler in the stern casts over his right shoulder over the star-
board (right) side and the angler in the bows, facing in the opposite
direction, again casts over his right shoulder but this time over the
port (left) side of the boat. Thus there is little chance of one angler
hooking the other with his flies and each angler fishes separate
sections of water.

Alternatively, the boat can be drifted side-on with the breeze, in
traditional loch-style, both anglers casting downwind, forward of
the boat. When doing this anglers need to exercise care in casting
and to co-ordinate each other's movements otherwise lines will
become tangled or, worse still, flies will become attached to a partner's hat, coat or person! It should be standard practice for an
angler to announce 'Casting now!' every time he casts, especially
when fishing with a new partner. If possible, the angler in the left
side of the boat should try to cast more over the left shoulder; it is
especially useful if you can find a left-handed angler to take this
position in the boat!

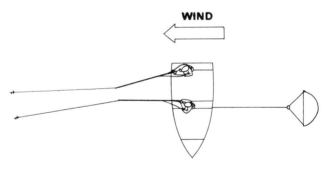

It is imperative that the angler in the bows (left in the diagram)
does not cast away to the left and *vice versa*, otherwise the back cast
be across or over the other angler and may have dangerous
consequences. Earlier writers have suggested that the two anglers
should imagine that there is a pane of glass between them which
extends out over the water in front and behind them and that they
should ensure that their lines and flies do not stray to this imaginary
barrier.

By far the best technique to use here is the standard three-fly lake
cast on a light, short line just three or four rod lengths long. The
flies are cast out, allowed a second or so to sink, and brought back
a little faster than the boat is drifting so that the bushy bob fly (e.g.
Blue Zulu) flickers through the ripple or makes a positive furrow
through the wave. With the combination of long rod and short line

very little line actually needs recovering. The angler casts, the rod ending up in the 'ten minutes to the hour' position. Any slack can immediately be pulled in, if necessary, and the rod raised slowly to the 'on the hour' or 'five minutes past' position. It is this rod movement that imparts life to the flies and moves them through the water. A quick flick, and the next cast is made.

The cast is made; the rod is at 10 o'clock

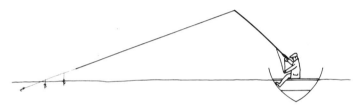

Slack line is recovered and the rod is slowly raised so that the bob fly flutters through the water surface

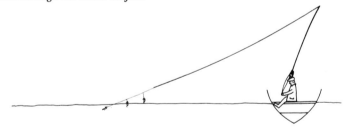

As the cast is fished out the rod is at the 1 o'clock position and is ready for the next forward cast

Such are the advantages of fishing from a drifting boat: only a short line is needed so less physical effort is required; new water is being covered by every cast; and the angler can approach the fish very closely, provided, of course, that (a) he has found the best fish-holding areas and (b) he fishes and handles the boat in such a manner that the fish are not scared away. I have had many trout take the bob-fly literally beneath the rod tip, no more than a couple of metres from the boat, i.e. there is no need for the sort of long casts that are often necessary when fishing from the bank.

Such a drifting style can also be used when trout are nymphing or taking the floating fly from the surface. Again, very short casts are made, with an appropriate team of nymphs or a dry fly, in front of the boat.

Speaking of dry fly leads onto dapping, the traditional way of fishing the floating fly on the Irish loughs and Scottish lochs. Some writers have considered this method tedious, but it is not as tedious as the mechanical cast and retrieve, cast and retrieve, *ad infinitum* of sunk line lure fishing! As a break from other styles it is relaxing and, when the offers come, extremely exciting. This is especially so when trout are taking big natural flies, such as daddy-long-legs or mayflies that are drifting and fluttering across the waves.

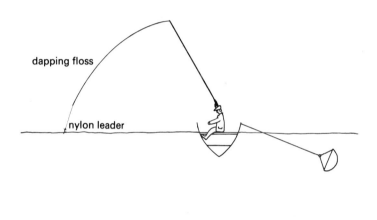

The rod is held high so that the breeze bellows the line and leader and only the fly touches the water. A big bushy dry fly, well soaked in flotant, such as a Daddy-long-legs, Red Sedge or Mayfly, is ideal

Line is lengthened and the dapping rod is raised and held stationary. The light line (dapping floss) carries the fly downwind on the water but, at the same time, it is kept afloat in the breeze. Only the fly touches the water surface.

The length of line to be used beyond the end of the rod and the angle at which the long dapping rod is held in the air are determined by the strength of the wind and the speed of the drift. In a high wind line length will be greater and/or rod-angle lower than when there is only a slight breeze. However, the two variables are adjusted so that, as the boat drifts, the fly will flutter on the water for a moment, lift off as the wind pushes against the line, and fall back on the water again a short distance further on. The fly will slowly make its way, a few metres in front of the drifting boat, across the lake as would a struggling, fluttering natural fly that is buffeted from wave to wave by the wind.

When the offers come one has to marvel at the speed at which the trout can see and respond to the fly, but though an offer is often bold and explosive, the strike must be leisurely and slow so that the fish is given plenty of time to turn down with the fly. Too quick a strike and the fly will be pulled from the trout's mouth.

Note on hooking offers to the dry fly or dapped fly

Some trout, especially rainbow trout, as I described in Chapter 7, will hook themselves on the dry fly if they are given enough slack line. It is fatal to be too quick on the strike when fishing the surface fly. Smaller trout tend to be faster than the larger ones, and brown trout are faster than rainbows. However, always err on the side of slowness. Some anglers are reputed to say 'God save the Queen!' when a fish takes the dry fly, and tighten on the word 'Queen'. I have conditioned myself to say, slowly and deliberately, 'And . . . strike!', tightening on the 'K' of 'strike'.

Oliver Kite used to say that he did not strike but simply felt for the fish, inferring that he slowly tightened the line until he felt the trout on the end of it. Far more trout are missed by the angler being too quick than are missed by him being too slow. Some anglers suggest that when they fail to connect with an offer to the floating fly it is due to the fish missing the fly or not taking the fly properly. This, I believe, is nonsense! It is far more likely that they snatched the fly out of the trout's open mouth!

Trailing the lure

The biggest problem with fishing from a moving boat is that, generally, it is very difficult to fish in a controlled way very deep below the surface for, as line and lure sink, the boat will be overtaking them. As I said earlier, the best way to fish a sinking line (especially a fast sinker) is to do so from an anchored boat, and if you want to drift, do it by progressing across the lake in fits and starts using the anchor.

However, there is another possibility *provided it is permitted by the fishery rules*—trailing the lure. This is a method that is especially effective for big trout that are patrolling deep in the epilimnion or where an angler wants to cover a lot of water quickly. Like dapping, it is an easy way to fish.

The angler rows to the top (lee shore) of the lake, puts out the drogue and then casts his lure, on a sinking line, into the wind (i.e. over the same side of the boat as the drogue). He strips off more line, allowing this slack to pass through the rod rings and thus letting the lure sink deeper. Then, as the boat drifts slowly across the lake he simply holds the rod, letting the lure trail behind. Depth can be varied by using lines of different densities or by varying the amount of line that is out. Even greater depth can be achieved by pinching one or two swan shots onto the leader or using a heavily weighted lure such as a Dog Nobbler.

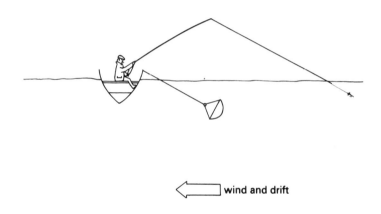

wind and drift

To all extents and purposes, this is the fly fishing equivalent of trailing a spinner behind a boat.

The leeboard

There is another technique of boat handling which is simple, yet effective: the leeboard. This is a piece of board which is attached vertically to the bow of the boat so that it hangs down beneath the boat into the water. I use one 5' × 6" × 1" (190 × 15 × 2.5 cm) which is attached by a big G-clamp.

Whereas the drogue when used alone will give just straight downwind drifts and the use of the rudder can be rather awkward, the leeboard is an excellent gadget to use when curved drifts down and across the wind are required. For example, suppose an angler

wishes to fish a narrow offshore reef across which the wind is
blowing. He positions the boat at A and attaches the leeboard as
shown. The boat then follows a curved drift across the reef. He rows
back to C with the leeboard removed, then replaces the leeboard
and drifts to D, and so on. This is a most effective way of fishing
such narrow bands of water.

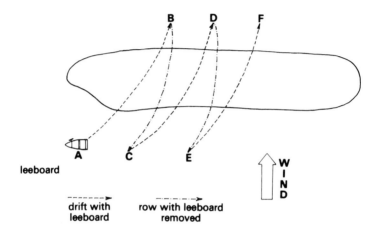

However, I must point out that a leeboard makes a boat very
unstable. Therefore:
1. do not use a leeboard in high winds or in a big wave;
2. do not use a leeboard with a drogue or rudder;
3. remove the leeboard when the boat is to be moved by either oars
or engine.
So potentially dangerous is the leeboard in inexperienced hands
that its use is banned by many commercial fisheries. I would recommend its use only in near calm conditions.

No matter what boat-handling technique is being used, you can
employ the full range of fly fishing methods. Lures and teams of
standard lake flies are probably the most frequently used styles but
there are many times, during a large hatch, when a team of imitative
nymphs or dry fly are more effective. As in fishing from the lake
bank, an angler who insists on persevering with just one style for
hours on end and finishes the day with an empty creel is an idiot. If
one method does not catch you a fish after it has been given a
thorough testing, try another. Experiment. If you don't catch on a
fly fished just beneath the surface, go deeper. And persevere.
Remember, variety is the spice of life!

It is especially important to pick up any clues that you can of what is going on beneath and on the water. I have already stressed the importance of spooning out the guts of fish as you catch them. By doing this you will have a good idea of whether there is a fall of land-bred flies that you had not noticed. There may be a lot of mature nymphs or pupae in the trout's stomach, indicating that a hatch is imminent, or a mixed collection of shrimps, snails and caddis will show that the trout was grubbing about the lake bed. If you have been struggling to catch with lure or standard lake flies, you can change to appropriate flies and technique to fit in with what you *know* at least one trout was feeding on.

There is one other point—the need for careful observation. You can have the best tackle and techniques but to exploit these to the full it is essential to keep your eyes open, to be aware of what is going on both in and on the water. Alas, it seems that many anglers fail in this respect.

One of the most amusing examples of this that I have come across was some years ago on a disused gravel pit that was stocked with rainbow trout. It was a hot summer day and I was sitting in the shade beneath some alders and birches that surrounded the wind-ward shore and overhung the water. Large numbers of trout were moving at the surface right underneath the overhanging branches. Two anglers were fishing a drift that started on the opposite shore and brought them across the middle of the lake close to where I was sitting. However, as soon as they approached within thirty or so metres of the bank they reeled in and rowed back to start a new drift. They actually stopped fishing just before they reached the fish! And their catch was nil! They were so intent on covering the vast open space that they had not thought where the fish might be lying, nor observed the water carefully as they fished. I found it quite amazing that they had not seen the trout wallowing and porpoising close to the wooded shore. What made the scene even more ridiculous was the arrival of a solitary bank angler who, by flicking his flies out beneath the trees, took a limit bag of four fish in quick time. Meanwhile our two boat anglers performed two more abortive drifts!

So remain alert. Study the water surface. Look out for fish and, if you see some, carefully move the boat around so that you can cover them.

Calm-lanes and algal-lanes   You should also be constantly on the look out for two special but transient fishing hot-spots—

calm-lanes and algal-lanes. Both depend on the wind and, whilst the bank angler can fish these when they are close enough, only the boat angler can take full advantage of them.

As the wind blows over the land towards the lake tall structures, such as buildings and trees or a smooth topographical outline broken up by a steep hill slope or rocky crag, produce calm-lanes: straight strips of calm, or almost calm, water that extend across the otherwise choppy lake surface. Of course, a change in wind direction will cause a change in the direction of the calm-lanes; should the wind drop, the calm-lanes might disappear altogether. Generally, the stronger the wind is, the more marked are the calm-lanes and the more important they are for trout and trout anglers. This is because food items accumulate in calm-lanes, so the trout will cruise along them in search of the food. A straight drogue-controlled or anchor-

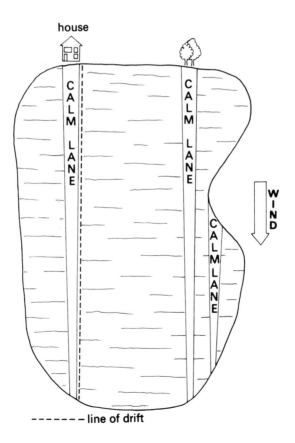

controlled drift, with the boat positioned just outside the calm-lane, is often a profitable way of catching these trout.

I remember fishing one Pennine reservoir on a warm, still, early May day for a gruelling three hours when, quickly, the wind freshened so that the lake became covered with good waves. Then I noticed, away to my right, a distant calm-lane caused by a copse of tall pines on the windward bank. I quickly rowed up and across the wind, finishing off a few metres from the strip of calm water. Earlier not a fish had stirred at the water surface, but soon I noticed that a lot of trout were feeding keenly at the surface in the edge of this calm-lane. After a few casts one came to the net on a Black Pennell. In its stomach were a few dark grey chironomid pupae. I kept the Black Pennell in place and put two small black Buzzer Pupae on the point and middle dropper. The result was another seven trout in two hours.

Algal-lanes are also an effect of the wind, but this time it causes a wave-drift that carries a band of algae or weed and associated invertebrates into the lake. Algal-lanes are not common, and are of greater significance in eutrophic waters where the affected margin holds a number of trout foods.

For instance, suppose a herd of cows come down to drink in a windward bay. They stir up the lake bed and the drift carries food items into the lake, attracting trout. Similarly, on the big English lowland reservoirs when the weed-cutter is in action the wind and wave drift clumps of weed, which hold shrimps, hog-lice, caddis and upwinged fly nymphs, into the lake. Trout will grub around these clumps of weed for food. So, a drift along these lanes will often find feeding trout. I suppose that it is akin to the river angler stirring up the gravel of the river bed and then casting a nymph downstream to the waiting trout.

Boat fishing is, in essence, a matter of working out where the fish are, of putting the boat in the right place, of having tackle that will catch the trout, and of using the tackle properly. That's all there is to it!

There is one other useful weapon in the angler's quest for lake trout, whether from the bank or boat, and that is experience. Experience is something which cannot be gained from reading a book. You have to go fishing to acquire it. However, an angler can pass on certain pointers that he has gained by experience, and one of these is the way trout fishing changes as the fishing season progresses. It is what Chapter 9 is about.

Safety and boats   It would be remiss of me if I did not stress the importance of safety when out in the boat. Every year many people who go out onto lakes in small boats get into difficulties and some drown. Even quite small lakes can be terrifying in some conditions: try rowing a square-bowed light fibreglass boat any distance into the teeth of a gale! Even on the calmest of days it is possible to get into trouble when fishing afloat and you don't need a depth of umpteen fathoms in which to drown. You will drown in water that is a little deeper than your own height; this depth will be less if hypothermia is setting in or you are exhausted. Therefore:

1. Go afloat only in good boats. It is rank stupidity to take a light, portable six-foot fibreglass or rubber dinghy onto a big lake: should the wind freshen, such craft are suicidal. Alas, some reservoir fisheries provide totally inadequate boats, sometimes with pathetic little electric engines. Avoid these at all costs.

2. Never go afloat, certainly on the bigger lakes, in very high winds. Rowing into a gale is physically and mentally exhausting. Should you be caught out by a sudden and violent change in the weather, something not unusual in the north and west of the British Isles, then make for the nearest bank. Either leave the boat there to be collected later or tow it by the painter along the shore back to base.

3. Make sure that you can swim, even when fully clothed. In *Sea Trout Fishing* Hugh Falkus, a great angler, a great writer, and a major contributor to the study of safety for anglers, wrote the following:

> 'In order to enjoy a feeling of security on or beside the water—whether river or lake—you should be able to paddle about fully clothed when out of your depth. If you can't practise until you can, paying particular attention to the backstroke. Most emergency swimming of this nature is (or should be) carried out on the back.'

Wear a buoyant waistcoat or life-jacket until you are really confident in the water.

4. If you fall into the water from a boat, climb back into the boat from the blunt end (stern)—anywhere else and the boat will probably capsize.

5. When getting into the boat at its moorings, step onto the floorboards as close to the middle of the boat as you can and sit down

immediately. Stand up in the boat only when it is essential. It is better to fish sitting down rather than standing up for then the fish will see less of you.

6. In a rowing boat make sure that the rowlocks are tied down with strong cord, and if they don't have some sort of clip that prevents the oars coming out of their own accord then tie them to the boat as well, again with strong cord. This may seem a bit niggling, but it is better to be niggling than having to row the boat back to base with only one oar!

7. If the boat has an outboard engine make sure that it is securely fastened to the boat. Carry an extra can of fuel. If you are going to a lake that is miles from civilisation learn the rudiments of servicing the engine: unblocking the fuel pipe, changing the plug, repairing the pull-cord, etc. Always carry oars just in case the engine fails and you cannot get it restarted. Drifting without control, in high winds and rough water, can result in the boat capsizing or being wrecked on rocks.

8. Wear adequate clothing. Even on hot summer days have spare pullovers and water- and wind-proof overtrousers and coat stowed in the boat.

9. Before setting out from the shore arrange everything in the boat so that important items are to hand. Set up rods on the shore: there is nothing more comical than watching two anglers in a small boat trying to thread line through the rings of a long rod! Open the landing net and tie it to the middle seat of the boat with a long cord that allows the net to be used over either side (I have known of at least three nets lost overboard!). Put boxes of flies where you can reach them easily. Stow food and drink in a convenient corner, and so on, to remove the temptation to stand up to reach out for something. Remember that most unavoidable boat accidents happen when people are moving about in the boat and an unexpectedly large wave hits them.

10. Have some emergency aids:

—an inflated rubber ring is an excellent padded seat which doubles as a lifebuoy;
—a rope with a secure loop tied with a bowline knot to act as a life-line;
—a baler (e.g. an old saucepan);
—some cream to prevent sunburn. Boat anglers receive a double-

dose of ultraviolet waves, both directly from the sun and indirectly, reflected from the water.

11. Keep a flask of hot coffee and some chocolate with you. Cold can kill, and there is nothing like hot fluid and high-energy foods to revive someone who has had a ducking and is chilled.

Never administer alcohol. Spirits such as brandy give a semblance of warmth but this is illusionary. In fact, alcohol causes a dilation of blood capillaries in the skin and therefore causes even more body heat to be lost.

12. Keep calm and think clearly in any emergency. Panic kills many people every year.

9
Fly Fishing
through the Season

'I'm not going fishing in this weather!'
The response from a friend on opening day in March 1984: it was pouring with rain and blowing a gale at the time!

'Can we wait until the weather improves?'
The response from another friend in mid-April 1985: the weather forecast predicted sleet and a cold north-easterly wind.

'For many seasons.. I had not fished for trout.. during September, having found September trout increasingly easy as the month advanced.. so my last visit was in the last week-end in August.'
G. E. M. Skues, *Itchen Memories*, 1951

The brown trout season is the shortest of all fishing seasons, usually starting in March and closing at the end of September, the actual dates varying from region to region. It is little more than half the year, with a close season that, though admittedly encompassing the worst part of the year as far as weather is concerned, seems to last for ages. Despite the brevity of the season, brown trout fishing lends itself to the more favourable time of the year when the warmer water, greater production of potential foods and hatches of fly result in more feeding activity by the trout than is the case in cooler conditions. Yet even in the short season the start can be very slow because of extremely low water temperatures which encourage the trout to stay deep and behave lethargically. In the British highlands, where some of the best wild trout waters are located, the month of September can be marked by the return of harsh winter weather.

There is no close season in the British Isles for the rainbow trout and American brook trout, though until recently almost all fisheries had a self-imposed one. However, the demand for an extended trout fishing season, together with great financial incentive, has encouraged more and more privately-owned fisheries to remain open throughout the year. So, it is now possible to fish for these two introduced species on just about every day of the year. Christmas

Day and periods when the lake is frozen over are the usual exceptions.

No matter what sort of water you fish, or what species of trout you fish for, the sport of trout fishing changes as the season progresses—sometimes dramatically and rapidly, sometimes slowly and almost imperceptibly. There is a pattern of change through the season and this is the subject of the chapter.

Sometimes no two consecutive days are identical. Take a day that is cool, overcast and with a strong south-westerly wind which has a hint of drizzle in it. Flies that hatch on the water surface must remain there, perched on the surface film, as their wings slowly dry. The low temperature means that their flight muscles warm up very slowly, prolonging the time before the flies can leave the water. On such a day the hatch will result in a lot of fish taking flies from the surface and dry flies will score heavily. However, the next day the weather may have changed: it may be warm, with a drying south-easterly breeze. The hatch may be as large as it was on the previous day, yet hardly a fly will be seen or a fish stir at the water surface. As the flies emerge from their pupal or nymph stage their wings dry almost immediately and they leave the water more or less straight away. Dry fly patterns will be largely a waste of time and subsurface nymph or pupal patterns will score more highly.

Heavy overnight rain, that turns feeder streams into silt-laden torrents which colour the whole of the lake, can make angling very difficult. So, too, can a change in wind direction and strength that may produce a day of frustratingly flat calm or impossible gale after one that was perfect. Of course, on stocked fisheries, angling will alter quite dramatically as new fish are put in the water and as the bulk of the trout are removed from it. Such factors will disrupt the pattern of the fishing season.

Furthermore, although this chapter will describe the way that trout fishing varies through the season, the pattern will change somewhat from year to year. For example, the seasons of 1975, '76, '82, '83 and '84 were marked by long summer droughts. In 1976 and 1984 hardly a drop of rain fell between March and September over much of the British Isles. Bright sunshine, very warm water and, in some reservoirs and smaller natural lakes, record low water levels made fishing extremely difficult. On the other hand, in 1973, 1985, and 1986 the other extreme prevailed. Higher than normal rainfall, high winds and low temperatures dominated the trout season, and in those two years, provided that you were prepared to get soaked through, fishing was very good.

Finally, the pattern of trout fishing through the season will vary from water to water. This will be most explicable in stocked waters. For instance, in a small water that is stocked weekly or several times per week the fishing should be fairly easy through the season (this, of course, will be reflected in the high ticket price). At the other extreme, a water that is stocked only once or twice during a season will be very difficult a few weeks after stocking because there will be few fish left. Even in natural wild brown trout waters there will be variations in the fishing pattern from one water to the next, possibly because of variation in water quality, the numbers and sizes of fish, the natural foods in the water, the intensity of fishing and a host of other factors. Anglers who fish just one water or one type of water lose out in experiencing such factors. The pattern that I will try to describe here encompasses all trout stillwaters in the British Isles, put together from my exieriences in a large number of fisheries from Ireland, England, Wales and Scotland—from tiny heavily stocked lowland pools to the highest tarns and lochans, from the big reservoirs of the English Midlands to the biggest lochs of Scotland, loughs of Ireland and lakes of Cumbria.

Early Spring: March and April

The opening days of the trout season in March are often dominated by high winds, heavy rainfall (or sleet and snow), and low temperatures. Occasional days may promise the coming of spring and summer, but a return to arctic severity or Atlantic depressions can be quick and dispiriting. For instance, on the opening day of the 1981 season in north-west England (15 March), the weather was superb. I sat by the water in my shirt-sleeves, sunning myself. The following day back came south-westerly gales and torrential rain. I sat in the fishing hut, hoping the rain would stop. It didn't. In desperation I went out to face the elements and got myself soaked through in only one hour's fishing.

Just as the weather can be so unpredictable in this first part of the season, so too can be the trout fishing. In the larger, deeper lakes the water will not be stratified, as is the case later in the year, and the water temperature will be at its coldest, often only two or three degrees centigrade. Thus the trout will have much less energy than they will have when the water is warmer. They will tend to stay deep and be less inclined to rise far through the water to take a lure or fly. The only exception to this are newly-stocked trout that will often swim around in shoals close to the surface in anticipation of a twice-daily helping of trout pellets. It is an interesting point to

note: these fish are most active at the times when they were accustomed to being fed at the trout farm, often in the morning at about
9 o'clock and in the afternoon at about 4 o'clock. For a few days
after stocking the trout are more likely to come to the lure at these
times than at any other time during the day.

Providing there is sufficient food in the lake, overwintered rainbow and brook trout (the latter, of course, will not breed in British
lakes, though the rainbow does so in a handful of British rivers) that
were stocked in the previous year will be in good condition and may
have gained weight over the winter. As an experiment, a few years
ago my local fishing club (Bowland Game-Fishing Association)
stocked one of its reservoir fisheries with brook trout after the end
of the season. These preyed heavily on the huge population of
stunted rudd which the reservoir contained and when we opened
the water for fishing the following April some of the brookies,
stocked at around the pound mark, scaled three pounds and were in
good fettle. Almost every one that was caught had its stomach
crammed with little rudd. Similarly, the over-wintered rainbows on
Rutland and Draycote, which averaged close to the two-pound
mark at the end of the season in which they were stocked, weighed
three pounds or more on opening day.

The same is not true of all put-and-take fisheries. In oligotrophic
waters where the food supply is very sparse rainbow trout from the
previous year will be mere shadows of their former selves when the
new season comes around. There is nothing so sad as catching one
of these pathetic specimens as the 'first fish of the season'. To
prevent this some owners of smaller fisheries that produce little in
the way of natural food try to have the bulk of the trout removed
before the winter by allowing bait-fishing at the end of the season
or they may provide a diet of trout pellets through the winter for the
remaining fish. Of course, in those fisheries which remain open
throughout the year the problem does not really exist as the vast
majority of trout are taken shortly after stocking, before they have
time to lose condition.

For wild brown trout the anglers' close season is the fish's breeding season. This is quite a long, protracted and physically demanding affair. Hence at the start of the new fishing season the brown
trout may not have regained the condition that was lost during
spawning, especially when the late winter and early spring are very
cold. The fish tend to be thinner and softer in the belly than will be
the case in late spring when they will have benefited from the
increasing food supply. However, not all wild brown trout will be

in this poor condition. Those in more eutrophic lakes tend to recover more quickly from the rigours of spawning and, therefore, are usually in better condition than those in oligotrophic waters, although even in one water some fish will be in better condition than others. For example, on waters as diverse as Loch Tay, Lough Mask and Windermere a large bag of trout in early spring will always include some that are of much better quality than the others.

There is no merit in killing trout that are in poor condition. They are not good to eat, which is the only reason for killing any fish (unless you come across a diseased or badly injured specimen). Yet, if returned carefully, within a couple of months the same trout could be perfection and excellent on the table.

The invertebrates and small fish that make up the diet of lake trout in early spring will be concentrated entirely in the lake margins or have their origins in the lake margins. Of course wind might drift them out across the lake from the lee shore, in which case the windward margins will always be a hot-spot where the trout will congregate. The only exception to this will be the new stockies that may roam in shoals, in the deeper water close to the steeper shelving shore and dam walls, or seek inflowing or outflowing streams or pumping towers. However, they *tend* to move fairly close to the surface. Therefore, a slow sinking or ordinary fast sinking line will often find them a few metres down. Overwintered stock fish *tend* to occur much deeper, close to the lake bed where a fast sinking line with a long sinking time from the bank, or a lead-cored line from an anchored boat, will be required. Wild brown trout will also tend to stay fairly deep and this is one time of the year when I would start a fishing day, for these wild trout, with a sinking line. The rest of the year I would stick with the floater. When the trout are grubbing deep in the lake they are not usually selective or fastidious feeders, so lures or standard wet flies are the most effective ways of catching with, as an alternative, a team of weighted, deeply fished shrimp or nymph patterns.

In stocked lakes white or black lures score heavily. For instance, I *always* start with a White Marabou, turn to a Black Marabou if that one fails and then, if need be, try white and black Dog Nobblers and the two more colourful Baby Dolls, Candy Doll and Barbara Cartland, ideally fished on appropriate sinking line. Nothing more is needed, despite the proliferation of lures each of which is said, by its inventor, to be better than all that have gone before!

In natural brown trout lakes the smaller wet flies are more successful at all times of the year. My son and I have experimented with the bigger lures for wild brownies and, except when they are feeding on minnows or fish fry in summer, find these lures far less effective than they are for stockies. So, an appropriate two- or three-fly cast should be used. In spring black flies are very good (actually, is there a time when a black fly is *not* good?) and at least one should be on the leader. I would recommend either Cast 7, which includes the leaded Cased Caddis, fished slowly on the floating line and long leader, or Cast 6 or 8 fished on a sinking line. Details of these casts are given in Chapter 4 (pp. 74–6).

Late Spring: May and early June

Beyond any doubt this is, or should be, the best time of the year for the trout fisherman. The weather tends to be warm, rainfall low and winds light. So the water warms rapidly, increasing the activity of both trout and trout foods. As yet the lake will not be stratified or stratification will just be becoming established and the epilimnion will not have had time to reach maximum productivity. The trout will still be concentrated in the shallower water or seeking foods that are being drifted across the lake by wind and wave.

In the shallows, weedbeds and algae will be growing quickly and on them will be feeding an increasing population of invertebrates —shrimps, water hog-lice, corixids, chironomid larvae, caddis, nymphs, toad tadpoles, insects and minnows. The list is long. From the shallows will emerge the first important hatches of the season.

Several species of upwinged flies are important on waters where they occur abundantly. The most widespread and numerous is the lake olive, the duns of which hatch in the late morning and early afternoon and the spent spinners fall, after egg-laying, in the late afternoon and evening. Of all upwinged flies this is the one that gives most anglers on most waters the opportunity of fishing the dry fly or nymph to rising trout. Less widespread, but very important where they do occur, are the true mayfly, claret, sepia, dark dun and dusky yellowstreak.

The appearance of the huge mayfly, which occurs throughout England, south Scotland and Ireland, on some lakes but not others, is the highlight of the year for many anglers. To see numbers of these huge flies perched on the waves as their wings dry and trout feeding on them demands the dry fly, fished either conventionally or by dapping. Then, late in the day, when there may be a big fall of spent female spinners, the trout can be almost suicidal as they take both natural and artificial with gay abandon! Every trout angler worth his salt should endeavour to fish, if only once, a mayfly lake at this time of the year. Incidentally, the emergence of mayflies occurs during only two or three weeks of the year, starting in the last few days of May, reaching a peak in the first fortnight of June, and tailing off thereafter. The main part of the hatch seems to yield the better results: it seems almost that the trout are slow to appreciate these big flies as food and later become satiated after a fortnight of sheer gluttony.

The claret dun is primarily a species of rocky peaty lakes and tarns and, though it occurs throughout the British Isles, is consequently commoner in Ireland and, to a lesser degree, northern England and parts of Scotland. The sepia is less common and occurs mostly in England and the south of Scotland. Both of these closely related, beautiful flies are of little interest to most trout anglers and their importance has been overstated somewhat by some earlier writers. However, where they occur in abundance the fish may take them selectively, to the exclusion of other foods, and when this happens imitative dry fly is the ideal and most satisfying method. However, I have personally experienced such large hatches on only a handful of occasions. The duns of both species emerge in the early afternoon; falls of spinners are rarely as large or important as the hatches of duns, and occur late in the evening.

I am tempted to dwell, at great length, on the hatches of upwinged flies and to go into raptures about all the species that might occur on a lake. To do so would be overstating the importance of this group. However, two other species ought to be mentioned. If an angler is fishing some of the Irish loughs in late May and June, then the dark dun (brown May dun) might be encountered in large numbers; similarly, on the upland tarns of northern England and lochs of Scotland the dusky yellowstreak will be very much in evidence. Woe betide the angler who encounters such a hatch, on which the trout are 'fixed', and has no reasonable imitation tucked away in the corner of the fly box!

Warm evenings in late May and early June see the first really big hatches of midges and sedges. Several species may be 'on' during a particular evening and the chosen fly pattern should reflect the natural fly, although there is not, in my opinion and from my experience, much need for especially careful imitation. Size, shape and general colouration of the artificial are all important, and presentation must be right. It is worth fishing a combination of nymphs or pupae on droppers with dry fly on the point and, when possible, continuing to fish well into the darkness.

May and early June sees the first really big falls of land-bred 'flies'. Of these beetles, from nearby woodlands, scrub and rough moorland, are probably the most important, but they are frequently overlooked by anglers. Often I have struggled away with fish that are obviously feeding at the surface, but on what I know not? Then, probably by luck, a fish has come to the net. An examination of the stomach contents has revealed masses of tiny beetles and, by turning to a Floating Beetle fished very slowly, with occasional little tweaks, offer after offer has come. For example, once on Draycote I had four fish in quick succession that had stomachs packed with ladybirds; on Cow Green seven fish had tiny olive-brown beetles predominating in their guts; on Loch Tay six trout had tiny black land beetles. Yet in none of these instances could I see the beetles on the water.

Just about any land animal might end up on or in the lake and be eaten by trout. The angler should be prepared for the commonest: to accommodate all contingencies would require literally thousands of fly patterns to be carried, just in case! In spring, therefore, only three more natural land flies need be considered: hawthorn flies, black gnats and dung flies. These sometimes occur in quite huge numbers on the water.

Remember: just because a fish is seen to take one fly from the surface does not mean that the trout will only take an artificial which imitates that species. A trout takes a stonefly which has happened to fall on the water. That fish will take just about any natural fly, for it is certainly not feeding selectively, that is, unless there are a lot of stoneflies on the water and the trout will look at nothing else— something I have never come across. I have seen a trout take a bumble bee, another a large white butterfly. Both were caught on flies that bore no resemblance to the last real mouthful consumed by those two fish. It is only when really large hatches or falls occur that lake trout become preoccupied with the one food and a very good imitation is needed (see Chapter 4).

The following is a useful ploy to try on smaller lakes on windy spring days when things are dour and you are fishing from the bank! Go to the lee shore, i.e. the shore from which the wind is blowing and which is usually the least productive. Find some thick vegetation by the lakeside, such as rushes, taller grass, and scrub, and kick your way through it. You will disturb flies that may be blown onto the water. Up will come the trout. Cast your fly and you will catch the fish! This can be very effective and can turn a tedious day into a very exciting one. Some might argue that it is unsporting and artificial groundbaiting, but I would strongly disagree. However, if you have any qualms then take the dog (if the rules permit it) and have Rover do the job for you. Occasionally a flock of sheep or herd of bullocks will oblige.

Of course, even in this most productive time of the year there may be no hatches or falls of fly at all. Then the margins and other shallow water hot-spots must be fished hard with appropriate flies. Whilst lures and standard lake flies will often yield success it is worth bearing in mind that, with the warming water and increased productivity of invertebrate life, there may be large populations of shrimps, hog-lice and corixids in weedbeds or amongst boulders on the lake bed. So, it is well worth using in your repertoire, increasingly as the season progresses, weighted nymph, shrimp or corixid imitations on a long leader and floating fly line. As I stressed in the last two chapters, to stick to one method for a long period when it is not catching you fish is idiotic especially when you know or have a good idea that the fish are there, in front of you!

Summer: mid-June to late August

From mid-June trout fishing becomes progressively more difficult through to the end of August except, possibly, on the put-and-take waters where there will be newly stocked fish that are relatively easy to catch. I say 'possibly' because it is foolish to make categorical statements or rules in angling. (That is why words like 'possible', 'usually' and 'often' figure frequently in this book.) I have been on some very heavily stocked waters where we all struggled to make a bag of fish in high summer. Indeed, no two waters are exactly the same and some become more difficult than others.

I could take you to a pair of small, apparently identical, Scottish lochs which are but a few hundred metres apart. From one you would have little difficulty extracting a dozen nice wild trout in an afternoon on a team of wet flies. On the other you would be lucky to get even one offer. Yet earlier in the season, in late April or May, there would be little to choose between them. Why? Goodness only knows! I have walked around them with a pond net and there seems to be no real difference in food availability. Depths and sizes are similar. There are no chemical differences between the waters.

Why should lake fishing tend to be a little more difficult through high summer? Several factors probably contribute. Firstly, the water in most larger lakes stratifies in summer and the warm epilimnion may hold huge concentrations of zooplankton and associated predatory invertebrates. The trout will feed on these, but whereas earlier the fish are concentrated in the narrower lake margins, shallow bays or offshore reefs, when they are feeding on zooplankton they may spread throughout the whole lake. Thus the trout might not occur in the sorts of high concentration in easily defined hotspots in summer as they do in spring. Certainly, the bank angler is at a great disadvantage over the boat angler at this time of the year, for the latter can slowly drift across what are probably the best areas and, by covering huge areas of lake, cover more fish. As I described earlier (Chapter 4, pages 62–80), large lures where there are rainbow trout or teams of standard lake flies are best in such a situation.

The second factor that makes summer angling that bit more difficult is the bright light intensity and, associated with this, high temperatures.

I will deal with the latter first. The higher the water temperature, the less oxygen that can dissolve in the water. It seems that once water temperature reaches about 18°C the fish become more lethargic or seek cooler water. In very hot weather that sort of temperature is often reached in the surface layer of many lakes so the fish descend to the thermocline where they can find cooler water which may have a higher amount of oxygen dissolved in it. This might also be linked to the daily migrations of zooplankton, outlined in Chapter 2, pages 24–48. The outcome of all this is that the trout may well be out of reach of the fly fisherman on hot, sunny days.

Furthermore, we all know that in summer cloudy days are usually better days than those with dazzling sunshine. Those of us who fish rivers regularly will know that in the brighter days the trout tend to seek out shaded seclusion beneath fronds of weed, under tree roots, beneath low overhanging branches. Similarly, in lakes although you cannot usually watch the trout as you can in the rivers it would seem logical for the fish to seek out the deeper, darker water during the day.

Of course, once the light begins to fall in the evening the trout will often return to the surface of the epilimnion or into the shallower water. They are encouraged to do this by the hatches that frequently occur around sunset, esecially of midges and sedges, and possibly of some of the upwinged flies. These hatches will often continue well into the darkness and anglers ought to be prepared, whenever possible, to continue fishing as late as possible. Unsocial hours are called for!

Suppose that you were planning a fishing trip in midsummer to a lake. Provided that you were not restricted in the hours of fishing by the fishery rules then, if the weather forecast predicted a swelteringly hot day, you would aim to be on the water after tea (say, about 7 o'clock) and be prepared to fish from about 8 o'clock, as the sun began to fall, to after dawn. Beyond any doubt the period up to about midnight would be your best chance, during the hatches of midges and sedges and the falls of spent spinners that had completed their egg-laying. You might rest for an hour or so after midnight, have a bite to eat, drink from the thermos flask and natter with other colleagues. From then until sunrise you would work hard once more, anticipating a lot of fish activity in the early hours in response to early morning hatches of fly and falls of spinners.

The technique and flies to use on such overnight jaunts depend, to some extent, on personal preference and to the natural insects that are about. You could choose to employ a team of standard lake flies or even a lure. On the other hand, many of us prefer, if one sort of food is being taken by the trout, to fish more confidently with imitative flies—possibly dry, possibly wet, possibly a combination of the two.

Four important species of upwinged flies may be encountered in summer. The pond olive is the most widespread species. The duns hatch in the afternoon, usually in the weedier bays on dull overcast days. Then the female spinners return to the water in the very late afternoon and the trout will feed on dead and dying spinners until the early morning.

On the lakes of upland Wales, the north of England, Scotland and parts of Ireland the large summer dun (actually two similar species) may emerge as the dun in the afternoon and be once more back on the water as the spent spinner in the late evening. This is a big fly which has been overlooked by the majority of angling writers who are based in the English lowlands. However, anyone going to a natural lake where this species occurs must take a suitable imitative fly pattern just in case there are a lot of large summer duns on the water, for the trout can be quite fastidious when they are taking these flies.

Also of local distribution is the yellow may dun, a common and important species on the Irish loughs which occurs on some lakes in the north of England and Scotland. As the name suggests, May is the month of the first hatches of this species, but the main, large hatches occur late in June or early July.

Alas, most stillwater anglers rarely experience a very big hatch of upwinged flies that turns the trout on, which is a pity for such a hatch can be quite exciting. The fish are feeding. The angler throws out his lure or wet flies amongst the feeding fish, but they are ignored. He turns to an imitative dry fly and success! I remember joining four anglers who were fishing a bay that was packed with a big hatch of pond olives. Scores of trout porpoised and splashed at the water surface, gorging themselves on their helpless prey. The four anglers, who later told me that they had never seen such a hatch before, just did not know what to do. They had tried a range of lures and lake wet flies with no success. Fortunately, I had my dry fly box and we all dipped in there and chose a suitable dry fly. The five of us then extracted fourteen trout in just over an hour, when the hatch ended, and every one had a stomach crammed with pond olive duns.

No matter how well an angler prepares, sooner or later he will get caught out by not having an appropriate fly in the box, but by careful planning it is usually possible to make sure that you are carrying flies suitable for a particular water at a certain time of the year. What really makes life difficult is when the trout become preoccupied with a food that is not easily imitated and for which there is no alternative to suffering! The final upwinged fly of summer, the *Caenis*, is a good example. 'Angler's Curse' is a fine epithet for this tiny fly that hatches out, mostly in the afternoon and evening but sometimes at dawn, in immense numbers. There are artificial patterns that will score, the tiny Grey Duster and my own Paythorne Caenis are two, but when literally millions of these tiny pests are on the water your artificial seems hopelessly outnumbered. It is a matter of plugging away with these patterns, or persevering with a range of large wet flies or lures in the hope that one or two stupid trout will lose their heads and grab hold. Sometimes they will. The other alternatives are to pack up and go home or, better still, to sit in the sun and watch!

It is not just the *Caenis* that presents this problem. Some waters, especially the very unproductive ones, often have hatches of extremely tiny midges that the trout will daintily sip down and ignore everything else!

Summer sees falls of many land-bred flies, especially during periods of strong wind. Beetles, dung flies, daddy-long-legs, ants, and, in the evening, moths can find their way onto the water in huge numbers. Trout will take them keenly. They will also hunt amongst the shoals of fry, minnows and sticklebacks in the shallow water when a flashy wet fly such as a Peter Ross or Bloody Butcher or a lure such as a Polystickle, cast down the shallow margin and tweaked back, will score. At this time of the year it is a very successful ploy. But let me stress again: the trout will be very close inshore, in very shallow water. So, approach cautiously. Stand well back from the bank. Ignore the vastness of the lake and concentrate on the margin, just as though you were fishing down-and-across a small stream. That is where the fry and minnows will be. That is where the trout will be—or ought to be! Too many anglers ruin their chance of catching trout that are feeding like this by wading into the water! Summer also sees the occasional mass migration of snails to the surface in eutrophic lakes. The fisherman ought to be prepared for all these.

Should there be no sign of fish feeding at the surface then to be afloat and fish a controlled drift with a team of wet flies or a lure will usually be the most successful way of catching fish. Alternatively, you could find a hot-spot where the trout *ought* to be concentrated, anchor up, and go through the repertoire of lure, wetfly and nymph. On very few days should any angler leave the water having failed to catch. Those that do are the ones who persist with one fly or one method, who don't try to work out where and on what the trout are feeding, who don't think!

Autumn: September

September often sees an improvement in lake trout fishing—an end-of-season revival, if you like. It is certainly true on the natural brown trout waters, but less so on the put-and-take fisheries if stocking has not been carried out for some time and the head of fish remaining is getting very small. The reason for the improvement is that, as the water cools and stratification breaks down, the trout move inshore once more to search through the day for food in the margins. By the end of the month they will begin to congregate close to their spawning becks, sometimes in quite huge shoals.

However, in September the wild trout are close to spawning. The testes in the male fish enlarge rapidly; the ovaries in the female fish quickly grow to fill the body cavity. It seems a pity, to me at least, killing fish that are on the point of breeding and thus restocking the water for us. Fair enough, take one or two for the table, but to make a big bag of easy fish, should a pre-mating congregation be found, is needless slaughter. I know that many will say, 'But the season has been so short, why reduce it further?'

I have not advocated a cessation of trout fishing, although some anglers, rather like G. E. M. Skues, do voluntarily stop fishing at the end of August. However, I do suggest that you use barbless hooks and gently shake back most of the wild brownies that you catch. Assuming, that is, that you happen to catch, by luck or design, a lot of fish. Indeed, to stop fishing at the end of August loses you the chance of hooking a really big fish for, during September, trout move up through the river and lake systems towards their spawning grounds, and that often includes many large fish—possibly the so-called slob trout that have been downstream as far as the river estuary since the previous breeding season, or possibly trout that have spent the spring and summer in a deep hole in the river or in an obscure lie out in the body of the lake.

September sees the last proper fly hatches of the season. Unless the weather turns very cold sedges and midges will be on or over the water during the afternoon and evening. A second hatch of lake olives might occur in the afternoon and, on upland lakes in northern and western Britain, there may be hatches of the autumn dun; and in windy, blustery weather land-bred flies such as daddy-long-legs may be blown onto the lake surface.

On many September days there will be little fish activity at the water surface. So, no matter what sort of lake is being fished, shallow water hot-spots must be found and fished thoroughly with a variety of techniques and flies.

Winter: October to February

This period, though it admittedly includes most of autumn as well as winter, is the brown trout close season. Trout fishing is thus for the introduced rainbow and brook trout. During October, if the weather is warm, there may be some hatches of fly, especially midges and sedges. On northern waters there may be sparse, late hatches of the autumn dun. However, as winter proceeds the trout will be less active, and the majority of fishing in this period will be based on the sinking line and large lures.

I suppose that one man's meat is another man's poison: some anglers delight in persevering at those fisheries which remain open through the winter. I must admit to hating trout fishing at this time of the year, preferring more seasonal sports such as grayling fishing on the rivers and sea angling for cod and whiting. Thus I feel really keen when at last the new season opens. You can't look forward with anticipation to a new season if, for you, there are no close seasons!

10
Spinning for Lake Trout

'There are of course many anglers who cannot use a fly rod .. the method to use is the one that gives the most pleasure.'

Norman Macleod, *Trout Fishing in Lewis*, 1977

'Apart from the fly rod there is really only one other type of rod which must of necessity be included in the 'complete trout fisher's' equipment and that is the spinning rod.'

H. D. Turing, *Trout Fishing*, 1943

Spinning for trout is as old a sport as fly fishing, possibly older. It is therefore a traditional way of catching trout. Today lots of anglers use the spinner* rather than any other method. Look at the catalogue of any major tackle manufacturer. A huge variety of spinners are available to the game angler, each bristling with a treble hook that will ensure a good hold on the fish. Each is easy to cast a long way on a light rod and fixed spool reel—much easier to cast, for a novice, than the fly. Each is so large that an angler can fish with them in the confident knowledge that the trout will see them clearly. In fact, on the face of it spinning seems the logical way to catch trout and those who use the fly are either forced to by stupid fishery rules or because they are faddy purists! That's true, isn't it? Look at it this way, would a fishery allow fly fishing if that was the most successful method of catching fish? No! It allows fly and bans the alternative methods because the others are the most successful! And where there is no ban on spinning, don't the spinners catch more than the fly-only men?

This sort of jumbled, ignorant gobbledegook has, for years, dominated the passions of many anglers who are not fly fishers and whose confidence lies in the use of spinning or bait fishing (see

---

*A spinner can be a bait (natural or artificial) cast out and retrieved so that it spins through the water to attract the fish. It can also be the final stage in the life cycle of the group of flies that includes the mayfly (*Ephemeroptera*): it is the sexually mature stage.

171

Chapter 11). I have come across it so many times. For instance, on the lakes of northern England and some of the Scottish lochs, where spinning and bait fishing are popular ways of catching trout, the feeling has often been expressed to me that the fly fisher is some sort of freak who is making life difficult for himself, and this attitude can be found in all game angling—trout, sea trout and salmon fishing. So, let me once and for all lay the record straight.

Firstly, the most effective way of catching trout, and for that matter sea trout and salmon, is the fly. It has got to be, for when fished properly the fly can provide the best of spinning—a flashy or coloured lure can be drawn through the water relatively quickly —whilst at the same time it is a method that can imitate the natural foods of the trout. Spinning can never achieve the latter, except when the trout are feeding on small fish which the spinner can represent.

The problem lies with the spin fisherman who has never given the fly a real trial. He has confidence in his spinners but his own personal experience of fly fishing has never given him any confidence in that method—a common occurrence amongst salmon anglers, but fortunately less so amongst sea trout and lake trout anglers. Many times I have known salmon that have ignored large Tobies and Devon minnows but have later taken a tiny fly first cast —and by tiny, I mean tiny: a size 12 Stoat's Tail!

One afternoon, for example, on the Ribble at Henthorn, one angler fished at least nine different spinners for over three hours over one salmon to no avail. It had my tiny fly second cast. On another occasion, on the river Hodder, Harry Duxbury had two salmon on a size 10 Peter Ross in something like a dozen casts when several spin and worm anglers had failed to catch in over six hours. The same principle is true in lake trout fishing. On many waters in North Wales, northern England and Scotland I have watched spin fishers fail to catch when fly fishers have had good bags. Again, some examples: firstly, on a Scottish loch, nine anglers fished spinners and had no trout; two anglers fished fly for 31 trout! Secondly, on a small Cumbrian lake, five anglers fished with spinners and had no trout; three fly fishers had 14 trout! Lastly, from a llyn in North Wales, three anglers fished spinners for no trout; two fly fishers had 9 trout!

Success of the fly   Fly is beyond any doubt the most successful way of catching trout, provided, of course, that the fly is fished properly. Why?

The reason for the fly usually being more successful than the spinner is that the fly can be fished with more control. Consider the use of the lure or flashy standard lake fly, the fly fisher's equivalent of the spinner. By using lines of different densities and allowing time for the fly to sink, the fly can be fished at precisely measured depths. By having such depth control the angler can retrieve his lures as slowly or as quickly as he likes. He can also achieve, by using weighted lures such as the Dog Nobbler series or semi-buoyant lures such as the Muddler Minnow, retrieves that fish the water in a most attractive sink-and-draw manner. Now consider the spin fisher. He can vary depth at which his spinner fishes only by allowing different sinking times, but, because of the high cost of his spinners, he is wary to fish them close to the lake bed in case they get hung up and he loses them. Then he must make sure that the spinner is retrieved at a speed which is fast enough to prevent it sinking to the lake bed and which produces the best 'action' of the spinner. He can rarely fish the spinner as slowly and with the control that the fly fisher can fish his lure.

The main problem is that nearly all spinners are too heavy—certainly the best are. Some lighter, more buoyant lures would be of great advantage but the nylon fishing line used in spinning would not pull them under the water in the same way that a high density fly line pulls down a Muddler Minnow or fairly light Marabou. Possibly it would be worth experimenting on the sorts of 'plugs' used in pike fishing which float until line is retrieved, at which point they dive to great depths and then, when no more line is retrieved, float back to the surface. These can be fished very slowly and with excellent control. However, none that I have found are suitable for trout fishing, because they are too large. I have tried small home-made ones that were barely over an inch long on perch with some success and have had a few trout on them. Perhaps a very keen trout spin angler might like to develop his favourite sport in this direction!

What certainly gives a lot of confidence to anglers who prefer spinning is the large treble hook that adorns their spinners. I have had such anglers look in my dry fly and nymph boxes, where there are flies tied on irons as small as sizes 16, 18 and even 20 and 22, and say, 'But don't you lose a lot of fish on these little hooks?' The answer to this is that, often, a large hook (even a treble) does not hold onto a fish as well as a deeply embedded small single hook. My old friend Pete Hemmings, who is primarily a sea trout and salmon angler, catches more than his fair share of these big fish (far bigger than the majority of trout) on flies tied on size 12, 14 and 16 hooks. He argues, rightly, that the fish can see them, will take them and, when hooked, rarely come off! So deeply embedded can a size 22 hook become in a trout's jaw that it has to be cut out. Bigger irons, including trebles, tend to wear a large hole in the flesh of the fish's mouth and thus will fall out more easily.

All that I have written here is true! It is just a matter of confidence. The spin fisher would generally be far more successful if he could use a tiny light spinner, say a centimetre long, armed with a single size 12 or 14 hook, than he will be with most conventional spinners. He would be even more successful if he turned to the fly! So successful is the fly that it would be more logical, if fishery rules were imposed to reduce the catch-rate, to ban the fly! Indeed, one of Britain's best game anglers, John Bettaney, said that if we wanted to make the stocked trout in a stillwater fishery last longer the easiest way would not be to reduce bag limits but to ban the fly! He wasn't joking!

The spinner

Despite what I have said so far, there are places and times when the spinner is the lure to use if you want to catch trout. The most obvious case is the angler who has not had the opportunity to learn or cannot, because of some physical disability, handle a fly rod. Such anglers have as much right to fish for trout as anyone else. Yet, mainly because of the damage that a treble hook can inflict on the mouth of a small trout, making it likely that the fish cannot be released to fight another day but has to be killed, the spinner is banned on most put-and-take fisheries. However, on waters where the angler has to kill each fish that he catches and must stop fishing once he has caught his limit bag (for example, at Draycote) then there is no good reason for preventing the use of spinning or, for that matter, bait. Incidentally, on waters where there are no rules, other than those set down by Act of Parliament, the spin fisher must accept that he may have to kill quite small fish due to the damage that can be caused by treble hooks.

Trailing spinners   The spinner is the method *par excellence* of catching very deeply feeding or swimming trout, including those that are referred to as *ferox*. No other method can succeed to the same extent. Trout may be feeding deep in the epilimnion or thermocline of oligotrophic lakes at a depth of possibly 20 metres or more: the fly fisher, even with his lead-cored line, will be hard put to fish *properly* at such depths, and a bait angler cannot hold his bait

SPINNING FOR LAKE TROUT

at that depth in mid-water. These trout may be few in number, large in size, and mostly piscivorous (i.e. fish-eaters). The stationary bait angler or anchored fly fisher will find their patience tested to the limit waiting for a trout to come along, even if they can manage to fish at the right depth. The system calls for a spinner, fished slowly across the whole surface of the lake. Such a method is termed trailing (often wrongly called 'trolling') the spinner.

One of the problems to be overcome when trailing spinners behind a boat is finding how deep the fish are. It is no use simply attaching an indeterminate amount of lead onto the line, tying on a spinner, casting and then rowing around in circles. Here we can learn something from the charr-fishers of the Cumbrian lakes, who also catch trout, and have this method off to a fine art. A keen spin fisherman could do worse than to emulate their technique.

Two trailing-rigs are set up (see diagram). Each consists of a long ash pole or 'spreader' from which is suspended an 80-feet length of main line. To the end of this is a heavy lead weight of about $1\frac{1}{2}$ lb which is of a special cone shape to prevent twisting as the rig is fished. Six droppers are fastened at about 12-feet intervals along the main line and to the end of the droppers are attached the spinners. A 'lazy-line' is attached to the main line just above the top dropper and, the other end, to the boat. A bell is attached to the end of the spreader which rings when a fish is hooked.

The fisherman slowly rows across the lake, covering the potentially best areas, and the series of spinners searches a wide range of depths. When a fish takes, the lazy line is pulled in by hand, followed by the main line and droppers until the fish is brought in. Obviously the very heavy lead used tends to deaden the activity of hooked fish. It is thus a method that lacks the finesse of real rod-and-line angling, but it is very effective. It is a technique that really demonstrates the importance of trailing spinners at quite precise depths. On bright days the bottom dropper may be the only one that is successful; on dull days the middle droppers may score; and during late evenings in wet blustery weather the fish might all come to the top dropper. Anyone interested in making a pair of these rigs should refer to Sea Trout Fishing (1976) by Hugh Falkus where full details are given. However, the problem with this method, for most anglers, is that it is not really worthwhile to acquire, transport and effectively use these rather complex rigs, especially for those, like me, who fish the spinner very rarely.

My alternative is as follows. Two rods are set up—ideally long, fairly stiff rods. I use 14-feet coarse rods (Bruce and Walker

CTM14 fibreglass, now obsolete). A fixed-spool reel is attached to each and the reel line (ideally 10 lb B.S., 4.5 kg) is threaded through the rod rings. To the end of the reel line is attached a ball-bearing swivel. A 4-feet (1.2 metres) length of 8 lb (3.6 kg) breaking strain nylon line is tied to the free eye of the swivel and the spinner is tied to the end of this short leader. Weight is now needed to sink the spinner and line to appropriate depth and the best type of weight to perform this task is, by far, the Arlesey bomb. These weights, invented by the great angler, the late Dick Walker, are required in a variety of sizes. On one line I would start with a smallish weight, on the other a larger one. The actual sizes will depend initially on the weather, time of the year and the depth of water to be fished: Spring: trout are concentrated in the shallower water, so weights are chosen to fish the spinners close to the lake bed.
Summer: trout are in the epilimnion or thermocline and their depth will depend to some extent upon the weather. The brighter the day, the deeper will be the fish and the greater the weight needed, and *vice versa*. I have not given precise weights of lead as this will vary from water to water and from day to day. The weights should be attached with 5 amp fuse wire to the top eye of the swivel (the eye to which the reel line is attached). Not only do these weights sink the spinners to the required depth, but they also act as an anti-kink lead, preventing excessive twisting of the line.

Once afloat, both lines are cast out and the weights and spinners are allowed time to sink. Then the boat is rowed slowly, trailing the lures behind. How quickly or slowly to row is a matter of experiment and experience, but as a general guide I would say row very *slowly*! When going with the wind it might be that the drift will be fast enough. When going into the wind a slight pull on the oars every few seconds if the breeze and drift are light, or a steady continuous pull if conditions are rough, may be required. If the area of lake to be fished appears fairly uniform, then a figure-of-eight track is always best as this will include stretches of margin as well as deeper open water.

If, after an hour or one circuit, nothing is forthcoming then a change is called for. You could change the spinner for another type but that rarely does more than raise the angler's confidence for a little while longer. It is far better to alter the speed the spinners are being fished (i.e. speed up or slow down the rowing rate) and/or to alter the amount of lead to search the lake at new depths. These ploys frequently work. For example, I fished Lake Coniston in this way for three hours. The result—blank! So I increased the amount of lead and in the next two hours landed four trout and two charr. On another occasion, this time on Ullswater, I had had just one fish for five hours' hard work. Then, whilst I had a coffee from the thermos as the boat drifted in the light breeze up the lake, I had three trout in quick succession. Earlier, it seemed, I had been fishing too quickly. I maintained the slow crawl and had another seven trout in the next three hours.

What sort of spinners are best for this type of fishing? You could do no better than consult the professional charr anglers of Cumbria for the answer, for trout comprise a large proportion of their catches. Small, silver or gold spoons—they use ones that are traditionally made with real silver and real gold! Many years ago I asked a couple of charr fishermen from Ambleside, the town at the north end of Windermere, to offer an opinion of the spinners in my boxes. They picked out two: a small silver Mepps Aglia (size o) and a tiny blue and silver 4g Toby. 'You'll catch charr and trout on them!' was their verdict. And they were right, for on these two I have had hundreds of both of these species from the Cumbrian lakes.

Mepps spinners   The Mepps series are excellent attractors of fish, each with a fluttering rotating fin that not only flashes nicely as the spinner is brought through the water but also creates a turbulence which must provide more attraction to the trout. This will be especially important at great depths where light does not penetrate, for the sensory system of the fish will pick up the vibrations of the revolving blade even though the fish cannot probably see the spinner. This is an interesting point, but predatory animals need not *see* their prey to catch it. I remember one blind otter on the Royal Society for the Protection of Birds Reserve at Leighton Moss that was skilled at catching eels even though it could not see them! I'm sure that trout often do the same, especially the *ferox* types which inhabit the dark depths. The only fault that the Mepps spinners are reported to have is a weak treble hook which bends straight when a big fish grabs hold. This, I am pleased to report, seems not to apply today. In recent years I have caught not only big trout but also salmon to 15 lb (6.8 kg) on the smaller sizes, with no hook-bending problem.

The Toby   The Toby is a splendid attractor of fish when used correctly. If retrieved too quickly it spins around. It should not do this! It should be fished very slowly so that its action is an erratic up-and-down flicker or wobble. Check that you are fishing your Tobies correctly! Trail the thing over the side of the boat and watch its action as the boat is rowed at different speeds.

The problem with all Tobies is a failure of the hook-hold. The hook attaches to one side of the trout's mouth. Then, as the fish turns quickly, the rigid spoon, pulled by the pressure on the line, levers out the hook. Alternatively, during the cast the hook flops back, jamming on its split-ring so that when the fish grabs, the hook cannot take a hold. So, never, ever, fish with a Toby (or Toby-type of spoon) without the following modification.

Remove the treble hook and rear split-ring. To the front split-ring tie a trace of heavy nylon or Alasticum wire (about 20 lb or 9 kg breaking strain will do nicely) and tie the hook to the other end of this so that, when the trace is extended alongside the spoon, the eye of the hook is level with the hole at the rear of the spoon. Then attach the hook to the rear hole of the spinner securely with 5 amp fuse wire. Wrap a little elastic band around the spinner to keep the trace close by the spoon. This may sound a bit fiddly, but the effort is worthwhile. You will lose less fish. The treble will stay firmly in place sticking out behind the spoon and, when a fish takes, the fuse wire will break and the fish will be attached to the free trace without the risk of the spoon levering the hook out. Since I began to use this modification I have lost only one fish on a Toby; before I used to lose about a third of the fish that I hooked.

Both of these spinners can also be used from the lake shore, cast out and retrieved in a style that most anglers would regard as proper 'spinning'. However, fishing *should* be regarded as an enjoyable pastime and personally I find this mechanical cast and reel-back style of spinning utterly boring, especially if I have not caught anything after a few minutes! True, one can fish the fly from a lake shore all day and catch nothing, but with fly fishing one can prevent flagging spirits by changing fly or style. Changing spinner does not elevate the spirits in anything like the same way. Use this method if you must! Nowadays I will try it only when I fancy a change from the fly and I have no bait (i.e. very rarely).

Tackle

The ideal tackle for spinning from the bank is a short spinning rod about 9 feet (2.7 metres) long with a fixed-spool reel filled with adequate strength of line. To the reel line is attached a ball-bearing swivel and then a short leader of lighter line. The spinner is attached to this leader. To prevent kinking of the line, one of the greatest problems of spinning, an anti-kink lead should be attached to the reel line above the swivel. Neglect of this apparently small detail can ruin the reel line in a matter of hours.

The final 'spinning' technique involves the use of the natural minnow, a much neglected technique. Other small fish can be used. Years ago even tiny brown trout and parr were used for this purpose! But from my experience there is nothing to beat the minnow. (Being also a useful natural 'bait', the catching and storing of minnows is dealt with in the next chapter.)

Earlier I criticised most commercially produced spinners on the grounds of weight and the concern, which anglers using them frequently have, that due to their high costs they must be prevented from fishing too deeply or too slowly lest they snag on the bottom and are lost. With the natural minnow such concerns are irrelevant. You can catch your own minnows and so the loss is inexpensive. Therefore, you can afford to fish them as slowly and as deeply as you wish.

Spun natural minnow can be fished from both bank and boat. In the former a short spinning rod is adequate but in the latter a longer rod is required to keep the line and spinner away from the boat. The rig is the same as for spinning with artificial baits.

Note: In all spinning rigs I have stressed the use of a lighter 'leader' beyond the swivel. I do this so that, should the spinner irretrievably snag on the lake bed, only the light leader will be lost and the reel line will remain intact. This is good for two reasons. Firstly, the repeated loss of reel line would reduce the amount of line on the reel spool and impair the distance that can be cast. Fixed-spool reels demand a full spool for effective casting. Secondly, monofilament nylon is environmentally a disaster. To risk the loss of huge lengths of line, as could happen if the spinner was tied directly to the reel line or the leader was the same strength as the reel line, is inexcusable, putting at risk waterside animals and, when strewn about the lake bed, possibly spoiling the sport of other anglers. I have often become entangled on the bottom of both lakes and rivers and have eventually found that the culprit has been huge lengths of lost line at the end of which is, invariably, a rusting lost spinner. The loss of a short length of lighter line is less potentially dangerous. So, when spinning *always use a lighter leader beyond the swivel!*

To attach the minnow, buy or make a 'baiting-needle'. A large darning needle mounted in a cork will do. Insert the needle into the vent of the minnow and push it through and out at the mouth. Insert the end of the nylon leader into the eye of the needle and then pull the needle back out of the fish. The nylon is then removed from the eye of the needle; it will be threaded through the minnow with the loose end protruding from the minnow's vent. Put a small shirt button into the nylon (this will prevent the hook cutting into the minnow) and tie onto the end a small treble hook (size 12–16, depending on the size of the minnow).

Finally, weight must be added. This can be done in two ways. Either use a heavy anti-kink lead (such as an Arlesey bomb) attached to the reel line eye of the swivel, the size of the lead being related to how deep the minnow is required to fish. Or, better, pinch one or two swan-shot to the leader and slide them down the line into the minnow's mouth. In this way the minnow can be fished like the Dog Nobbler series of lures in a superb sink-and-draw manner (see Chapter 7). By putting a bend in the minnow's body an erratic wobble can be imparted on the way the minnow fishes through the water. Special 'spinning vanes' and 'minnow mounts' are available. These are unnecessary and their expense removes some of the advantage of using these cheap, freely available spinners.

From the bank the minnow can be fished in the usual spinning cast-and-retrieve style. However, it is best to retrieve as slowly as possible. Remember, no minnow ordinarily covers 30 metres or more in a matter of seconds! Alternatively, it can be brought back in a slow sink-and-draw manner by making very short retrieves, followed by long pauses when the minnow is allowed to sink. From the boat the minnow can be trailed like other spinners (see above) or fished sink-and-draw on a very slow drift, controlled either by a drogue or the anchor (see Chapter 8). This is spinning at its best! Exciting, interesting, demanding in ingenuity, something that is not quite so when solid metal spinners are being used.

But beware! Trout hit the natural minnow very, very hard. Always make sure that the line you are using is strong enough to withstand the sudden impact. If there are pike, salmon or sea trout in the lake these, too, will take the natural minnow. It is an excellent method, provided you are fishing it properly and you know where the fish are!

11
Bait Fishing
for Lake Trout

'The trout is usually caught with a worm or a minnow (which some call a penk) or with a fly...And, first, for worms...'

Izaak Walton, *The Compleat Angler*, 1653

'Sir, your methods are damnable, and I have a great distaste for your personality, so now let us discuss the question of 'fly versus bait'.'

H. T. Sherringham, *Trout Fishing Memories and Morals*, 1920

There is no doubt that fly fishing is the most effective way of catching lake trout and that spinning is, with some exceptions, a poor second. With the fly it is possible to cover a wide range of depths, save for the deepest water where spinning has the advantage and, from a boat, large areas of lake can be covered in the space of a day by both of these methods. However, there are a lot of anglers who fish bait for trout, possibly because they prefer to, or because they want a change, or because they have never learned to handle the fly rod and they don't like spinning. But bait fishing is often, as a fish-catching technique, grossly inferior. Let me give a couple of examples. Peter and I were fishing a small Scottish loch from the bank where seven other anglers were fishing the worm. Peter had 8 brown trout and I had 7 through the evening; the worm anglers had not one between them. On another occasion, this time on a Pennine reservoir that was stocked with brownies, brookies and rainbows, five fly fishers had 17 trout between them in the course of the afternoon and six bait fishers caught but four. Such are a couple of instances amongst many that I could quote. On the loughs of Ireland, lochs of Scotland and many Welsh llyns and English lakes the rules allow the use of any legal method, even in some stocked fisheries. However, just about every competent fly fisher and spin fisher who fishes from a boat and who has regularly fished such waters could tell of days where they were far more successful than the bait anglers.

For many fly fishing purists the thought of bait fishing for trout will be horrific and considered a less sporting method than the fly.

However, to argue that one legal method of angling is more or less sporting than another shows a priggish and narrow mentality. One man's opinion as to what is sporting can be completely different from another's. Yet, provided that the sport of other anglers is not impeded by the use of one type of angling, that the method does not damage the fishery and, most important, that the standing and future of this great sport is not put at risk, then *any method is sporting*!

What is *not* sporting is the fly fisher who damages the fishery for others by taking more than his quota of trout. He is the fisherman who stands in what is patently the best trout lie and refuses to let others have a go there, or the boat angler who cuts through the swim being fished by anglers restricted to the bank, or the fisherman who does not kill his fish humanely or leaves monofilament nylon strewn about the countryside. Such anglers put a nail in the coffin of the sport of angling by antagonising the observant non-angling public and converting them to anti-angling fanatics.

A trout taken from the water is a fish removed, whether on dry fly, nymph, wet fly, lure, spinner, worm or maggot. No matter what the method, that dead fish provided sport.

However, it is reasonable for commercial stocked fisheries, which are heavily fished, to impose restrictions to make it harder to catch the fish. Thus, the argument goes, the stocked fish will last much longer into the season and provide more sport than if, by allowing any method, they could be caught easily and quickly. It would be much better to reduce the bag limit on such waters and to insist that anglers, once they have taken their limits, leave. This is because, by allowing fly fishing, the fishery permits the most effective way of catching trout! It would be far better to insist on, say, worm fishing only (with no groundbaiting), for this is a very unproductive way of catching trout. Then the stocked fish would last much longer, but the air of superiority and mystique that encumbers fly fishing renders this an improbability, especially when one considers that fly fishers tend to have the loudest voices on fishery committees!

There are ways, however, that render the use of bait unsporting; for example, to fish with a slack line or to give slack line when a fish nibbles the bait so that the hook is taken into its stomach. The latter fish must be killed, even if it is undersize, or it will almost certainly die when released due to the traumatic handling needed to remove the hook or due to a fungal infection where it was injured.

Also unsporting is the use of masses of loose-feed or groundbait that affects the normal feeding behaviour of trout over a large part of the lake. In one small Welsh llyn that I visited a few years ago I could not get the trout to take my flies, nor would they look at a big hatch of lake olives that were on the water. Eventually I was lucky to catch one fish. I spooned it—dozens of maggots thrown in as groundbait! This should not prevent the better angler from using a *little* loose-feed, where such is permitted, to encourage the fish to take the hook-bait. Knowing when and how much loose-feeding is required is one of the bait fisher's arts. As a coarse-fishing friend used to say, 'When we groundbait we should give the fish just enough to entice them to the baited hook. We should not be aiming to give the fish a free meal!'

Types of bait

There are four major baits used in trout fishing (worm, maggot, caster and natural minnow), though trout can be caught on a much wider variety. I have caught them also on bread (including an unexpected four-pound rainbow trout!), crayfish, creeper (the nymphs of the larger species of stonefly), cheese, cigarette ends, pork luncheon meat and sweet corn when I have been fishing for coarse fish in waters that also held trout.

Worm There are several species of earthworm, varying in size from the large lobworm to the tiny redworm found in compost heaps. Trout can be caught on them all. However, the best, beyond doubt, are the blue-headed lobworm, that can be obtained from around old cowpats or dug from the garden vegetable plot, and the smaller red-and-cream banded brandling, obtainable from the oldest compost heaps or the soil around rotted lawn clippings.

Earthworms should be carefully looked after once they have been collected, especially during prolonged summer droughts when they can be hard to find, or during trips to the Scottish Highlands, an area where worms are more precious than gold! So, make sure that there are no damaged ones in the box, as injured worms quickly die and the others soon die in sympathy! Old books used to recommend storage in moss. Even better is moist (not sodden) crumpled newspaper. Especially important is temperature. High summer temperatures kill earthworms rapidly, so do as I do—keep them in their box in the vegetable compartment at the bottom of the fridge. The family do not mind for I have convinced them, over many years, that this is quite normal! (Quite honestly, kept thus, your earthworm supply will keep fit and healthy for many weeks.) If the weather is very hot don't take all your stock down to the lake. Just take the few you will need and leave the rest in the cool.

Maggot and Caster I put these together for, as the maggot is the larva of the blue-bottle, the caster is the pupa. Both are excellent baits, much used by coarse anglers.

You can breed your own maggots but it is much more convenient to buy them from fishing tackle shops. However, if you live in an area where tackle shops do not sell maggots (and this is the case over much of upland Britain where there is very little coarse fishing) you must breed your own. Simply buy a sheep's heart from the butcher and put it in a biscuit tin on a bed of sawdust. Then put the tin in the middle of the lawn on a summer's day. Allow between six and ten blue-bottles to enter the tin and lay their eggs on the heart and then put a perforated lid on the tin. Put it in the shed and wait for the maggots to develop. In warm weather this might take only a week or so.

As with earthworms, keep the maggots cool. Again, if you can, persuade the family to let you use the bottom of the fridge. This might be difficult, I know! But there they will remain as maggots for weeks. If kept warm they will rapidly metamorphose into the brown cigar-shaped caster which itself is a good bait.

If you want to fish the caster, beware! Some casters will float and others will sink, providing problems of presentation to the fish. So, never buy casters (which are, in any case, very expensive) but allow your maggots to turn. Then, as the maggots pupate take off the casters, put them into a jar of water and separate into floaters and non-floaters. Keep the non-floaters, wrapped tightly in a polythene bag, in the fridge. Then you really have two baits: the sinking caster for conventional use, fished deep below the surface, and the floating caster which can be used, with no weight on the line, as a floating bait. I suppose that this latter is the bait fisher's equivalent of the dry fly! And like the dry fly for trout and the floating crust for carp, the floating caster is an exciting bait to use. It is also an under-used bait.

A word of caution! Some anglers may still have stocks of maggot dyes such as chrysodine that can be used to colour maggots bronze or yellow. These dyes are very nasty carcinogens. If you have any, burn it now! As far as trout fishing at least is concerned, I have no evidence that having different colours of maggots confers any real advantage over the plain natural creamy-white ones.

Natural Minnow Natural minnow is also a spinning bait (see Chapter 10). However, trout will keenly take dead minnows as pike will take a deadbait herring or mackerel.

Never, ever use live minnows as a bait. To insert a hook into a live fish, even though only a tiny one, and have it swimming around tethered to a float, is inhumane. The live minnow is a traditional bait for trout and many coarse fish; and the minnow *may* not feel pain, but in the eyes of the non-angling public at least there seems to be a degree of cruelty. For this reason alone such live baits should have no part in the sport of angling.

It is possible to buy minnows, but it is easier to catch your own and prepare them as you want. Ignore the old bottle minnow trap. Take a fine micromesh net (e.g. a landing net) down to the river or lakeside on a warm summer day. The minnows will be congregated in the shallows. Find a shoal and lie the net flat in the water close to the shoal. Then put some flaked white bread over the net and wait. Within a few minutes the minnows will be over the net, eating the bread. Quickly raise the net and you have your minnows. Kill them by tapping them on the head. Then drop them into a 70% formalin solution (7 parts formaldehyde, obtainable from the chemist's, to 3 parts tap water) and leave them for a week. (Formaldehyde is poisonous so keep it away from children.) After the week drain the minnows in a colander and wash thoroughly under a running tap. Store them permanently in screw-top jars containing a strong sugar solution made by dissolving about a pound of sugar in one pint of hot water (but allow the sugar solution to cool before you add the minnows or you will cook them). When you go fishing take enough minnows for the day and wash the preserving sugar away under the tap. This method of storage results in baits without the obnoxious taste and smell of formalin that might otherwise dissuade the trout from taking them.

Bait-fishing techniques

The two techniques of bait fishing for trout are:
1. float fishing, and
2. ledgering.
Float fishing is the method to use where long casts are not needed, when the trout are only a few metres offshore, whereas ledgering allows for much longer casts due to the heavy ledger weights that are used. Ledgering is also preferable in deep water where the bait must be presented close to the lake bed, though some anglers use a sliding-float to fish at these depths, a more tiresome technique which I do not use.

Float fishing Float fishing requires the longest manageable rod, usually 14 feet (4.2 metres) long, preferably made of carbon- or boron-fibre. A fixed-spool reel filled to the rim with a suitable monofilament line completes the basic tackle. It is important that the reel line is of a reasonable strength—5 or 6 lb (about 2.5 kg) is probably optimal. To this line is tied a short length of lighter line, 3 or 4 lb (about 1.5 kg) B.S. This lighter hook length allows better bait presentation than the thicker reel line and should the hook become snagged on the lake bed only the short hook length will be lost. A float is slipped onto the line by the float-ring and a hook is tied to the end of the line.

Coarse anglers frequently use tiny floats, but generally these have no place in trout fishing. Far better are the bigger floats that take a fair amount of shot, at least 3BB, preferably two swan or more. Such weight allows for longer, easier casting. Also the large size of the float holds better in choppy water and is more visible in a wave. Incidentally, having mentioned split shot let me encourage the use of non-lead weights which I find just as effective as the old ecologically doubtful lead shot.

Hooks depend on the bait to be used. When maggot or caster fishing I would stick with a size 14 or 16 forged spade-end hook. Beware of fine-wire hooks which are meant to be used where tiny roach are the quarry. A biggish, quick-moving trout will straighten these hooks, as I have learned to my cost! When fishing the worm a size 10 or 12 specimen bait hook is ideal with brandlings; with lobworms I use either a single size 8 specimen hook or a double Pennell-tackle made from two size 10 specimen hooks tied in tandem onto a short length of heavy nylon. With the minnow a single hook of appropriate size (size 8 for a big minnow, size 12 for a tiny one) hooked through the body will suffice.

Coarse anglers, especially those who enter fishing competitions in heavily fished waters, have all sorts of intricate rigs, finely balanced arrangements for different situations. This is not necessary in lake trout fishing, where the fish will probably have never seen a hook before. All important is the depth the bait lies and the way the bait falls through the water after casting.

To start with I would suggest the following arrangement:
The float is fixed in position by the bulk of the shot so that the length of nylon beneath the float is a little more than the water depth. This should never be more than about three metres. If you don't know the water depth then find out! Attach an Arlesey bomb to the hook and cast it in. Adjust the shot and float until you have the right depth:
By having the float fixed in place by shot on the line it is an easy matter to alter depth of the float by sliding the shot and the float one way or the other.

Bait up and cast in. Stick the rod tip deep underwater and quickly reel back to recover any slack and to sink the line between rod and float. This will prevent the floating nylon drifting on the water surface, pulling the float and hook out of position, and improves sensitivity of the float to offers from the fish. With the shot concentrated around the float the unweighted hook length will slowly sink, carrying the baited hook down slowly and naturally. Trout that take 'on the drop' do so boldly and little effort is usually needed to hook them. This is also the set-up to use with the floating caster, the single shot a few centimetres below the float keeping the nylon beneath the surface and therefore preventing Floating Nylon Syndrome.

Often, however, the trout will not rise to the bait and it must be presented very close to the lake bed. This is done by sliding all the shot, other than the two that lock the float in position, down the hook length to within about 25 centimetres (10″) of the hook. Trout taking the bait at this depth will feel the weight soon after they have taken the bait and they may quickly reject it. Thus a rise or fall or jerk of the float tip must be responded to immediately by the strike. It is no good sticking the rod in a rod rest and sitting back as you wait for the offer. A rod rest can be used but the rod butt must be held all the time. Of course, trout are sometimes very obliging and persistent, especially when taking the worm, but then they tend to swallow the bait. To prevent this, strike at the first sign of an offer and the trout will be lip-hooked and can, if you wish, be returned carefully to fight another day.

If no offers result then *a little judicious* groundbaiting is reasonable. When fishing sinking caster make sure that those you use as loose-feed are not floaters, and *vice versa*. Restrict yourself to no more than 10–20 maggots or casters, or four or five chopped-up earthworms per hour as loose-feed. There is never any need to groundbait when fishing a minnow under the float. Remember: the aim of loose-feeding is to attract the trout to take the baited hook, not to feed the fish until they are full!

Ledgering Ledgering is the best way of fishing close to the lake bed in deep water or where the trout are some way out.

A shortish rod of about 9 feet (2.7 metres) is standard, usually with a quiver-tip or swing-tip attached at the end. These are bite indicators, the quiver-tip being better in choppy water whereas the swing-tip is better in calm water because it is more sensitive than the quiver-tip. A fixed-spool reel filled with suitable monofilament is attached to the rod and the line is passed through the rod rings

and the rings on the bite indicator. At the end of the line is tied an
Arlesey bomb. About 18″ (45 cm) from this weight a small loop is
tied in the reel line and to this is attached, by a tucked blood knot,
a hook length of about 4 feet (120 cm) of slightly lighter nylon. An
appropriate hook is attached (see *Float Fishing* above).

The weight and baited hook are cast out, allowed to settle on the
lake bed and the line is then tightened so that it is straight between
bite indicator and ledger weight. This may be quite a large amount
of line—a surprisingly large amount if you have never fished this
technique before—but tightness is important in bite detection.
With this rig the baited hook will drift around, independently of the
tight reel line, on or very close to the lake bed.

Bite indication is easy. When a trout takes the bait the swing-tip
may rise or fall and the quiver-tip may just twitch or bend quite
violently. In all cases an immediate rapid strike is essential.

An alternative and just as effective a bite indicator, should the
angler not have a rod with a quiver- or swing-tip, is the butt-
indicator. This may sound a bit stylish for the top off a plastic
washing-up liquid bottle filled with plasticine, but that is all it is!
Otherwise the rig is exactly the same. After the cast is made and the
line is tightened between rod tip and ledger weight, the plastic top
from a washing-up liquid bottle, weighted with plasticine, is
clipped round the line between butt-ring and reel. When a fish takes
the bait the washing-up bottle top will rise or fall jerkily—an immediate strike is needed to set the hook.

Once more, the judicious use of groundbaiting can improve the
catch rate without detriment to the fishery or other anglers. This
can be provided as loose-feed (propelled at a distance with a bait
catapult). Alternatively, a swim feeder containing ground bait can
be used in place of the Arlesey bomb so that the loose-feed ends up
exactly where it is needed, around the baited hook. This is important. Too many anglers sling in their loose-feed with no regard to
accuracy so that it may entice the fish *away* from the hook!

Locating the fish is important when bait fishing, just as it is in fly
fishing and spinning. It is possibly more so for the bait fisher, as he
and his bait tend to be fairly static. What the bait fisher must do is
look for areas where trout will find a lot of food in the lake margins.
Water depth is critical for, as described in Chapter 2, most lake-bed
trout foods will be concentrated in water up to two or three metres
deep. There is, for instance, no point hurling a ledger out into vast
depths where the lake bed is relatively sterile and, possibly,
anaerobic. Hot-spots can be identified around the lake in the same

way that the bank fly fisher does (see Chapter 7). On some of the more popular lakes for bait fishing the newcomer will have little difficulty finding the hot-spots. Other anglers will be there already!

Bait fishing has much to commend it. Small children who are still too young to fish the fly enjoy it, especially when they catch something, even if it is nothing more than a slimy eel. Many adults come into game angling via the use of coarse angling techniques. Bait fishing is restful, particularly on a hot day when you can lounge in the deckchair, be served with iced drinks, and keep an eye on the float or rod tip. And you just don't know what will grab the bait even though you are after trout. In Ireland it might be a big bream or a pike, in the Cumbrian lakes, a charr or big perch. In some Scottish lochs you may find yourself attached to a salmon or big sea trout. Of course, it might be just a trout! When a restful day is called for and you want to go fishing, bait provides the perfect answer. I would go further than this. Any angler who cannot fish successfully with fly, spinner and bait cannot call himself a *compleat angler*!

12
Trout for the Table

'Fish, fish, fish, fish, fish, fish . . .'
The words of an I.B.A. Television advert promoting the virtues
of fish (April–May 1986)

Trout are good to eat! This has been known by anglers and the
friends and relations of anglers for many years. Indeed it was, for
many people, regarded as a rich man's food up to the 1950s, because
it rarely figured in the fishmonger's shop and you had to be or know
a fisherman to eat one. However, in recent years the great increase
in the number of trout farms has put the trout on the fishmonger's
slab at a very low cost and it is available to all.

Most trout fishermen catch a lot of fish in the course of the
season. Some sell their surplus. Most give away their surplus. The
rest they and their family eat, and overall, in Britain, probably more
trout are eaten that have been caught by anglers than are sold by
fishmongers. So, the angler is in a fortunate position. He can pass
on fish to those who have never eaten a trout before and this will
encourage them to go and buy trout from the shop. By so doing he
will increase the quality and variety of the recipients' diets.
Remember, trout is a very rich food. Like mackerel, herring and
salmon, trout are oily fish. By this is meant that the oils produced
by the body of the fish are stored in the muscle or meat. This
contrasts with 'white fish', such as cod, plaice and halibut, that store
their oils in the liver. As most of us know, these oils are rich in
vitamins, notably A and D. Trout meat is therefore rich in energy,
protein, most vitamins and many important mineral salts.

To eat trout frequently when it is cooked by the same method
(e.g. grilled) becomes rather tedious. To get children to eat trout at
all can be difficult—they prefer fish fingers or chip shop fish! However, with the minimum of effort you can turn the trout caught into
a very wide range of fish dishes, acceptable to all who profess to like
fish in some shape or form.

This chapter provides a guide to storing, preparing and cooking the trout you catch. Some of the recipes are easy. Others convert the trout into 'convenience food'. Others are real gourmet dishes suitable for the special occasion.

Storage

As soon as a trout is caught that you want to keep, kill it. Then spoon out its stomach contents so that you can see what it has been feeding on. As soon as you have done this put the fish into either a wicker creel or wet rush fish-bass so that air circulates and, by the evaporation of dampness from the creel or bass, the fish will remain cool for a few hours.

If it will be several hours before you can get the fish home it is worth having, in the boot of the car, a cold-box packed with special ice-packs. These can be obtained from suppliers of camping equipment. They can also be used to keep drinks cool on hot days by the river! I have one which will keep trout that I have caught over a two-day weekend in good condition until I get them home. Try to put the trout into this cold store as soon as you can.

When you arrive back home, if you are going to eat the trout within about 24 hours, store them in the refrigerator. Do not gut them at this stage. Simply wash them in cold water, wrap in kitchen-paper, and store at the bottom of the fridge.

Remember, uncooked trout will possibly have dangerous bacteria that might drip down onto other foods. Always store uncooked meats of any type with a covering at the bottom of the fridge.

Deep-freezing   Many trout are stored in deep-freezers and yet most are stored incorrectly. Again, do *not* gut the fish that you want to freeze. Wash them in cold water, wrap individually in aluminium foil and put them into a freezer bag as soon as you can. Gutting and open-freezing fish results in the meat becoming dehydrated. Label the bag with the date, type and sizes of the fish and freeze them as quickly as you can. Use the fast-freeze compartment if you have one. I freeze larger trout, over about 2 lb (1 kg), separately so that I can use them one at a time without disturbing others in the same bag.

Fish such as salmon, sea trout and lake trout should not be stored in the freezer for more than six months, as their meat will deteriorate even when properly stored. Check the freezer carefully from time to time and use those that are nearing their 'eat-by' date.

Preparation of the trout for cooking

For this you will need a very sharp knife with a pointed blade about
10″ (25 cm) long.

For small trout, up to $1-1\frac{1}{2}$ lb (1 kg), the preparation need be
nothing more than removing the head, tail and guts. Some people
prefer to keep the head and tail in place and simply gut their fish.
To gut a trout, insert the knife point in the vent and cut through the
body wall to the head and pull the guts away. Also make sure that
you remove the large blood vessel and kidneys that lie at the back
of the body cavity along the backbone. A teaspoon is a useful
scraper for this job.

For larger fish preparation can be the same or you can fillet them.
This is easy to do. Take the whole fish and lie it on its side. Make
a long incision the length of the dorsal side, taking a line that runs
straight down the body parallel with, but a few millimetres away
from, the dorsal and adipose fins. Slowly cut deeper, alongside the
backbone and down by the side of the ribs that are attached to the
backbone (thus the large bones will be missing from the fillet). This
may sound tricky, but the knife will follow the correct line as it
follows the bones. Keep on cutting until you reach the ventral side
of the trout. Detach the fillet, turn the fish over and repeat for the
other side. Until you have learned to do this properly, *go slowly*.
After half a dozen trout, filleting will be easy, but remember the
need for a very sharp knife!

To skin the fillet simply lie it on a board, skin-side down. Start at the tail end and make a little cut between skin and meat. Then insert the knife into the little gap that you have made, hold onto the small flap of skin, and force the blade through between fillet and skin, keeping the blade pressed downwards onto the skin and underlying board. Again, go slowly until you have the hang of it and, with a little perseverance, you will be producing fillets that would enhance the fishmonger's slab!

These fillets are especially useful for those who do not like to see a 'real fish' on the plate. Children love them fried, or turned into fish cakes, fish fingers or fish pie.

Recipes

The recipes that follow are for four people, unless otherwise stated.

Fried Trout 1 (Truites à la Meunière)

4 small trout or fillets
Seasoned flour
Butter
Lemon
Parsley

1. Coat the trout with seasoned flour.
2. Fry gently in the melted butter, turning frequently, for 10–15 minutes.
3. Serve, garnished with chopped parsley and wedges of lemon.

Fried Trout 2

An alternative when using fillets. Instead of flour coat the fish in oatmeal and continue as in Recipe 1. Quite a superb, simple dish.

Grilled Trout (a traditional recipe)

4 medium-sized trout or fillets
4 oz (115 g) butter
Salt and pepper
Lemon

1. Put the trout on the grill pan and coat with melted butter.
2. Put under a hot grill, turning after 5 minutes when the other side should be coated with butter and grilled for 5 minutes. If necessary continue cooking a little longer, turning so that both sides are cooked evenly. The actual cooking time depends on the thickness of the fish.
3. Season and serve with slices of lemon.

Baked Trout

When I was a small boy one of the delights was baking freshly caught fish (wrapped in tin foil) in the embers of the fire. Here is the same recipe, but the oven is used rather than the fire. It is also a good way to cook trout over the home barbecue. This is a simple, uncomplicated recipe and what is especially good is that is makes little washing up!

4 medium-sized trout or one large trout
4 oz (115 g) butter
Black pepper
Lemon
Garlic (optional)

1. Put a knob of butter into the body cavity of the fish together with the garlic (optional). (I recommend one clove of garlic per medium-sized trout and two cloves for a bigger fish.) Dust with black pepper.
2. Wrap the fish individually in baking foil ensuring that all the seams are well sealed.
3. Bake in a fairly hot oven at 200°C (400°F, Gas Mark 5) for 20 minutes (for medium-sized trout) or 30 minutes (for large trout).
4. Remove the fish from their wrappers, season and serve with slices of lemon.
This is a good way to prepare a dish of cold trout (allow them to cool sealed in their wrappers).

Poached Trout 1 (supper for one!)

1 small freshly caught trout
Salt and pepper
Vinegar
Parsley
2 oz (60 g) butter

1. Drop the cleaned trout into a pan of boiling water that contains a little salt and a dash of vinegar. Reduce the heat and simmer gently for ten minutes.
2. Drain and garnish with parsley and butter, and season with pepper.

Poached Trout 2 (trout in cider)

1 large trout of at least 3 lb (1.4 kg) or 4 fillets
1 pint (570 cc) dry cider
2 tablespoons cider vinegar
2 cloves crushed garlic
Paprika
Parsley
1 bouquet garni (sachet)
1 bay leaf
Salt and pepper

1. Put the trout into a casserole dish with the cider, cider vinegar, garlic, bouquet garni, bay leaf and salt and pepper seasoning.
2. Place in a pre-heated oven at 200°C (400°F, Gas Mark 5) and cook for 15 minutes per pound of fish.
3. Drain and serve dusted with paprika and garnished with chopped parsley.

Trout Pie

(A recipe that children love, that is good for a large gathering who have called in for supper, or for lunch.)

1 large baked trout (see recipe above)
Boiled potatoes (well mashed)
1 pint (570 cc) parsley or cheese sauce
Salt and pepper
Parsley

1. Remove all the meat from the fish, making sure that there are no bones in the meat. Flake the meat.
2. Put a 1″ (2.5 cm) layer of potatoes in the bottom of a deep dish. Cover with a 1″ layer of flaked trout, season with salt and pepper and pour over a coating of the sauce. Repeat with alternating layers of potatoes, fish and sauce until the dish is full (or you have run out of ingredients), ensuring that the last layer is of potatoes.
3. Brown the top of the pie under a hot grill, garnish with chopped parsley, and serve.

Trout Cakes

(Again, a good recipe for the children or for lunch.)

1 large baked trout (see recipe above)
Boiled potatoes (well mashed)
1 beaten egg
Salt and pepper
Breadcrumbs

1. Remove and flake the fish as in the last recipe.
2. Put trout and potatoes into a mixing bowl in approximately
50 : 50 proportions. Season and mix thoroughly.
3. Mould into flat round cakes about 1″ (2.5 cm) thick on a greased
baking tray. Coat with beaten egg and cover with breadcrumbs.
4. Put under a hot grill until heated thoroughly and serve.

This recipe is a good one to use up any trout left over from other
dishes. Alternatively, a large number can be made and put in the
freezer and used as required. Don't de-frost them; cook them under
the grill for ten minutes or in the microwave for 3 minutes on full
power.

Trout Bits

(Fish fingers are difficult to make at home. This is a good alternative, resulting in a scampi-like bar snack dish. Excellent for
lunches, supper dishes and the children will like them.)

4 trout fillets
1 beaten egg
Breadcrumbs
Salt
Lemon (vinegar for the children)
Tartar sauce

1. Cut the fillets into small pieces, about 1″ (2.5 cm) square.
2. Coat with beaten egg and breadcrumbs.
3. Deep fry until cooked (keep checking carefully as it will be a
matter of minutes; the exact time will depend on the thickness of the
fillets). Make sure that each piece remains separate.
4. Drain on kitchen paper and serve with salt, lemon slices (or
vinegar) and Tartar sauce.

Trout Grenoblaise

4 medium-sized trout
2 oz (60 g) sliced mushrooms
Breadcrumbs
Salt and pepper
4 oz (115 g) butter
Lemon

1. Remove the backbones from the cleaned, beheaded fish. This is easy to do. With a sharp knife continue the incision into the body cavity, which extends to the backbone (see '*Preparation of the trout for cooking*' on page 192), down to the tail and open up the fish like a kipper. Press the hand down hard on the back (skin-side) of the fish, crushing it slightly along the backbone. Turn the fish over so that the meat side is uppermost and the backbone and associated ribs will peel away, with a little encouragement and a sharp knife, from the flesh.
2. Fry the prepared trout in the butter for ten minutes.
3. Remove the fish from the frying pan and keep warm.
4. Fry the mushrooms and breadcrumbs for five minutes.
5. Serve the trout garnished with the mushrooms and breadcrumbs, and with a wedge of lemon.

As an alternative fried, blanched almonds can be used instead of the mushrooms.

Truites au Vin

4 medium-sized trout
$\frac{1}{2}$ pint (285 cc) dry white wine
$\frac{1}{2}$ oz (15 g) flour
Salt and pepper
1 oz (30 g) butter
Lemon
Parsley

1. Prepare the trout as for Trout Grenoblaise.
2. Put the fish into a casserole, season and add the wine.
3. Bake in a pre-heated oven (190°C, 375°F, Gas Mark 4) for 12 minutes per lb of prepared fish.
4. Remove the fish to a hot dish.
5. Put the butter into a frying pan, melt over a low heat and stir in the flour. Cook for 3 minutes, stirring all the time.

6. Pour the wine from the casserole dish into the frying pan, stirring all the time, and cook until the sauce thickens.

7. Serve the trout with the sauce poured over them, garnished with chopped parsley and wedges of lemon.

Bowland Trout

A very large trout at 4 lb-plus (1.8 kg) or 2 large trout at 2 lb (900 g) each
$\frac{1}{2}$ pint (285 cc) single cream
1 small chopped onion
$\frac{1}{2}$ bottle dry white wine
Chopped parsley
Pinch of chopped thyme
Salt and pepper
1 lb (450 g) sliced mushrooms
4 medium-sized sliced carrots
12 asparagus tips (tinned if you cannot get fresh)
1 bay leaf

1. Place the cleaned whole fish into a large casserole or roasting tin.
2. Add cream, mushrooms, onion, carrots, wine, herbs and seasoning.
3. Cover with baking foil and cook in a pre-heated oven at 190°C (375°F, Gas Mark 4) for 15 minutes per lb of fish.
4. Add the asparagus tips 20 minutes before the end of the cooking time.
5. Serve on a large plate, with the sauce poured over.

This is a rich dish for special occasions.

Smoked Trout

The most convenient way of having smoked trout at home is to use a portable smoke-box or smoke-cooker. They turn ordinary trout into the most delightfully flavoured food. There are several makes of smoke-box, the one I have being a *Smokit*. This came with a recipe book and all materials (except, of course, the trout!). Not only can you smoke your own trout but also salmon, chicken, cheese, sausages etc. I recommend you to buy one.

Accompaniments   Trout, like most fish, have a mild, subtle flavour. It is essential, therefore, that the accompaniments do not overpower the flavour of the fish, but complement it with their own fresh, subtle flavours.

Sauces   Some recipes have sauces included. If they have not, can I recommend Hollandaise sauce or, for fried trout recipes, Tartar sauce.

Vegetables   Salads, with a mild dressing, are the best vegetable accompaniment with trout, as their cool, fresh crispness keeps the palate fresh and enhances the flavour of the trout. For cooked vegetables garden peas, runner beans and asparagus are hard to beat and are at their best, fresh, during the trout season.

Though potatoes are a staple diet ingredient for most British people, often not enough care is taken in their cooking. New potatoes, perfectly boiled, so that they are cooked but not breaking up, are best. Do not peel or scrape them, because the outer skin has the best of the flavour. Just give them a good washing.

Most people automatically think of chips with fish. Good chips are fine, poor ones (the majority!) are an abomination! To cook good chips is easy. Get the fat or oil in the chip pan as hot as you can and lower the chips, in the frying basket, into the fat. When the chips are cooked (i.e. soft) lift them in their basket out of the fat, let the fat get really hot again, and put the chips back in. They will puff out and the outside of the chips will crisp up. Drain off surplus fat, dry quickly on kitchen paper and serve immediately.

Drink   Once more, the drink that accompanies a good trout dish should complement it, not overpower it. Very sweet or strong flavoured drinks will hide the flavour of any fish. Try a dry or medium dry cider or white wine, well chilled. If you do not partake of alcohol, then try chilled Perrier Water or a glass of plain water with a couple of ice cubes and a squeeze of lemon.

Bon appetit!

Appendix

In Chapter 4 I presented my list of flies for stillwater fishing in the British Isles. I decided to leave out details of dressings as many anglers would already know them and to put such details in there would have crowded up the chapter needlessly. However, there will be many who would benefit from having details of the fly dressings in one place, so here they are.

Until fairly recently all my flies were tied on hooks sold by Peter Mackenzie-Philps of Wetherby. Alas, he has retired from the retail tackle trade. I have thus turned to Partridge Hooks which used to make some of those supplied by Peter. They are excellent in every way. It is essential to use hooks of their quality for it is, after all, the hook that ultimately catches the trout. Too often I have been let down by cheaper, shoddy hooks. Once, on Loch Smaisaval, I lost a massive trout when the hook I was using straightened out.

There is less of a problem with the furs, feathers, silks and tinsels that are used to tie flies. There are a *few* sharks in the tackle industry who will try to offload poor materials to the unsuspecting. I would recommend all would-be serious tiers of flies to cultivate one of the established retail suppliers. Again, since Peter Mackenzie-Philps retired I have stuck with Veniard; they have not let me down.

Fly patterns

These are given in the categories in which they were presented in Chapter 4. This seems much more logical than alphabetical order where lures, nymphs and wet flies appear all mixed up!

Lures

1. *Marabous*

Body	Chenille, ribbed round silver tinsel.
Hackle	False hackle from dyed cock spade feather.
Wing	Marabou.

The Marabou wing and Chenille body should be the same colour, and that by which the particular lure is named (e.g. White Marabou has a white body and wing). In the White and Black Marabous the hackle is crimson, in the Yellow and Green Marabous, hot orange.

2. *Dog Nobblers*

Head	Either a swan shot securely pinched and tied in or several turns of lead wire. I use a swan shot and then paint it silver.
Tail	Bunch of Marabou fibres.
Body	Marabou fibres wound round the hook shank, ribbed round silver tinsel.

Again, the colour of the Dog Nobbler is the colour of the Marabou used in the tail and body.

3. *Whiskey Fly*

Body	Gold lurex.
Hackle	Hot orange cock.
Wing	Buck tail dyed hot orange.

4. *Baby Dolls*

The two I find most useful have a white Doll body and a back and tail of fluorescent pink (in the Barbara Cartland) or fluorescent lime green (in the Candy Doll).

5. *Polystickle*

Body	Rear $\frac{2}{3}$ silver lurex, front $\frac{1}{3}$ red floss overwound with clear polythene strip to give a fish shape.
Back and Tail	Raffine strip—any colour may be used but dark brown seems the best.
Hackle	False hackle of crimson cock.
Head	Black tying silk, large.

6. *Muddler Minnow*

Body	Gold lurex.
Head	Large head of spun deer hair, trimmed to shape with some of the hairs left untrimmed to provide a sort of collar hackle.
Wing	Brown Turkey quill slips.

7. *Floating Beetle*

Body	Made of small spheres of Plastazote, coloured as required, enclosed in ladies' tights material, and tied to the hook. Two spheres, one larger than the other, are most commonly used to represent the thorax and abdomen of a beetle. Sometimes several spheres are tied in to produce a longer segmented body.
Hackle	Dark red or brown cock, long in the fibre.

Lure hooks: Except for the Floating Beetle, size 6, 8 or 10 long shank hooks are usual, the best being Partridge Streamer Hooks. Some anglers prefer lured ties on two- or three-hook tandem mounts. However, these are a bit more fiddly to tie to no real advantage and, in any case, these are not permitted on many stocked rainbow trout fisheries where big lures are mostly used. In the Floating Beetles a whole range of sizes should be tied on hooks varying in size from 12 to 8 (standard wet fly hooks with a wide gape) and, where many plastazote spheres are incorporated, a slightly longer shank nymph hook.

Standard lake/loch flies

1. *Black Pennell*
Silk	Black.
Tail	Golden Pheasant tippets.
Body	Black floss silk ribbed silver tinsel.
Hackle	Black henny-cock.

2. *Bloody Butcher*
Silk	Black.
Tail	Small red ibis substitute feather.
Body	Flat silver tinsel ribbed (optional) round silver.
Hackle	Dyed bright red hen.
Wing	Blue mallard.

3. *Blue Zulu*
Silk	Black.
Tail	Short red wool.
Body	Black floss silk.
Body hackle	Black henny cock wound in palmer fashion, ribbed silver.
Head hackle	Cock dyed gentian blue.

4. *Butcher*
Silk	Black.
Tail	Small red ibis substitute feather.
Body	Flat silver tinsel ribbed (optional) round.
Hackle	Black hen.
Wing	Blue mallard.

5. *Cased Caddis*
Silk	Brown.
Under-body	Fine lead wire.
Body	Spun fur from hare's mask with a turn of cream wool behind the head.
Hackle	Natural red hen, sparse.

6. *Connemara Black*

Silk	Black.
Tag	Silver wire and yellow floss.
Tail	Crest feather of golden pheasant.
Body	Black seal's fur ribbed fine oval tinsel.
Hackles	Black hen with a false hackle of blue jay tied in front.
Wing	Bronze mallard.

7. *Fiery Brown*

Silk	Brown.
Tag	Yellow floss.
Tail	Golden Pheasant tippets.
Body	Fiery brown seal's fur ribbed oval gold tinsel.
Hackle	Natural red hen.
Wings	Bronze mallard.

8. *Golden Olive Bumble*

Silk	Golden olive.
Body	Golden olive seal's fur ribbed oval gold tinsel.
Body hackle	Golden olive and natural red cocks tied palmer fashion.
Throat hackle	Blue jay.

9. *Kehe*

Silk	Brown.
Tail	Golden Pheasant tippet tied above short tail of red wool.
Body	Bronze peacock.
Hackle	Natural red hen.

10. *Kingfisher Butcher*

Silk	Black.
Tail	Fibres of cock dyed kingfisher blue.
Body	Flat gold tinsel.
Hackle	Cock dyed kingfisher blue.
Wing	Blue mallard.

11. *Mallard and Claret*

Silk	Black.
Tag	Crimson floss.
Tail	Golden Pheasant tippets.
Body	Dark claret seal's fur ribbed oval gold tinsel.
Hackle	Hen dyed claret.
Wing	Bronze mallard.

12. *March Brown*

Silk	Orange.
Tail	Fibres of brown partridge.
Body	Hare's ear fur ribbed yellow silk.
Hackle	Brown partridge.
Wing	Partridge tail.

13. *Peter Ross*

Silk	Black.
Tail	Golden Pheasant tippets.
Body	Rear $\frac{2}{3}$ silver tinsel, front $\frac{1}{3}$ red fur, all ribbed fine round tinsel.
Hackle	Black hen.
Wings	Barred teal flank.

14. *Silver March Brown*

As for March Brown but with a body of flat silver tinsel.

15. *Soldier Palmer*

Silk	Red.
Body	Red floss silk.
Body hackle	Natural red cock, ribbed fine gold wire.
Front hackle	Natural red cock.

16. *Straggly Spider*

Silk	Black.
Body	Black seal's fur ribbed narrow flat silver tinsel.
Hackle	Black henny cock.

17. *Teal and Black*
>   Silk   Black.
>   Tail   Golden Pheasant tippets.
>   Body   Black seal's fur ribbed oval silver tinsel.
>   Hackle   Black hen.
>   Wing   Barred teal flank.

18. *Teal and Green*
As for Teal and Black but with a green seal's fur body.

19. *Treacle Parkin*
>   Silk   Red.
>   Tail   Yellow wool.
>   Body   Bronze peacock herl ribbed with tying silk.
>   Hackle   Natural red hen.

20. *Williams's Favourite*
>   Silk   Black.
>   Body   Black floss silk ribbed fine silver wire.
>   Hackle   Black hen.

21. *Woodcock and Yellow*
>   Silk   Yellow.
>   Tail   Golden Pheasant tippets.
>   Body   Yellow seal's fur ribbed fine gold oval tinsel.
>   Hackle   Natural red hen.
>   Wing   Slips from woodcock secondary quills.

22. *Zulu*
>   Silk   Black.
>   Tail   Red wool.
>   Body   Black floss silk.
>   Body hackle Black henny cock wound in palmer fashion, ribbed silver.
>   Head hackle Black henny cock.

Hooks: These should be tied in sizes 8–14, with 10 and 12 being possibly most useful. As well as being tied onto standard wet fly hooks it is worth tying some on Caddis or Shrimp Hooks (e.g. Straggly Spider and Keke). Their curved shape gives more of an insect look to the fly!

Imitative Flies
Corixa

Corixa
Silk	Black.
Body	Underbody of lead wire flattened to shape and with an overbody of flat silver tinsel. The back is made by tying in at front and rear a slip of rook secondary. This whole is then varnished.
Legs	Four short stiff lengths of peacock herl, two at each side, tied back at an angle.

Chironomids (Midges)

Buzzer Pupa
Tail	Filaments from pale grey mallard flank cut short.
Body	Floss silk, ribbed finest round silver tinsel or wire.
Thorax	Peacock herl.
Breathing tubes	As tail, cut very short.

Buzzer pupae should be tied in a wide range of colours (i.e. body floss silk and tying silk). Traditionally, these are tied on standard hooks; far better are curved grub or sedge hooks, sizes 10–16.

Suspender Buzzer Pupae
These are tied as for the ordinary Buzzer Pupae but at the head, in front of the peacock thorax, is tied a small polystyrene bead enclosed in ladies' tights material.

Floating Midge
Body	Floss silk of an appropriate colour wrapped over by clear polythene strip.
Hackle	Blue dun cock.
Wings	White cock hackle points tied back.

Grey Duster
Silk	Grey.
Body	Rabbit fur spun on tying silk.
Hackle	Cock badger.

The ideal hook for the last two species is the Hooper Short Fine Dry Fly, size 14–18.

Land flies

Ants (Black and Red)
      Silk   Red or black.
      Body   Tying silk built up to give an ant's body shape, i.e. large abdomen and thorax with a narrow waist.
      Hackle   Blue dun cock.
      Wings   White cock hackle points.
Hooks size 14–16 Dry Fly.

Black Gnat
      Silk   Black.
      Body   Floss silk ribbed one strand of peacock herl which is used, after ribbing the abdomen, to give a large thorax.
      Hackle   Black cock.
Hooks size 12–16 Yorkshire Sedge or Partridge Grub Hooks to give a natural curved body outline.

Brown Moth
      Silk   Brown.
      Body   Brown seal's fur.
      Hackle   Red cock.
      Wings   Brown turkey, large.
Hook size 10–12 Partridge Up-eyed Mayfly.

Daddy-long-legs
      Silk   Brown.
      Body   Pheasant tail herl.
      Legs   Eight fibres of pheasant tail herl, knotted three times each to imitate the joints of the natural leg, tied in and splayed out behind hackle.
      Hackle   Honey cock.
      Wings   Cree cock hackle-point wings, one on either side, splayed out.
Hook size 10–12 Partridge Up-eyed Mayfly.

Green Caterpillar
    Silk   Green.
    Body   Green seal's fur ribbed tightly with tying silk.
    Head and Olive ostrich herl.
      Thorax
Hook size 10–12 Yorkshire Sedge Hooks.

Wickham's Fancy (Hackle Pattern)
    Silk   Brown.
    Body   Flat gold lurex.
    Body   Natural red cock wound palmer fashion along the
      hackle   body and ribbed with fine gold wire.
    Hackle   Natural red cock.
Hook size 10–14 Dry Fly.

Sedges

Sedge Pupa

Silk	Brown.
Body	Swan herl dyed appropriately, ribbed fine gold wire, and with a thorax of ostrich herl of the same colour.
Hackle	Brown partridge, long in the fibre.

Body colours olive, orange and brown. Hook sizes 10–12 Yorkshire Sedge.

Suspender Sedge Pupa

These are tied exactly as the plain pattern but with a polystyrene bead attached (as in the Suspender Buzzer) at the head.

Deer Hair Sedge

Silk	Brown.
Body	Deer hair spun the full length of the hook shank, trimmed to a sedge outline. Beneath this, below the hook shank, is tied in a band made up of green seal's fur spun on tying silk.
Hackle	Light honey cock. I use two hackles and leave the hackle-stalks pointing forwards to imitate the antennae.

Palmer-hackled Sedge

Silk	Brown.
Body	Seal's fur—a variety of colours can be used but brown is as good as any.
Hackle	Natural red cock tied palmer fashion along the body and ribbed in with fine gold wire.
Wing	Brown turkey.

Hooks size 8–12 Partridge Up-eyed Mayfly.

Shrimps

Lane's Shrimp

Silk	Medium olive.
Tail	Bunch of brown partridge hackle fibres $\frac{3}{16}''$ long, pointing downwards.
Body	Dubbed hare's ear wound over an underbody of fine lead wire.
Hackle	Brown partridge tied palmer fashion. The fibres above and at the sides are trimmed away and the exposed quills strengthened with a touch of varnish.

Sawyer's Killer Bug

A simple pattern to tie! A fat underbody of fine copper wire is built up (no silk is needed). A length of wool is then tied in with the wire and wrapped over the wire underbody, the loose end of the wire being used to tie off the wool at the 'head' of the Bug. The colour of the wool is all-important—Chadwick No. 477 was the shade that Sawyer insisted upon but this is no longer manufactured. Basically, it was a soft grey with a pink caste. Some retailers sell a good subsititute.

In both these shrimp patterns I would suggest a curved Shrimp Hook which helps in giving the pattern a realistic shape, sizes 10–12.

Snail

Floating Snail

A piece of cork is cut to the shape of a snail and tied to the hook with silk. The whole is then coated with black nail varnish. Hooks size 10–12 Wet Fly. Easy to tie and effective in the right circumstances!

Upwinged flies—wet flies and nymphs

Greenwell's Glory (Spider Variant)

Silk	Yellow or, as an alternative, primrose.
Tail	Bunch of fibres from hen Greenwell spade hackle.
Body	Waxed tying silk ribbed fine gold wire.
Hackle	Hen Greenwell.

Olive Spider

Silk	Light olive.
Body	Tying silk.
Hackle	Olive Hen.

Sawyer's Pheasant Tail Nymph

No silk is used. Some fine copper wire is used to form an underbody with a pronounced thorax. A bunch of cock pheasant tail fibres are then tied in so that their tips form the nymph tail filaments. Then the pheasant tail fibres are twisted around the wire and wound over the wire underbody. The nymph wing cases are accentuated by folding the dark base of the herls back and forth over the thorax before tying off at the head with the wire.

These should be tied in a range of sizes (12–16), either on standard wet fly hooks or Yorkshire Sedge Hooks.

Upwinged flies—floating dry flies

Greenwell's Glory (Dry Fly)

Silk	Yellow or, to give an alternative, primrose.
Tail	Bunch of fibres of Greenwell cock spade hackle.
Body	Tying silk ribbed fine gold wire.
Hackle	Cock Greenwell (these can come in a variety of shades, allowing a variety of flies—this is one great advantage of this traditional pattern as a dry fly).
Wing	Starling wing slips, tied upright and split.

Hook sizes 12–14 Captain Hamilton Dry Fly Down-eyed.

Mayfly Dun

Silk	Black.
Tail	Fibres of cock pheasant tail fibres.
Body	Buff raffine ribbed black and red silk, the two lying side by side.
Hackles	Olive cock and hot orange cock wound separately with the orange one at the front.

Mayfly Spinner

Silk	Black.
Tail	Fibres of cock pheasant tail fibres.
Body	Palest natural raffine ribbed black silk.
Hackle	Blue dun cock.
Wings	Iron blue dun hackle points.

Hooks for both Mayfly patterns size 8–10 Partridge Up-eyed Mayfly.

Norris Sepia

Silk	Brown.
Tail	Bunch of fibres of natural red cock spade hackle.
Body	Heron herl dyed in red, ribbed fine gold lurex.
Hackles	Two, natural red cock and brown cock, wound separately.
Wing	Mallard secondary wing slips tied upright and split.

Hook sizes 12–14 Dry Fly. This is one of the great dry flies devised by Jack Norris, an outstanding dry fly angler.

Paythorne Caenis

Silk	Black.
Tail	Fibres from blue dun cock spade hackle.
Abdomen	Stripped white hen hackle stalk with one turn of black silk showing at tip.
Thorax	Peacock herl.
Hackle	Blue dun cock.
Wing	White cock hackle tips tied spent.

Hook sizes 16 and smaller, down to 26 if you can tie it on this size!

Pheasant Tail Spinner

Silk	Brown.
Tail	Fibres from honey cock spade hackle.
Body	Cock pheasant tail fibres ribbed fine gold wire.
Hackle	Honey cock.

This pattern can be tied on a range of hook sizes, 12–16. There can also be variations in the pattern by using different shades of hackles. An excellent fly!

Yellow Spinner

Silk	Yellow.
Tail	Fibres of blue dun cock spade hackle.
Body	Swan herl dyed yellow ribbed fine gold wire.
Hackle	Two, golden olive cock and blue dun cock wound separately with the blue dun in front.

Hook sizes 12–14 Captain Hamilton Featherweight Down-eyed Hooks.

References

BARKER, Thomas, *The Art of Angling*, 1651

BERNERS, Dame Juliana, *A Treatyse of Fysshynge with an Angle*, 1496

BRIDGETT, R.C., *Loch-Fishing in Theory and Practice*, 1924

BUCKNALL, Geoffrey, *Modern Techniques of Stillwater Fly-Fishing*, 1980

BULLER, Fred, and FALKUS, Hugh, *Freshwater Fishing*, 1975

CALVER, Jim, *Bank Fishing for Reservoir Trout* (2nd Ed.), 1979

CHURCH, Bob, *Reservoir Trout Fishing*, 1977

CONDRY, W.M., *The Snowdonia National Park*, 1966

FALKUS, Hugh, *Sea Trout Fishing* (2nd Ed.), 1975

FROST, W.E., and BROWN, M.E., *The Trout*, 1967

GODDARD, John, *The Super Flies of Stillwater*, 1977

GODDARD, John, *Trout Fly Recognition* (3rd Ed.), 1976

GODDARD, John, *Trout Flies of Stillwater* (4th Ed.), 1979

HARRIS, J.R., *An Angler's Entomology* (Rev. Ed.), 1956

HEWITT, R., *A Trout and Salmon Fisherman for Seventy-Five Years*, 1948

HILLS, John Waller, *A History of Fly Fishing for Trout*, 1921

IVENS, T.C., *Stillwater Fly-Fishing* (Rev. 2nd Ed.), 1973

KITE, Oliver, *Nymph Fishing in Practice*, 1963

MACAN, T.T., *A Guide to Freshwater Invertebrate Animals*, 1959

MACAN, T.T. and WORTHINGTON, E.B., *Life in Lakes and Rivers* (Rev. Ed.), 1972

MACLEOD, Norman, *Trout Fishing in Lewis*, 1977

MALONE, E.J., *Irish Trout and Salmon Flies*, 1984

MOON, H.P., *J. Anim. Ecol.* (1934), 3: 8–28

MOORE, T.C. Kingsmill, *A Man may Fish* (2nd Ed.), 1979

PEARSON, Alan, *An Introduction to Reservoir Trout Fishing*, 1984

RANSOME, Arthur, *Rod and Line*, 1929

RITZ, Charles, *A Fly Fisher's Life*, 1959

SAWYER, Frank, *Nymphs and the Trout* (2nd Ed.), 1970

SANDISON, Bruce, *The Trout Lochs of Scotland*, 1983

SHERINGHAM, H.T., *Trout Fishing Memories and Morals*, n.d., (1920)

SKUES, G.E.M., *Itchen Memories*, 1951

TURING, H.D., *Trout Fishing*, 1943

ULLYOTT, P., *Int. Rev. Hydrobiol* (1939), 38: 262–4

WALKER, C.F., *Lake Flies and their Imitation*, 1960

WILLIAMS, A. Courtney, *A Dictionary of Trout Flies* (5th Ed.), 1973

'Simon Peter said, 'I go a-fishing': and they said, 'We also will go with thee.'   John, xxi, 3

Index